Family Mediation Handbook

Related Titles of Interest

1) British Columbia Family Law Quantum Service

2) Butterworths Ontario Family Law Quantum Service

3) Ontario Annotated Family Law Service

4) Klein: Family Law Awards in Canada

5) Wilson: Children and The Law, 2nd Edition

Family Mediation Handbook

Barbara Landau
Ph.D., LL.B., LL.M.
Psychologist and Member of the Ontario Bar

Mario Bartoletti
M.A., Ed.D.
Marriage and Family Counsellor

Ruth Mesbur
B.A., LL.B.
of the Ontario Bar

Butterworths
Toronto and Vancouver

Family Mediation Handbook

Printed and bound in Canada

The Butterworth Group of Companies

Canada:
Butterworths, Toronto and Vancouver
United Kingdom:
Butterworth & Co. (Publishers) Ltd., London and Edinburgh
Australia:
Butterworths Pty Ltd., Sydney, Melbourne, Brisbane, Adelaide and Perth
New Zealand:
Butterworths (New Zealand) Ltd., Wellington and Auckland
Singapore:
Butterworth & Co. (Asia) Pte. Ltd., Singapore
South Africa:
Butterworth Publishers (SA) (Pty) Ltd., Durban and Pretoria
United States:
Butterworth Legal Publishers, Boston, Seattle, Austin and St. Paul
D & S Publishers, Clearwater

Canadian Cataloguing in Publication Data
Landau, Barbara.
  Family mediation handbook

Bibliography: p.
Includes index.
ISBN 0-409-81161-0

1. Family mediation – Canada. 2. Divorce
mediation – Canada. 3. Domestic relations –
Canada. 4. Domestic relations – Ontario.
I. Bartoletti, Mario Dante, 1933-
II. Mesbur, Ruth.   III. Title.

HQ838.L36 1987   306.8'9   C87-093351-5

Sponsoring Editor: Paul Truster
Managing Editor: Linda Kee
Supervisory Editor: Marie Graham
Freelance Projects Coordinator/Cover Design: Joan Chaplin
Editor: Anne Butler
Production: Jill Thomson
Typesetting and Assembly: Computer Composition of Canada Inc.

Preface

Over the past decade, judges, lawyers, mental health professionals and disputing spouses have all become disillusioned with the adversarial approach to resolving family disputes. Conflicts among family members are different than most other legal challenges in that the relationship between the warring parties does not end with the judge's decision. Unlike other civil litigation cases in which the disputants go their separate ways after an adversarial court battle, parents must continue to cooperate in the interests of their children for years following the court proceeding. Recent research has shown that children are the real victims of family breakdown and the more intense the parental conflict following separation, the more likely it is that the children will be torn apart by a conflict of loyalties over their parents. Also, the more adversarial the struggle to end the marriage, the more difficult it is for parents to work cooperatively in the future.

Mediation is a method of dispute resolution which has as its objective a cooperative, voluntary and equitable outcome to a dispute. Agreement is reached by the parties themselves with the assistance of an impartial professional. The emphasis on improved communication and cooperation between the parties is attractive to the legal profession, the mental health profession and parents, because a mediated solution is more likely to be honoured, tension between the parties usually diminishes and the children often benefit from a more meaningful relationship with both parents. Over the past several years mediation has attracted considerable interest as an alternative to litigation, particularly for disputes involving children.

The *Family Mediation Handbook* is a comprehensive Canadian text that explains the process of mediation, distinguishes mediation from other forms of dispute resolution such as litigation, counselling or arbitration, and reviews the ethical issues that must be considered by all professionals involved in this field. This book covers the mediation of family law disputes involving property and support issues, as well as disputes with respect to custody of and access to children.

The *Family Mediation Handbook* is a handy reference tool for mental health professionals, lawyers, family doctors and clergymen who intend to practice as mediators or who are in a position to refer clients for mediation services. This book could also be read by potential clients who wish to evaluate the alternatives of mediation, litigation and other methods of dispute resolution.

The *Family Mediation Handbook* contains a great deal of practical advice and information as to the procedure followed in mediation, communication skills, methods of dispute resolution, ethical standards and the effects on children of separation and divorce. In addition the book contains a detailed Appendix with samples of forms, agreements and correspondence that will be particularly helpful to the beginning mediator.

The *Family Mediation Handbook* offers a summary of law in Canada, with special reference to the Province of Ontario. Mediation has been described by Professor Robert Mnookin of Stanford University as a process of "bargaining in the shadow of the law" and therefore it is essential to include both the law and the clinical practice of mediation.

Finally, the *Family Mediation Handbook* is a useful reference for professionals who deal with either children or adults who are undergoing separation and divorce and who wish to be more sensitive to this process. For example, teachers, family physicians and clergymen are often looked to for assistance during a marital crisis. This book provides an understanding of the mediation process so that these professionals can offer guidance to families experiencing a marriage breakdown.

Chapter 1
Provides the historical background to mediation from both a legal and a mental health perspective. Information is provided about the development of mediation services in both Canada and in the United States.

Chapter 2
Examines alternative methods of dispute resolution, such as counselling, mediation, arbitration, litigation and assessments as methods of resolving family law problems.

Chapter 3
Sets the stage for mediation by outlining the role of referral sources, clients and the mediator in the mediation process. Practical information is provided to assist in initiating the mediation, arriving at interim arrangements and terminating the mediation. The emphasis is on ethical issues that might arise at various points in the process.

Chapter 4
Focusses on the mediation procedure and sets out in detail the objectives for meetings with counsel, the parties, children and other significant individuals during the course of mediation. It is expected that there will be considerable differences in procedure between mediators depending on the nature and complexity of the problems as well as the experience of the mediator.

Chapter 5
Examines the clinical skills associated with mediation. In this chapter the mediator is seen as an educator, a fact gatherer and a communicator. The chapter offers considerable information as to the responses of children to separation and divorce, as well as specific suggestions for information gathering. In addition, the chapter contains practical ideas for dealing with serious communication problems during the mediation process. This chapter will be of interest to both mediators and non-mediators as it provides extensive background material for anyone dealing with families who are experiencing marital difficulties.

Chapters 6 and 7
Both chapters 6 and 7 set out the relevant family law in Canada and more specifically in Ontario with respect to custody and access (Chapter 6) and property and support (Chapter 7). These chapters will be of particular interest to non-lawyers who are looking for a clear, concise and readable outline of the most important features of family law for the purpose of mediating matrimonial disputes. Although non-lawyers cannot give legal advice, it is important for the mental health professional who is acting as a mediator to understand the legal context relevant to the issues in dispute.

Chapter 8
Discusses in some detail the rules of professional conduct which have been adopted by the Ontario Association For Family Mediation. In addition this chapter explores the areas of conflict between mental health professionals and lawyers as well as within the legal profession with respect to lawyers acting as mediators. This chapter demonstrates the direction mediation is taking in its efforts to become a recognized profession. All mediators and those referring to mediators need to be aware of the ethical code of conduct expected from those who practice.

Chapter 9
Contains practical information with respect to preparing agreements, minutes of settlement or a report in cases where the parties have arrived at a full agreement, a partial agreement or in some cases no agreement at all. This chapter clarifies the differences in reporting requirements for mediators depending on whether the mediation is a closed or open process.

Chapter 10
Compares the procedure in custody assessments with that of mediation of custody and access disputes. This chapter explores the purpose of a custody assessment, the differences between mediation and assessments and the procedure to be followed. In addition, specific information is given as to the contents of an acceptable custody assessment report.

Chapter 11
Sets out specific, detailed information with respect to the role of the mediator/assessor as expert witness. The difference between privilege and

confidentiality are discussed, and the guidelines for giving testimony in court, including the qualifications of an expert witness, are explored in some detail. Practical suggestions are given for those mental health professionals who are to appear as an expert witness and for the lawyer who requires the services of an expert witness in a family law trial.

* * *

Each chapter contains an annotated bibliography, a handy reference for the reader who may wish to explore particular subjects in more detail. In addition, precedent material is provided for all steps in the mediation process and will be particularly helpful for those who are new to mediation. Copies of the standards of professional conduct adopted by Family Mediation Canada, the Ontario Association for Family Mediation, the Law Society of Upper Canada and the American Bar Association are included. This information will be useful for mediators in other jurisdictions who are presently developing a code of conduct for practicing mediators.

The *Family Mediation Handbook* clearly sets out the purpose of mediation, the procedure followed and all of the material necessary to inform clients about mediation services or carry out these services as part of a professional practice. The format adopted can be easily used for lectures, quick reference or a practical guide. It covers both custody and access mediation as well as comprehensive financial mediation and will be of interest to a variety of audiences.

Acknowledgements

The authors are grateful to many individuals who contributed their ideas and efforts toward the preparation of this book. Particular thanks go to Simone Johnston, Maureen Holder, Lili Bartoletti, Jane Dewar and Debra Brick for their patience, creativity and tremendous organizing skills. Many thanks are also due to the editorial staff at Butterworths, notably Linda Kee, Lebby Hines, Paul Truster and Joan Chaplin. Without the considerable efforts of all these individuals, this book would not have become a reality.

The authors wish to acknowledge the contribution made by our colleagues on the Board of Directors of the Ontario Association for Family Mediation for their considerable contribution to mediation as a profession. Working together as colleagues has enriched our ideas and clarified important concepts with respect to mediation as a profession.

Finally the authors wish to thank their spouses and children for their patience and emotional support in the lengthy process from conception to delivery of this book.

Table of Contents

Table of Statutes

1. Statutes re Property and Support

Canada
Divorce Act, 1985, S.C. 1986, c. 4

Alberta
Maintenance Order Act, R.S.A. 1980, c. M-1
Maintenance Recovery Act, R.S.A. 1980, c. M-2
Matrimonial Property Act, R.S.A. 1980, c. M-9

British Columbia
Child Paternity and Support Act, R.S.B.C. 1979, c. 49
Family Relations Act, R.S.B.C. 1979, c. 121

Manitoba
Child and Family Services Act, S.M. 1985-86, c. 8 (C.C.S.M. c. C80)
Family Maintenance Act, S.M. 1978, c. 25 (C.C.S.M. c. F20)

New Brunswick
Family Services Act, S.N.B. 1980, c. F-2.2
Marital Property Act, S.N.B. 1980, c. M-1.1

Newfoundland
Children of Unmarried Parents Act, 1972, S.N. 1972, c. 33
Maintenance Act, R.S.N. 1970, c. 223
Matrimonial Property Act, S.N. 1979, c. 32

Northwest Territories
Maintenance Act, R.S.N.W.T. 1974, c. M-2

Nova Scotia
Children's Services Act, S.N.S. 1976, c. 8
Family Maintenance Act, S.N.S. 1980, c. 6

Ontario
Family Law Act, 1986, S.O. 1986, c. 4
Child and Family Services Act, 1984, S.O. 1984, c. 55

Prince Edward Island
Family and Child Services Act, S.P.E.I. 1981, c. 12
Family Law Reform Act, S.P.E.I. 1978, c. 6

Quebec
Civil Code, Book II

Saskatchewan
Deserted Wives' and Children's Maintenance Act, R.S.S. 1978, c. D-26
Matrimonial Property Act, S.S. 1979, c. M-6.1

Yukon
Children's Act, S.Y.T. 1984, c. 2
Matrimonial Property and Family Support Act, S.Y.T. 1979 (2nd), c. 11

2. Statutes re Custody

Canada
Divorce Act, 1986, S.C. 1986, c. 4

Alberta
Domestic Relations Act, R.S.A. 1980, c. D-37

British Columbia
Family Relations Act, R.S.B.C. 1979, c. 121

Manitoba
Child and Family Services Act, S.M. 1985-86, c. 8 (C.C.S.M. c. C80)

New Brunswick
Family Services Act, S.N.B. 1980, c. F-2.2

Newfoundland
Child Welfare Act, 1972, S.N. 1972, c. 37

Northwest Territories
Domestic Relations Act, R.S.N.W.T. 1974, c. D-9

Nova Scotia
Infants Custody Act, R.S.N.S. 1967, c. 145

Ontario
Children's Law Reform Act, R.S.O. 1980, c. 68

Prince Edward Island
Custody Jurisdiction and Enforcement Act, S.P.E.I. 1984, c. 17

Quebec
Civil Code Book II

Saskatchewan
Infants Act, R.S.S. 1978, c. I-9

Yukon
Children's Act, S.Y.T. 1984, c. 2

Chapter One

Historical Overview of Mediation

A. LEGAL ASPECTS: The Evolution of Non-Adversarial Dispute Resolution in Family Law and Other Legal Areas

The 1960s were a catalyst for many major innovations in our cultural traditions, social mores and legal framework. One of the innovations that emerged in North America in the 1960s was the use of mediation for family law disputes. Mediation, a non-adversarial method of dispute resolution, has been used for many years to settle labour problems, community conflicts, religious disputes and international disputes; however, in the 1960s mediation began to be used with families in conflict.

Family mediation is a process whereby an impartial professional, usually a mental health professional, but sometimes a lawyer, helps the parties negotiate a voluntary settlement to the family law issues in dispute. The mediator does not act on behalf of either party and does not impose a settlement, but rather acts as a facilitator, an educator and a communicator who helps parties clarify issues, identify and deal with feelings, generate options and, it is hoped, arrive at a settlement without the need for an adversarial court battle.

Before we can discuss meaningfully the process or procedures used in family mediation, it is essential to understand something about the historical context for dealing with family law disputes, the perceived problems with the approach of the past and then how and why mediation emerged as an alternative approach for assisting disappointed spouses. The history of family law for the past century reflects an enormous social change in our values and our cultural mores. As our assumptions about the family, the permanence of marriage and the role of mothers and fathers change, so do the laws and the legal procedures for handling family problems.

In the past, the primary objectives of the law in family law matters was to preserve marriage, and therefore divorce was either prohibited or socially shunned. Until recently, divorce was only granted on fault-oriented

1

grounds. For example, in Canada, generally speaking, the only ground for divorce prior to 1968 was adultery. The courts showed their disapproval of marriage breakdown by inflicting a punitive consequence on the party who was guilty of destroying the marriage. The guilty party was usually denied custody of the children and received limited or no access. In addition, the criteria for obtaining support or custody of the children were not based on present-day concepts of fairness and equity, but rather were tied in with moralistic judgments and judicial retribution. If the "guilty spouse" was a man, he would usually be obligated to pay support indefinitely, regardless of the wife's needs, while a wife who committed a single act of adultery could lose support for life.

Because of the very serious consequences of divorce, both in the courts and in terms of society's reaction, family law cases were handled in an intensely adversarial manner. The objective of each lawyer was to present his or her client as morally pure and blameless while alleging immoral conduct by the other spouse. This resulted in highly polarized morality plays that were staged in the courtroom and were usually emotionally destructive to both participants.

Present-day family laws reflect the change in social attitudes to marriage breakdown. In the first place, the law no longer provides strong protection for marriage or a bulwark against divorce, but rather reflects the concept that adults should be free to choose whether or not to remain in the marital union. Fault is no longer a necessary ingredient for being granted a divorce, and support and custody are no longer used as part of the social sanction against divorce.

Today the laws are far less arbitrary and reflect such concepts of equity and fairness as marriage is a social and economic partnership. That means that the product of the marriage should be shared between the spouses at the time of breakdown. Custody laws are now tied to the needs or best interests of children and economic support is determined on the basis of financial need and ability to pay, with conduct explicitly excluded as a criterion.

With the change from a moralistic, fault-finding approach to a less judgmental legal framework, the procedures in family law cases have also shifted considerably. Today the emphasis is on negotiation, pretrial conferences, mediation of matrimonial disputes, the use of expert assessment reports and other techniques designed to assist couples in reaching an early resolution of the issues in dispute. Particularly where children are involved, the courts and the legislature now seem to understand that while the spousal relationship may come to an end, the need to continue in a co-operative framework for the sake of children may continue for many years. An adversarial procedure leads to bitterness and hostility and undermines the co-operation required for parenting. Also, research has demonstrated that the persons who suffer most as a result of an adversarial divorce are those who are totally faultless, namely the children.

Clinical research has not only demonstrated the need for parents to co-operate in the interests of their children, it has also demonstrated that divorce is a complex clinical problem, with individuals going through stages that are somewhat similar to a grieving process. The research of Drs. Wallerstein and Kelly that followed 60 families over a ten-year period documents the long-term emotional repercussions for both parents and children. Litigation exacerbates and prolongs the emotional strain on all parties, and therefore non-adversarial alternatives are being encouraged to limit the harmful emotional consequences.

Further impetus for changing the procedure in family law cases has come from the tremendous increase in the number of divorces in recent years, the backlog of cases in the courts, the great expense of family law litigation, as well as the tremendous increase in the number of children affected by marriage breakdown. It is estimated that each year approximately one and one-half million children in the United States and an additional one hundred and fifty thousand children in Canada experience separation. To deal with the problem, a number of jurisdictions in the United States have reduced trial lists by requiring at least one mandatory meeting with a mediator prior to litigating custody and access issues. For example, California requires mandatory mediation in their conciliation court. In Canada, mediation can be ordered or arranged on consent in many provinces, but only in Winnipeg and Edmonton can couples be ordered to attend at least one meeting with a mediator.

In summary, the chief precursors to family mediation are the shift from fault-oriented to no-fault divorce, the great increase in numbers of people divorcing, the exorbitant costs of a divorce, the emotional strain for both adults and children and the long delays in the courtroom that keep people's lives in limbo for several years prior to litigating their family law matters.

It is important to note that mediation has been used to resolve matters other than family law problems and was used in other cultures prior to its use in North America. For example,

- Non-westernized cultures such as China, Japan and Africa have long traditions of using mediation and conciliation as preferred methods of resolving neighbourhood disputes.
- In many cultures, respected elder members of the extended family have acted as mediators for resolving conflicts within the family.
- Religious leaders, priests, ministers and rabbis have often served as mediators in family disputes. They encourage family members to use religious principles to resolve conflicts rather than take family problems to court.

One of the first areas of law to use mediation for the resolution of disputes was labour law. Mediation has been used largely to resolve labour-management conflicts, such as disputes with respect to working conditions, pay scales, hiring and firing practices and employee benefits.

Family law and labour law share an important common feature that lends itself to mediation, as opposed to an adversarial method of dispute resolution. That is, both in labour-management conflicts and in family conflicts, individuals are usually in a relationship that will continue in some form following the resolution of the dispute. Unlike criminal cases or other civil matters where the parties may have no further contact after one party is declared the "winner" and the other the "loser", in family law and labour law cases the parties usually have to be able to co-operate with each other on an ongoing basis. The need for continuing co-operation between the parties makes mediation a more suitable process for dispute resolution than an adversarial method.

In mediation, an experienced, impartial professional helps the parties reach a voluntary settlement that has been designed by them. Ideally the settlement is a fair and reasonable resolution of their competing needs and interests such that neither party is a complete winner and neither party suffers a humiliating loss. Because the settlement is reached voluntarily by the parties themselves, it is more likely to be carried out without the need for external enforcement or further litigation. The non-adversarial nature of the process and the emphasis on co-operation are likely to reduce tension and encourage future co-operative behaviour. This is an important objective where children are involved.

The success of non-adversarial techniques, such as mediation and pretrial conferences, in addition to the continuing shift in philosophy away from fault and toward a more co-operative approach to family law problems, has stimulated the recent reforms of family law, both federally and in many provinces.

(1) FAMILY LAW

(a) Federal Legislation

(i) The Divorce Act, 1985

- The *Divorce Act, 1985,* S.C. 1986, c. 4, encourages a no-fault approach to divorce by stating that the sole ground for a divorce is "marriage breakdown". A divorce can now be obtained after a one-year separation (rather than the three- or five-year separation period required under the previous *Divorce Act* (R.S.C. 1970, c. D-8)) or more quickly if one spouse alleges adultery or cruelty as the basis for the marriage breakdown.
- This Act requires lawyers to advise their clients to consider mediating any issues in dispute (including custody and child and spousal support) prior to litigating these issues. Lawyers must also inform

clients about mediation services that are available in the community. In addition, lawyers are obligated to try to resolve matrimonial issues through negotiation rather than litigation.

- The best interests of children is the sole criterion for determining custody of and access to children. Any person can apply for custody of or access to children; that is, persons other than biological parents or relatives can apply if they have a meaningful relationship with the child.
- Joint custody is an option for judges to consider in custody awards. The principle of encouraging maximum contact between the child and both parents is set out in the legislation. The judge must consider which parent will facilitate maximum contact with the other parent when determining who will be awarded custody. Also conduct, except ability to parent, is not considered when determining custody and access.
- Need and ability to pay are the sole criteria for determining awards for child and spousal maintenance. Fault or matrimonial misconduct is expressly excluded in determining entitlement to and quantum of support.

(b) Provincial Legislation

(i) The Ontario Children's Law Reform Act and The Ontario Family Law Act, 1986

In Ontario, on the consent of the parties, the court can order mediation with respect to custody and access: (*Children's Law Reform Act,* R.S.O. 1980, c. 68, s. 31 (en. 1982, c. 20, s. 1)), as well as for child and spousal support and the division of assets (*Family Law Act, 1986,* S.O. 1986, c. 4, s. 3).

(ii) The Manitoba Queen's Bench Act

In Manitoba, the court can make a referral to a conciliation officer to resolve any matter without a formal trial. The judge or master can make this order at any stage of the proceedings and can appoint either a conciliation officer or any other person on the consent of the parties. In practice, the Unified Family Court in Winnipeg requires that every couple attend at least one mediation session in cases where there is an application for custody of or access to children. That is, the couple must attend at least one mandatory mediation session before they will be permitted to litigate custody and access issues. (*Queen's Bench Act,* R.S.M. 1970, c. C280).

(iii) The British Columbia Family Relations Act

The *Family Relations Act* of British Columbia permits the court to appoint a family court counsellor to assist in the resolution of family law matters. This is not restricted to custody and access issues. (*Family Relations Act,* R.S.B.C. 1979, c. 121, s. 3).

In addition, in most provinces:

- The best interests of children is the sole criterion for determining custody of and access to children.
- Need and ability to pay are the criteria for determining child and spousal support.
- Matrimonial misconduct is specifically excluded from determinations of custody, access and support.
- The value of all assets acquired during the course of the marriage (with certain exceptions, such as gifts or inheritances from third parties) is divided equally at the end of the marriage, based on the philosophy of marriage as an economic and social partnership. The trend is toward sharing all assets with very limited judicial discretion to vary the 50-50 split. Limiting judicial discretion reduces the likelihood of an adversarial battle, because the more accurately the parties can predict the outcome in court, the easier it is to arrange a settlement.

The trend in family law is toward less adversarial procedures that encourage early settlement on a co-operative basis, with the assistance of an impartial professional, as well as independent legal advice. The legislation, by moving away from fault and toward more consistent, predictable and objective criteria, is highly compatible with a more co-operative approach to dispute resolution in family law cases.

B. MENTAL HEALTH ASPECTS: The Evolution of Mediation from Models of Clinical Intervention

Mediation bills and procedures have evolved from clinical psychology as well as from labour negotiations. It is important to review the clinical roots of mediation to understand the similarities and differences between mediation and other forms of clinical intervention.

(1) MODERN INTERPERSONAL PSYCHOLOGY

Modern interpersonal psychology as a mental health discipline has its origins in the theories of Sigmund Freud. An understanding of the significance of his psychological concepts is important for seeing their relation to the evolution of mediation.

Freud's concept of a human unconscious, his hypotheses about infant sexuality and his dividing of mental functioning into three distinct yet interrelating parts have all had a significant impact on the field of human relations. That is, according to Freud:

- Human functioning is not entirely a rational, conscious process. There are areas of mental functioning that become overladen with fear and guilt, and become lodged in the unconscious because they are too painful to be confronted. Nevertheless, they affect personal decision-making and behaviour.
- Infant sexuality is a powerful force in the emerging personality. It is important to understand this aspect of childhood development and its role in adult emotions.
- The human mind can be conceived as a tripartite construct of the id (instinctual impulses), the ego (the self as distinguished from the environment) and the super-ego (the conscience or counterbalance to the id). Functionally, the ego is the mediator between primal drives and society's expectations.

As part of his study of human behaviour, Freud developed clinical means for assisting emotionally disturbed persons:

- free association, whereby the unstructured verbal ramblings of an individual begin to assume some cohesion and relevance;
- individual psychotherapy, often extending over many months of confidential, regular visits, wherein a trusting and accepting relationship with the counsellor is developed.

The clinical treatment Freud developed is termed *psychoanalysis.* It produced several important contributions to the understanding of human behaviour.

One of the more significant contributions is the process by which the human mind defends itself against painful confrontations. Collectively they are described as *defense mechanisms,* being the psychological armour that individuals use to protect themselves from rejection, real or imagined:

- *projection* — a process wherein the individual unconsciously attributes to another person his or her own thoughts and feelings;
- *repression* — a process wherein there is an unconscious denial of painful or traumatic experiences;
- *suppression* — a process wherein the individual consciously denies experiences that cause him or her pain.

(2) NEO-FREUDIAN THEORIES

Later, there were significant departures from Freud's theories. In particular, the neo-Freudians represented a strong rejection of his focus on instinctual and intrapsychic functioning.

The neo-Freudians placed much greater emphasis on interpersonal behaviour, specifically parent-child interactions:

- *Harry Stack Sullivan* contributed greatly when he emphasized that personality is made manifest through interpersonal relations.

- *Alfred Adler* postulated that the child becomes emotionally "stuck" at an infantile stage as the result of an overbearing parental focus on discipline and punishment. He emphasized the need for nurturing parental behaviours.
- *Eric Fromm* developed the concept of "social character", a core of social behaviours resulting from parental influence during childhood.

Concurrent with the work of the neo-Freudians, *Carl Rogers* was independently pursuing careful research into counselling methodology. That is, Carl Rogers:

- took the position that counselling should focus more on the healthier drives within the individual than on negative instinctual impulses.
- placed greater emphasis on the present than on past experiences.
- developed a positive, supportive "client-centred" approach to psychotherapy that tended to shift some responsibility from the counsellor to the individual.

A further theoretical shift of power from the counsellor to the client occurred with the development of *group therapy*. The focus then changed from primarily intrapersonal issues to interpersonal relationships, with an added emphasis on problem-solving in the present.

Group therapy was first used by *Jacob Moreno* as a means of dealing with large numbers of patients in institutional settings. He soon came to recognize that groups provided several advantages over one-to-one counselling, namely:

- Group therapy provides the opportunity for peer input and more closely approximates the real world.
- Personal conflicts are often dealt with more quickly through group interaction than in individual counselling.
- The members of the group function as a support system and also as models for each other in attempting to resolve current conflicts both within and outside the group.

(3) CONJOINT FAMILY THERAPY

The next major theoretical advance was an increased emphasis on the family unit, not only as a key factor in personality development, but also as an important element in counselling intervention. The counselling process became known as conjoint family therapy.

There were rapid strides in the study of the family unit and its method of communication. A number of innovative people from a variety of professional backgrounds helped develop new approaches to the family unit as a means to understanding and changing behaviour.

- *Virginia Satir* demonstrated the importance of involving every family member when dealing with the behaviour of one family member.
- *Jay Haley* provided important mechanisms for assessing the non-verbal and verbal behaviour of all family members as part of the process of changing the family system.
- *Nathan Ackerman* helped family members understand how individual dysfunction is tied closely to family dysfunction.
- *Salvador Minuchin* was instrumental in developing the enmeshed-disengaged continuum for explaining the preferred transactional style of a particular family.

The majority of researchers and practitioners in family therapy have integrated the concept of the normative family. It is important that family counsellors recognize that most families have strengths and areas of healthy functioning despite the problems and crises that bring them into counselling. Often, one of the most important services the counsellor can provide is to help the family members identify and apply those strengths.

- *Don Jackson* integrated the work of Satir, Haley and Ackerman and used family systems as a means to improve family therapy.
- *Carl Whitaker* explored how the therapist's "use of self" can help the family take more responsibility for therapeutic change.

(4) FAMILY MEDIATION

Family mediation can be represented best as the flip-side of the professional coin to family therapy. Both share the historical antecedents described earlier; however, each has a very different theoretical objective. Whereas family therapy is a process to assist families working to remain together, family mediation is a process to assist families where there has been a decision to separate and/or divorce.

- *James Coogler,* a lawyer, was one of the first professionals to question the advisability of using the traditional legal/judicial process for handling marital and family conflict during separation and divorce. He became active in advocating that family law lawyers apply non-adversarial or mediative techniques rather than adversarial techniques. He advocated a system of comprehensive mediation for resolving all issues in dispute, such as support, property division and custody of and access to children.
- *Howard Irving* and *John Haynes* were also among the early researchers and proponents of family mediation as an effective alternative to litigation.
- At about the same time, other mediators were focusing on the effect of separation and divorce on parents and children. Their work had important implications for the resolution of custody and access

issues. The work of *Judith Wallerstein* and *Joan Kelly* confirmed the value of regular involvement by both parents in the lives of their children after separation.

- *Donald Saposnek's* work has supported the value of resolving parent-child disputes outside the court, confirming the earlier work of *Meyer Elkin* and *Hugh McIsaac* at the Conciliation Court program in Los Angeles.

As mediation continues to develop, integrative work is being done that is blending family therapy objectives with family mediation. The awareness that there really is no such thing as a "single parent family", in the sense that both parents from broken marriages continue to function in important ways in the lives of their children, has resulted in continued innovative approaches:

- The usefulness of an approach that provides mediation of all issues combined with a separation contract that includes ongoing monitoring and support of all family members after the separation is being applied by *Mario Bartoletti* and his associates within a private practice setting.
- The integration of family mediation and family therapy techniques is also emerging quite naturally in the work of *Lillian Messenger* with remarriage families following divorce.

The historical sequence of events, from Freud's focus on the individual's intrapsychic processes, through the interpersonal and parent-child theories of the neo-Freudians, to the increasing interest in and involvement of the whole family in both counselling and mediation, has been briefly chronicled in this section. Of particular importance for mediation is the fact that:

- Mental health professionals have been moving toward techniques that encourage clients to take more personal responsibility for decision making.
- Resolutions worked out in a co-operative atmosphere by family members produce the most stable and long-lasting results.

Set out below is a chart containing some of the significant developments in family mediation in North America, with particular emphasis on Canadian initiatives. The list is not exhaustive but does include a number of important events in the relatively brief history of family mediation. Today most provinces have developed or are in the process of developing a provincial mediation association, and Family Mediation Canada, which was established in 1984, is encouraging the use of mediation on a national level.

C. CHRONOLOGICAL DEVELOPMENT OF FAMILY MEDIATION IN NORTH AMERICA

	Organization	Developers	Year
(1)	Conciliation Court Los Angeles County	Meyer Elkin Hugh McIsaac	1961

– The first court-based mediation service in North America.

(2)	Association of Family and Conciliation Courts	Judge R. A. Pfaff Meyer Elkin	1963

– The first international association of family mediators. Initially directed at court-based services, more recently it has included private mediation as well.

(3)	Divorce Counselling Unit Health and Welfare Ottawa, Ontario	Gerry Gaughan	1969

– The first initiative by the federal government, following the enactment of the *Divorce Act* (S.C. 1967-68, c. 24) in 1968, to encourage established counselling services to offer conciliation services to divorcing couples.

(4)	Supportive Separation System Family Life Centre Markham, Ontario	Mario Bartoletti Judge T. Moore	1971

– The first non-court-based family counselling agency in Ontario offering comprehensive conciliation services to separating couples.

(5)	Conciliation Services Family Court Edmonton, Alberta	Judge M. Bowker	1972

– The first court-based conciliation service in Canada.

(6)	Conciliation Counselling Family Court Hamilton, Ontario	Judge David Steinberg	1973

– The first court-based conciliation service in Ontario.

(7)	Conciliation Project Provincial Court, Family Division Toronto, Ontario	Howard Irving Judge H. T. Andrews	1974

– A three-year demonstration research project, funded by Health and Welfare Canada, examining the effectiveness of family conciliation services.

(8)	Family Mediation Association Bethesda, Maryland	O. J. Coogler	1975

– The first mediation association focused on private mediation.

(9)	Frontenac Family Referral Services, Family Court Kingston, Ontario	Judge G. Thomson	1975

– The first court-based, comprehensive mediation service in Ontario, offering assistance with such issues as that handled custody, access, property and financial support.

(10)	Conciliation Service Unified Family Court Hamilton, Ontario	Judge J. VanDuzer	1977

– The first federal-provincial venture establishing a court-based conciliation project.

(11)	Academy of Family Mediators Claremont, California	John Haynes	1978

– An association of family mediators that encourages a more clinical approach to mediation.

(12)	Family Conciliation Service, Superior Court Montreal, Quebec	Chief Justice Jules Deschenes	1981

– The first court-based conciliation service in Quebec offering comprehensive mediation.

(13)	Ontario Association for Family Mediation Toronto, Ontario	John Goodwin Mario Bartoletti Ellen Macdonald	1982

– The first provincial family mediation association in Canada (OAFM).

(14)	Family Mediation Services of Ontario Toronto, Ontario	James MacDonald Philip Epstein	1982

– The first court-based conciliation service in Ontario, established specifically for the Supreme Court.

(15) The Family Mediation   Fran Kitely   1984
      Project Law Society of Upper   Barbara Landau
      Canada Legal Aid; Sub-   Craig Perkins
      Committee on Mediation
      and Assessments

– The first research project to evaluate the cost-effectiveness and social benefits of mediation services for legally aided clients.

(16) Family Mediation Canada   Howard Irving   1984
      Toronto, Ontario   Audrey Devlin

– The first national mediation association in Canada, with representatives from every province. Established by the Department of Justice.

(17) Code of Professional   Barbara Irving*   1986
      Conduct
      Ontario Association for
      Family Mediation

   – The first code of conduct for family mediators established in Canada.
   *(Chairperson, Standards and Ethics Committee: OAFM.)

Note: The data cited are the authors' best estimates of when significant developments in mediation occurred. The list does not presume to be complete, but rather is a list of highlights in family mediation across North America.

D. PROVINCIAL MEDIATION ASSOCIATIONS IN CANADA

	Organization	Developers	Year
(1)	Ontario Association for Family Mediation (OAFM) Toronto, Ontario	John Goodwin Mario Bartoletti Ellen Macdonald	1982
(2)	Alberta Arbitration and Mediation Society Edmonton, Alberta	David G. Elliott William Geddes Nanette Moreau	1982
(3)	Alberta Family Mediation Society Edmonton, Alberta	Renee Cochard Kent Taylor	1983
(4)	Mediation Association of British Columbia Victoria, B.C.	Catherine Scambler Andrew Pirie Dinah Stanley Jerry McHale	1985

(5)	Family Mediation Association of New Brunswick Moncton, N.B.	Louis Richard	1985
(6)	Ass'n de Mediation Familiale de Quebec	Linda Berube Audrey Wise Andre Murray	1985
(7)	Nova Scotia Association for Divorce and Family Mediation	Susannah Starnes	1986
(8)	Yukon Public Legal Education Association Mediation Committee	Steven Smyth Lynn Gaudet Trish Archibald	1986
(9)	Family Mediation Newfoundland and Labrador	Rick Morris Rick Browning Dennis McKay	1985
(10)	Family Mediation Manitoba	Justice A.C. Hamilton Shirley Smith Marta Smith	1987
(11)	Family Mediation Saskatchewan	Daniel L. Hamoline Francine D'Aoust Elaine Lund	1986

ANNOTATED BIBLIOGRAPHY

Abella, Judge R. "Procedural Aspects of Arrangements for Children Upon Divorce." (1983), 61 *Canadian Bar Review* 443. This article examines the present adversarial system and recommends non-adversarial refinements to the present process, such as pre-trials, mediation, expert assessments and independent legal representation for children for the adjudication of custody and access disputes.

Bartoletti, M. "Separation: Perspective on the Couple, the Counselor and the Lawyer." (1974), 17 *The Single Parent Journal* 4. This paper describes the procedures developed for helping separating couples to mediate all issues and arrive at an interim separation memorandum.

Bartoletti, M., Bourke, P., and Macdonald, E. M. "The Supportive Separation System: A Joint Legal and Marital Counselling Alternative." In *Therapy with Remarriage Families,* edited by L. Messinger. Rockville: Aspen Publications, 1982. In this chapter, the authors (trained respectively in psychology, social work and law) present a collaborative approach to comprehensive mediation within a private practice setting.

Breuer, J., and Freud, S. *Studies on Hysteria.* New York: Basic Books, 1957. This work represents the cornerstone of modern psychoanalytic theory. Translated with the collaboration of Anna Freud.

Brown, D. "Divorce in Family Mediation: A History, Review, Future Directions." (1982), 20 *Conciliation Courts Review* 1. This article outlines the history of the divorce mediation movement and discusses significant issues in the mediation process.

Camozzi, D. "Divorce Mediation: A Perspective From Quebec." (1985), 11 *Therapy Now* 20. This article looks at the history of mediation in Quebec.

Chalke, D. "Family Mediation in British Columbia: A Struggle to Get Out of the Starting Gate." (1985), 11 *Therapy Now* 22. This article examines the history of mediation of family disputes in British Columbia.

Coogler, O. J. *Structured Mediation and Divorce Settlement: A Handbook for Marital Mediators.* Toronto: D. C. Heath & Co., 1978. This was the first major textbook on family mediation and outlines the author's procedure known as *structured mediation.*

Elkin, M. "Conciliation Counseling: A Moral and Ethical Responsibility of Conciliation and Family Courts." (1981), 19 *Conciliation Courts Review* III. A description of conciliation counselling with separating couples.

Evans, B. "Volunteer Court Conciliation Services: A Dream Becomes Reality in Durham Region, Ontario." (1985), 11 *Therapy Now* 16. This article describes the court conciliation services in Durham Region, Ontario.

Folberg, J. "A Mediation Overview: History and Dimensions of Practice." (1983), 1 *Mediation Quarterly* 1. This article sets out the evolution of mediation and its use as a tool for resolving neighbourhood and intra-family disputes in different cultural groups.

Folberg, J., and Taylor, A. *Mediation: A Comprehensive Guide to Resolving Conflicts Without Litigation.* San Francisco: Jossey-Bass Publishers, 1984. The first chapter of this excellent book on mediation contains a discussion of the development of mediation, what mediation means and what the objectives of the mediation process are.

Haley, J. *Strategies of Psychotherapy.* New York: Grune & Stratton, 1963. The author's insights from communication analysis are used to discover the common factors in various forms of psychotherapy.

Haley, J. *Problem-Solving Therapy.* San Francisco: Jossey-Bass Publishers, 1976. This book explores the author's communication systems approach to family therapy.

Haley, J., and Hoffman, L. *Techniques of Family Therapy.* New York: Basic Books, 1969. A collection of papers by the pioneer family therapists of the 1960s and 1970s.

Haynes, J. M. *Divorce Mediation: A Practical Guide for Therapists and Counsellors.* New York: Springer Publishing Company, 1981. The author presents a description of his model of mediation designed for clinicians practising mediation.

Irving, H. *Divorce Mediation.* Toronto: Personal Library, 1980. The first text on mediation published in Canada. It presents the results of a court-related mediation project directed by the author.

Irving, H. "Family Mediation — Coming of Age." (1985), 11 *Therapy Now* 7. The author explores the history of family mediation in Canada.

Jones, E. *The Life and Work of Sigmund Freud.* 3 vols. New York: Basic Books, 1957. A comprehensive biography of Freud based upon interviews with the famed psychoanalyst's family and access to many thousands of private letters and unpublished records.

Lemmon, J. A. *Family Mediation Practice.* New York: Macmillan Publishing Inc., 1985. A guide to mediation within a variety of family and marriage scenarios, including conflicts that may occur at different stages of the family life cycle.

McIsaac, H. "Mandatory Conciliation, Custody/Visitation Matters." (1981), 19 *Conciliation Courts Review* 73. This is an in-depth review of

California's mandatory mediation law and how the Los Angeles Conciliation Court functions within that legislation.

McWhinney, R. "Family Mediation in Ontario: Origins and Development." (1985), 11 *Therapy Now* 18. This article traces the history of family mediation in Ontario.

Messinger, L. *Remarriage: A Family Affair.* New York: Plenum Press, 1984. The author considers "the new American extended family" and presents a refreshing and sensible account of the complex issues facing partners marrying for the second or third time.

Minookin, R., and Kornhauser, L. "Bargaining in the Shadow of the Law: The Case of Divorce." (1979), 88 *Yale Law Journal* 950. This thought-provoking article discusses the role of law in the private settlement of legal disputes and presents the arguments in favour of "private ordering" of dispute resolution over the results of litigation for family law matters.

Minuchin, S. *Families and Family Therapy.* Massachusetts: Harvard University Press, 1974. This is an excellent text, which presents the author's strategies for using a family systems approach.

Moreno, J. L., ed. *International Handbook of Group Psychotherapy.* New York: Philosophical Library, 1966. This book provides a thorough historical review of the development of group psychotherapy internationally from its inception to the mid-1960s.

Payne, J. "Aspects of Mediation: Mediation in Canada and the United States." (1985), 11 *Therapy Now* 4. This article examines the evolution of conciliation and mediation as methods of dispute resolution in both Canada and the United States.

Rogers, C. *Client-Centred Therapy.* Boston: Houghton-Mifflin Company, 1951. This book is the most complete text written by Rogers on non-directive client-centred therapy.

Saposnek, D. *Mediating Child Custody Disputes.* San Francisco: Jossey-Bass Publishers, 1983. This book is a practical and comprehensive approach to the resolution of child custody disputes.

Satir, V. *Conjoint Family Therapy.* Rev. ed. California: Science and Behavior Books, Inc., 1967. This book makes a very important contribution to marital therapy and was one of the earliest books advocating that marital and family problems be dealt with conjointly rather than individually. The book contains a number of strategies for dealing with marital problems.

Sullivan, H. S. *The Interpersonal Theory of Psychiatry.* New York: W.W. Norton & Co., 1953. This book contains a systematic presentation of

Sullivan's theory, which emphasized the importance of broad social factors in mental health and mental disease.

VanDuzer, Judge J. "Mediation: A View from the Unified Family Court, Hamilton, Ontario." (1985), 11 *Therapy Now* 24. The author describes the mediation services offered by the Unified Family Court in Hamilton, Ontario.

Wallerstein, J. S. "Children of Divorce: The Psychological Tasks of the Child." (1983), 53 *American Journal of Orthopsychiatry* 230. This paper discusses the major coping tasks faced by children who are experiencing parental separation and divorce.

Wells, J. G., ed. *Current Issues in Marriage and the Family.* New York: Macmillan Publishing Co. Inc., 1979. The editor presents a variety of papers on such current issues as marriage vs. cohabitation, monogamy and marital fidelity, divorce reform and the future of the North American family.

Whitaker, C. "The Growing Edge." In *Techniques of Family Therapy.* New York: Basic Books, 1969. A graphic description of the author's "administrative battle", that is, the interface between the family and the therapy team over responsibility for movement in family therapy.

Chapter Two

Dispute Resolution: Alternative Methods

A. METHODS OF DISPUTE RESOLUTION

(1) NON-ADVERSARIAL METHODS

There are many methods for resolving conflict. Some methods are distinguished by their non-adversarial nature. Clients may be involved with more than one method; therefore, it is important to understand the range of options available for non-adversarial dispute resolution. This information is helpful in advising clients about the most appropriate method(s) for their particular situation.

(a) Counselling

Counselling is a process whereby clients are assisted in dealing with their personal and interpersonal emotional conflicts. The approach used will depend upon the theoretical orientation of the counsellor. It may be brief or long-term, depending upon the severity of the problem and the commitment of the client. Counselling is intended to assist clients in learning and applying improved problem-solving techniques.

- *Individual counselling* is a process whereby the client is seen alone for one or more of a variety of problems.
- *Marital counselling* is a process whereby a couple is seen together, in most instances. The emphasis is usually on communication and relationship difficulties between the two partners.
- *Reconciliation counselling* is a process whereby the counsellor sees the couple together, although some individual sessions may be needed. The emphasis is on helping them to re-establish communication and trust after an intense conflict. Often, separation has been either contemplated or attempted for a brief period.
- *Separation counselling* is a process whereby the partners may be seen individually, together, or both. The emphasis is on helping each

19

person through a re-positioning process from living together to living apart. The sessions identify the partner initiating separation and the partner responding to that initiative and then provide appropriate supportive intervention. Provision of information about mediation is usually made available during the latter stages.

(b) Conciliation

Conciliation is a process whereby separating partners are helped to deal with their issues in a non-adversarial manner. Conciliation is a term that is often used to refer to a court-based service.

(c) Mediation

Mediation is a process whereby an impartial third party is retained to effect a resolution of issues between two or more disputants. There are several important elements in mediation:

- It is a voluntary, non-judgmental process.
- If the parties reach an agreement, then there will not be conclusions or recommendations from the mediator as part of the written report.
- All agreements in mediation arise from the parties to mediation themselves.
- If the parties fail to reach an agreement, then it will be so stated in the written report, which may include further steps recommended by the mediator.

With specific reference to separation and divorce, *family mediation* is a voluntary procedure that offers four major advantages to the couple:

- The whole decision process remains in the hands of the two parties, who best know their needs and resources and those of their children.
- The parties can avoid the trial process, which is often traumatic to both the parents and their children, as well as their extended family.
- Mediated settlements generally work better and are more stable than court-ordered dispositions.
- Parties who have succeeded in reaching resolutions once are more likely to deal successfully with differences that develop later.

There are two basic forms of family mediation that separating partners may choose, *open* or *closed*. There are some essential differences between the two:

(i) Closed Mediation

With closed mediation:

- The mediator's report includes only the issues that the parties themselves have resolved.

- If the parties fail to obtain a resolution on one or more issues, then the mediator's report will contain a description of where agreement was reached, as well as a statement specifying which issues remain unresolved.
- All other information disclosed to the mediator remains confidential and unreported (with the exception of child abuse data).

(ii) Open Mediation

With open mediation:

- The mediator's report may include any information that is considered relevant to the issues being mediated.
- If there is a resolution of the issues, the report will usually be restricted to a description of the agreement reached.

In choosing between open and closed mediation, the parties will want to consider the following factors:

- Some mediators restrict their practice to either open or closed mediation.
- With closed mediation, there is an assumption that the total confidentiality of the process may make the parties less apprehensive about disclosing personal information. (That impression is not supported by research at the present time.)
- With open mediation, if the process breaks down and an assessment is required, the disclosed information can be used. That eliminates the need to commence a new process from the beginning, which is a saving of time, money and effort.

There are several common ways in which parties are referred to mediation. The following is a listing of the more frequent sources of referral:

- *Self-referral* is a process whereby a couple comes voluntarily into mediation, usually as the result of recommendations by family or friends, or in response to the media. Within this referral source, it is not uncommon for the couple to be assisted through a resolution of all the issues pertaining to their separation.
- *Referral by lawyer(s)* is a process whereby both lawyers and their clients agree on mediation to resolve specific issues. Most often, those issues are the custody of, residency for and access to the couple's children, but financial and property issues may also be mediated.
- *Referral by mental health professional(s)* is a process whereby family physicians, psychiatrists, social workers or family counsellors recommend a couple into mediation to resolve any issues related to a decision to separate or divorce.

The marriage or family counsellor may refer the couple to another professional for mediation or, if the counsellor is a trained mediator, may ask both parties if they wish to continue with the counsellor as the mediator. This option provides several advantages:

- The parties remain with the same professional throughout the whole process of marriage counselling, separation counselling and mediation.
- It thus facilitates the emotional transitions being experienced by both parties.

There are cautions that need to be considered, however. This process should be undertaken only if the parties have discussed the option of mediation at the outset with the counsellor and confirm in writing that they accept the change in professional role. Please note that it is inappropriate for the mediator to provide personal counselling to either partner during or after mediation.

(d) Arbitration

Arbitration is a process whereby a neutral third party who is agreeable to both sides functions in a quasi-judicial capacity. It differs from mediation in that decisions may be made by the neutral party on behalf of the disputants. In binding arbitration, the decisions and recommendations of the arbitrator are final and cannot be appealed.

(2) ADVERSARIAL METHODS

There are also adversarial methods for resolving conflict that are supported and practised in society:

(a) Litigation

Litigation is a process whereby the judicial process is used to arrive at a legal resolution of the differences between the opposing parties (or litigants). There is a growing set of opinions and body of evidence indicating that litigation should be used only as a last resort for resolving family disputes. Recent legislation is supportive of that view.

(b) Custody-Access Assessment

Custody-access assessment is a process whereby a trained professional prepares a report about the parenting arrangements that may best meet the child's needs, given the capabilities of the parents. Information is obtained through a variety of sources, and recommendations are then made for a parenting plan that is seen to be in the best interests of the child. If the parties and both counsel agree, the assessor should attempt mediation at the outset of the process.

Note: *Negotiation* is a bargaining process that can be utilized in any of the non-adversarial or adversarial methods of conflict resolution. It basically involves the exchange of something by one of the parties in return for something else by the other party, which both perceive to be fair and equal.

Negotiation can occur between the parties, or between their counsel, with or without the assistance of an intermediary. It may occur face-to-face, by letter or by telephone, and is frequently applied to resolve a broad range of deadlocks.

(3) COURT-ORDERED METHODS

Either party may apply to the court for an order appointing a mediator or an assessor.

(a) Court-Ordered Mediation

(i) The Ontario Children's Law Reform Act

Legislation in Ontario provides for court-ordered mediation upon the consent of the parties.

- In Ontario, mediation with respect to custody and access disputes can be ordered under the *Children's Law Reform Act,* R.S.O. 1980, c. 68, s. 31 (en. 1982, c. 20, s. 1).
- Section 31 provides as follows:

  31(1) Upon an application for custody of or access to a child, the court, at the request of the parties, by order may appoint a person selected by the parties to mediate any matter specified in the order.

- The mediator must consent to being appointed and must agree to file a report with the court within a time period specified by the court.
- Before beginning the mediation, the parties must decide whether they wish:
  open mediation or
  closed mediation.
- The mediator shall file his or her report with the clerk or registrar of the court and the clerk or registrar shall give a copy of the report to each of the parties and to any counsel representing the child.
- If the parties have agreed to closed mediation, then evidence of anything said or of any admission or communication made in the course of the mediation is not admissible in any proceeding except with the consent of all parties to the proceeding in which the mediation order was made.
- The court shall require the parties to pay the fees and expenses of the mediator and shall set out in the order the proportions to be paid by each party.

(ii) The Ontario Family Law Act, 1986

Section 3 of the revised *Family Law Act, 1986*, S.O. 1986, c. 4 permits the court to order mediation on the consent of the parties for resolving disputes involving property division, child and spousal support and custody of and access to children. The provisions of this statute are similar to the court-ordered mediation under s. 31 of the *Children's Law Reform Act*, as described above. That is, mediation is only ordered on the consent of the parties and when the parties agree on a mediator.

(iii) The Manitoba Queen's Bench Act

The rules of the Unified Family Court in Manitoba permit the court to order mandatory mediation with respect to any of the issues in dispute. Section 52(4) (re-en. 1984-85, c. 3, s. 3) states as follows:

> 52(4) Where a judge or a master considers that an effort should be made to resolve any issue otherwise than at a formal trial, he may, at any stage of the proceedings, refer the issue to a conciliation officer or to any other person agreed to and engaged by the parties.

Section 52(5) (re-en. 1982-83-84, c. 81, s. 4) sets out the duties of the conciliation officer, namely:

> 52(5) Where an issue is referred for conciliation, the conciliation officer, with the assistance of such other conciliation officers, or a judge, as may be required, shall attempt to resolve the issue but where the conciliation officer concludes that a settlement cannot be reached, he shall report that the case is ready for trial.

In Manitoba, the legislation provides for closed mediation, unless the parties otherwise consent. That is, s. 52(6) (re-en. 1982-83-84, c. 81, s. 4) states:

> 52(6) Unless the parties otherwise agree, no conciliation officer or other person who renders services to a person pursuant to subsection (4)
>   (*a*) is competent to give evidence in respect of
>   (i)   written or oral statements made to him by any party during the provision of the services,
>   (ii) knowledge or information acquired during the provision of the services; or
>   (*b*) shall be required to produce any written statement mentioned in subclause (*a*)(i) at a trial, hearing or other proceeding.

- It would appear that legislation in Manitoba does not even permit the conciliation officer to submit a report if a settlement is reached, unless the parties consent to such a report being prepared and submitted to the court.
- There is no provision in the legislation with respect to an order for payment of the mediator's services.

(iv) The British Columbia Family Relations Act

The *Family Relations Act,* R.S.B.C. 1979, c. 121, of British Columbia permits the court to appoint a family court counsellor for the purpose of resolving family law issues that are in dispute.

- The family court counsellor is authorized under the legislation to offer the parties to the dispute any advice and guidance that he or she believes will assist in resolving the dispute.
- In British Columbia, the *Family Relations Act* protects information from disclosure in mediation cases unless the parties consent otherwise. That is, s. 3(3) states:

> 3(3) Subject to the law of Canada, where
>> (*a*) a family court counsellor receives under subsection (2) evidence, information or a communication in confidence from a person who is a party to the proceeding, or from a child; and
>> (*b*) the person who gave the evidence, information or communication to the family court counsellor under subsection (2) does not consent to the family court counsellor disclosing the evidence, information or communication,
>
> the family court counsellor shall not disclose the evidence, information or communication in a proceeding in a court or tribunal, and no person shall examine him for the purpose of compelling him to disclose that evidence, information or communication.

The British Columbia *Family Relations Act* does not provide for an order for payment of fees, and a report cannot be prepared, even if a settlement has been reached, unless the parties consent.

(b) Court-Ordered Assessments

(i) The Ontario Children's Law Reform Act

In cases where either the parties themselves or the court wishes an assessment in relation to custody of or access to children, the court may order a custody assessment pursuant to s. 30 (en. 1982, c. 20, s. 1) of the *Children's Law Reform Act.* The parties may agree that open mediation be attempted at the outset of the assessment. This can be made part of the court order.

The provisions of s. 30 are as follows:

> 30(1) The court before which an application is brought in respect of custody of or access to a child, by order, may appoint a person who has technical or professional skill to assess and report to the court on the needs of the child and the ability and willingness of the parties or any of them to satisfy the needs of the child.

- Where possible, the court will appoint a person who is agreed upon by the parties, but if the parties are not able to agree on an assessor, the court will choose and appoint a qualified person.
- The assessor must consent to carry out the assessment and to report to the court within a specified time period.

- The court has the power to order the parties, the child and any other person who has been given notice of the order for assessment to participate in the assessment.
- In the event that one or more of the persons who have been ordered to participate in the assessment refuses to participate, the court may draw a negative inference with respect to the ability and willingness of any person to satisfy the needs of the child. That is, a judge may order an assessment to be performed without the consent of one or both parties.
- The assessor may begin the assessment process by attempting to mediate the custody and access issues. It is not necessary to have a court order to incorporate mediation as part of the assessment process. It is the practice of many assessors to try to reach a mediated solution, that is, one that the parties agree to voluntarily, before preparing an assessment report with their own recommendations.
- The assessor is required to file his or her report with the clerk or registrar of the court and the clerk or registrar must give a copy of the report to each of the parties and to any counsel representing the child.
- The assessor's report is admissible as evidence on the application.
- Any of the parties and counsel representing the child may require the assessor to attend as a witness at the hearing of the application.
- The court will require the parties to pay the fees and expenses of the assessor and will specify the proportion of the assessor's fees and expenses to be paid by each party.

(ii) The Manitoba Queen's Bench Act

The legislation in Manitoba permits a judge to order a family investigation with respect to the issues of custody, access or other family-related matters. In this case, the family investigator must submit a report to court.

Section 52(7) (re-en. 1982-83-84, c. 81, s. 4) sets out the court's jurisdiction as follows:

> 52(7) If a report is required for the trial of a proceeding a judge of the court may request a family investigator to interview the parties, and such others as may be necessary, to provide the court with information and opinions upon which a determination of custody, access and other family-related matters may be made.

(4) Open Mediation, Closed Mediation, and Custody Assessments

There has been considerable confusion about the essential differences between open and closed mediation and custody assessments. The following chart sets out the similarities and differences between the three procedures.

Closed Mediation	Open Mediation	Assessments
This is a non-adversarial method of dispute resolution that parties participate in voluntarily in the hope of avoiding an adversarial court proceeding.	This is a non-adversarial method of dispute resolution that parties participate in voluntarily in the hope of avoiding an adversarial court proceeding.	This is an adversarial process, in that it contemplates adversarial court proceedings and may be entered into voluntarily or by court order.
The parties in dispute meet with the mediator.*	The parties in dispute meet with the mediator.*	The parties in dispute usually meet with the assessor*.
Discussions are confidential, and it is agreed that the parties will not subpoena the mediator to court.	Discussions are not confidential, and it is agreed that the mediator can be subpoenaed by the parties to court.	Discussions are not confidential, and it is agreed that the assessor can be subpoenaed by the parties to court.
Usually no conclusions or recommendations are made by the mediator to the court.	Usually no conclusions or recommendations are made by the mediator to the court.	The assessor makes recommendations and arrives at a conclusion that may be communicated to the court.
All agreements arise from the parties themselves on a voluntary basis.	All agreements arise from the parties themselves on a voluntary basis.	There is no requirement that the parties reach an agreement.
Only the terms of an agreement or the fact that there is no agreement is disclosed.	The terms of the agreement, or the fact that there is no agreement, is disclosed, and the mediator may report on the mediation process.	The assessor puts forward recommendations for a court-ordered agreement.
The parties, and usually the children, are seen by the mediator in a combination of individual and group sessions for the purpose of assisting the	The parties, and usually the children, are seen by the mediator in a combination of individual and group sessions for the purpose of assisting the	The parties, and usually the children, are seen by the assessor in a combination of individual and group sessions. In addition, extensive investigations

Closed Mediation	Open Mediation	Assessments
parties to arrive at a mediated agreement on the parenting arrangement that is in the best interest of the children.	parties to arrive at a mediated agreement on the parenting arrangement that is the best interest of the children.	are carried out and information is collected from collateral sources, for example, visits and discussions with teachers, family doctors, other relevant professionals, etc. This information is used for the purpose of evaluating parenting capacity and helping the assessor to arrive at a recommendation.

*Some mediators prefer to begin the mediation process by meeting with each party individually prior to a joint meeting.

ANNOTATED BIBLIOGRAPHY

Bartoletti, M. "Separation Is a Time for Working Together." (1975), 1 *One Parent Family Journal* 2. A critical appraisal of a non-adversarial approach to separation using mediation compared to the traditional contested litigation process.

Corsini, R.J., ed. *Current Psychotherapies.* Itaska: F.E. Peacock Publishers, 1973. This book contains a collection of chapters written by a number of leading psychotherapists describing their theories and therapeutic approaches.

Gaughan, L.D. "Toward a Structural Theory of Family Mediation." In *Therapy With Remarriage Families,* edited by L. Messinger. Rockville: Aspen Publications, 1982.

Goldstein, J., Freud, A., and Solnit, A. *Beyond the Best Interests of the Child.* New York: Free Press, 1973.

and

Goldstein, J., Freud, A., and Solnit, A. *Before the Best Interests of the Child.* New York: Free Press, 1979. These books sparked a great deal of interest, particularly among the judiciary who were dealing with family law matters. The books contain important concepts such as the child's sense of time in custody decisions and the need to provide the least detrimental alternative. However, some of the books' recommendations have been discounted by other professionals, in particular the recommendation that the custodial parent have a controlling influence on access to the non-custodial parent.

Haley, J. *Problem-Solving Therapy.* San Francisco: Jossey-Bass Publishers, 1976. This book explores the systems approach to family therapy and contains many helpful suggestions for interviewing family members.

Keeney, B.P., ed. *Diagnosis and Assessment in Family Therapy.* Rockville: Aspen Publications, 1983. A collection of papers by some of the foremost family therapists and diagnosticians in the United States and Canada describing how to make family assessments more comprehensive.

Langsley, D., and Kaplan, D. *The Treatment of Families in Crisis.* New York: Grune & Stratton Inc., 1968.

Minuchin, S. *Families and Family Therapy.* Massachusetts: Harvard University Press, 1974.

and

Minuchin, S., and Fishman, C.H. *Family Therapy Techniques.* Massachusetts: Harvard University Press, 1981. These two books describe a number of strategies for dealing with families from a family systems approach.

Satir, V. *Conjoint Family Therapy.* Rev. ed. California: Clients and Behaviour Books Inc., 1967. This book makes a very important contribution to marital therapy and was one of the earliest books advocating that marital problems be dealt with conjointly rather than individually. The book contains a number of strategies that are useful for handling marital problems.

Shipley, A. "Custody Law Reform in Ontario: The Children's Law Reform Act." In *Children's Rights in the Practice of Family Law,* edited by B. Landau. Toronto: Carswell Publishing Co., 1986. This chapter contains a detailed discussion of the Ontario *Children's Law Reform Act* and makes special reference to the provisions with respect to mediation and assessment of custody and access cases.

Chapter Three

Mediation in Practice: Issues

A. EXPECTATIONS OF REFERRAL SOURCES

Referrals for mediation come from a variety of sources. The expectations of the referral sources are not the same. Therefore, the response of the mediator must be specific to the referral source. The following guidelines will assist the mediator in establishing a more useful and practical relationship with the referral sources:

Referral Source	Expectations
(1) Judge	(a) Confirmation from mediator of readiness to proceed with mediation.
	(b) Agreement as to date when mediator's report can be expected. (If additional time is required, the mediator will make a request in writing to the court for an extension.)
	(c) Receipt of report, by court and counsel, at least two weeks prior to the date of the hearing.
(2) Lawyer	(a) Agreement by both parties to enter into mediation. (If only one client, or lawyer, is supporting mediation, it cannot proceed.)
	(b) Confirmation from mediator of readiness to commence mediation of stated issues.
	(c) Clarification on fees regarding proportion to be paid by each party and when due.

	(d) Clarification regarding open or closed mediation.
	(e) Receipt of up-to-date copy of *curriculum vitae* from mediator.
(3) Family physician	(a) Acknowledgement confirming referral.
	(b) Feedback by letter regarding whether mediation was successful or not.
(4) Counsellor	(a) Acknowledgement confirming referral.
	(b) Clarification regarding any ongoing professional involvement by the counsellor.
	(c) Feedback by letter regarding whether mediation was successful or not.
(5) Family or friend	(a) Normally, contact from the mediator is neither required nor recommended.

Feedback to the referral source, within the guidelines suggested, is not only a professional courtesy, but also serves to educate other professionals about the mediative process. It also encourages a more co-operative approach with other professionals involved.

B. EXPECTATIONS OF CLIENTS

Expectations of the clients coming for mediation can vary greatly. There may be expectations that: mediation has as its objective reconciliation; mediation is similar to personal and marital counselling; or mediation will vindicate the position of one or the other partner through assignment of blame. It is very important that the mediator explain the purpose and function of mediation carefully to correct such misconceptions. The following issues should be covered with all clients contemplating mediation:

- The mediator is an impartial professional who will remain unaligned with both parties. (There is often a tendency by the parties to want to convert the mediator into an ally.)
- Mediation is not the same as counselling; that is, discussions will be focused on reaching a settlement of the issues in dispute.
- Mediation is not a process for venting anger or blame by one party on the other, and such verbalizing will be interrupted by the mediator.

- The time period for issues to be addressed in mediation is understood and agreed upon by both parties and their lawyers.
- The nature of the mediator's report will be determined by the issues under discussion and which type of mediation, open or closed, is being done.

C. EXPECTATIONS OF THE MEDIATOR

The mediator will want assurances on the following factors prior to commencing mediation:

- Both parties and their lawyers are agreeable to proceeding with family mediation and are satisfied with the mediator selected.
- Responsibility for payment of the mediator's fee is agreed upon.
- A decision has been made on whether the mediation will be open or closed and the implications of both types of mediation are fully understood by the parties and their lawyers.
- The mediator will be provided with full disclosure of all information pertinent to the issues in dispute.
- Permission is granted to contact or see any persons relevant to the issues under mediation.
- A mediation contract integrating the foregoing will be signed by both parties prior to commencing mediation.

D. ESTABLISHING THE MEDIATOR'S IMPARTIALITY

It is important for the mediator to be impartial and for both parties and their solicitors to see the mediator as impartial in order to accomplish the following objectives of the mediation process, namely, that the parties feel that:

- any agreement reached was reached voluntarily, that is, without duress by either party or the mediator;
- they were the prime architects of any agreement, that is, the agreement reached was their agreement;
- the agreement was fair and reasonable;
- in cases where children are involved, the agreement was in the best interests of the children;
- the agreement was reached after each party had an opportunity to explain his or her views and after full disclosure of all relevant information had been made.

Agreements reached when the mediator is not seen as impartial are:

- less likely to be implemented following the mediation process;
- less likely to be followed voluntarily;
- more likely to be questioned in the future, either in a subsequent mediation process or in a court application.

For an agreement to last and to be carried out in a spirit of co-operation, both parties must feel that the procedure and the outcome are fair and reasonable.

In addition, for a court to enforce an agreement made outside of court, the agreement must be reached voluntarily, without coercion, with full disclosure and preferably with independent legal advice.

For these reasons, it is essential that the mediator establish his or her impartiality with both clients and solicitors from the outset.

(1) ESTABLISHING IMPARTIALITY WITH THE LAWYERS

If the initial contact for mediation is made by a lawyer for one party or if both parties are represented by solicitors from the outset, the mediator should contact both solicitors, by telephone or letter, and indicate that the mediator :

- will be acting as an impartial person as between the parties;
- will help the parties to focus on the best interests of their children, if custody of or access to children is being mediated;
- will require full financial disclosure from both parties as early as possible in the mediation process, if financial matters are being mediated.

(2) ESTABLISHING IMPARTIALITY WITH CLIENTS

In some cases the clients will contact the mediator directly. One or both parties may not as yet be represented by solicitors.

If the initial telephone call is from a client, the mediator should indicate at the outset that he or she will be acting in an impartial manner as between the two parties. To ensure this impartiality the mediator should explain that:

- The mediator will act as a facilitator, that is, an impartial person who is helping the parties arrive at their own voluntary settlement of the issues in dispute. The mediator is not acting as a judge, but rather hopes that the parties will reach their own solution.
- The mediator will place a call to the other party following this initial telephone conversation.
- The mediator will call the solicitor for one or both of the parties if solicitors have been retained.
- The mediator will discourage any discussion of the client's position or any detailed description of the case until the initial interview (either held with the parties together or with the parties individually).
- Both parties will have an opportunity to explain their position to the mediator in either joint or individual sessions and will have an opportunity to respond to any allegations or issues raised by the other party.

It is important that the mediator maintain his or her impartiality and not mislead either client into believing that the mediator will be his or her ally.

To ensure that the clients see the mediator as impartial, it may be desirable to meet with both clients together initially. Some mediators prefer to meet with the clients individually first, and if this is the case, the mediator should explain carefully to both clients that this does not suggest a preference for either client. The mediator could ask the parties to suggest which party should be seen first, in order to avoid the appearance of partiality.

Whether the parties are seen together initially or separately, if children are an issue, the mediator should help both parties to focus on the best interests of the children, rather than each party's individual interests.

If financial matters are an issue, then the mediator should encourage each party to give prompt and full financial disclosure to the other. Both parties should be encouraged to be fair and reasonable in their proposals with respect to support or division of property, on the basis that a fair settlement is more likely to last and to lead to less litigation in the future.

The mediator should explain to both parties that:

- There will be open communication with both parties. The mediator will not have a confidential relationship with either of the parties and may in fact share whatever information the mediator feels is relevant with either party. If serious allegations are made that could affect the welfare of the children, this information will be shared with both parents and will likely be discussed with the child protection authorities. This is an example of the mediator's impartiality and underlines the mediator's concern for the best interests of the children. The parties should be told that the mediator has a statutory duty to report all cases of alleged child abuse to the appropriate child protection agency.
- He or she will be seeing both clients for approximately equal periods of time. If there is a valid reason why one party should be seen on more occasions than the other, this matter should be drawn to the attention of the other party, so that the mediator is not perceived as biased.
- He or she will advise both clients to get independent legal advice before signing an agreement on any of the issues resolved in mediation.

E. INTERIM ARRANGEMENTS

(1) DURING MEDIATION

It is important that the status quo be maintained, to the extent possible, during the course of the mediation to ensure fairness to both parties. In order to achieve this goal, the following steps should be taken:

- In the first meeting with counsel and/or with the parties, the mediator should help the parties come to an agreement on the specific arrangements that will prevail during the course of mediation with respect to those issues that have been sent to mediation. That is, if custody of or access to children is an issue, an interim plan should be arrived at as soon as possible in order to offer the parties and children some stability. It should be clear that whatever arrangement is agreed upon on an interim basis will not necessarily be the final arrangement, and both parties should be assured that they will have an opportunity to obtain independent legal advice prior to agreeing to even an interim plan.
- If financial matters are an issue, then parties should agree not to change their wills or beneficiaries on their life insurance policies and not to close out or make substantial withdrawals from any bank accounts or otherwise dispose of assets. That is, the parties should not dissipate or remove assets during the course of mediation in a way that would prejudice the other party without prior consultation and agreement.
- If spousal or child support are issues, an interim agreement should be reached, in consultation with the parties' solicitors. The parties should agree that these arrangements are "without prejudice" to any final agreement (see (2), "Without Prejudice").
- If the parties are still living together but want to separate, an important issue to be decided in an initial meeting may be who will live in the matrimonial home. Should both parties remain in the matrimonial home? Should the home be put up for sale? Should one party be granted interim exclusive possession? Should both parties live in the home on some alternating basis? The determination of who has exclusive possession of the matrimonial home is often a significant factor in cases where custody of or access to children is an issue. Also, the matrimonial home may be the largest or only asset of the parties, and therefore its disposition is extremely important.

The mediator should determine from both counsel and the parties whether there is a particular urgency to arrive at an interim arrangement with respect to one or more issues. These issues should be given priority in order to:

- prevent litigation during the course of the mediation process;
- build the clients' confidence in the mediation process as a method of quickly, efficiently and co-operatively dealing with issues of prime concern to the parties;
- build the confidence of counsel in the mediation process. It is important that counsel be assured that the parties will be referred to them for independent legal advice before implementing any interim arrangements.

Interim arrangements are extremely useful in that they allow the parties and the mediator to try out and evaluate possible alternative arrangements. Parties often decide to try an interim arrangement and evaluate it with the assistance of the mediator before coming to a final agreement, particularly in cases where:

- the parties have not as yet separated or have separated only recently and therefore have not had experience with alternative solutions to their difficulties;
- the parties are highly suspicious of each other and do not trust each other enough to come to a final decision without some trial period;
- one or more issues are in dispute and the resolution of one key issue affects the others. For example, if custody of and access to children, possession of the matrimonial home, support and division of property are all in issue, it may be essential to resolve the question of custody of and access to children before the other issues can be satisfactorily dealt with. In such a case, the parties may wish to try out one or more parenting plans before coming to a final decision on the other matters.

If an interim plan is being considered, the mediator and the parties should work out in advance the objective criteria that are going to be used to evaluate the arrangement. A time limit should also be set, at which point the arrangements should be reviewed.

In addition, the mediator and the parties should agree on the consequences in the event that one or both parties fail to live up to the terms of the interim agreement.

The parties should agree that either party can return the issue to mediation prior to the review date if he or she has some serious concerns.

(2) WITHOUT PREJUDICE

The term *without prejudice* is usually used to refer to an agreement that is privileged or confidential. It also carries the implication that an agreement will not be detrimental to the rights of either party. It is important for the mediator to explain to both parties that it is not really possible to have a "without prejudice" agreement in mediation. That is, any interim arrangements that are arrived at by the parties will affect the parties' positions at the end of mediation, particularly if mediation fails and the matter is returned to court.

For example, if custody of or access to children is an issue and if the parties have not as yet separated, it may be determined that it is in the children's best interests and even the spouses' best interests for a separation to occur (for example, if there is continual bickering or physical violence in the home). However, if the children remain in the home, the spouse who leaves will be at a disadvantage with respect to custody of the children and exclusive possession of the matrimonial home. Any arrangement whereby one parent has *de facto* custody of the children and the other parent is absent from the matrimonial home is prejudicial to the absent parent, at least in a court of law. This would be particularly true if the *de facto* custody arrangement continued for some period of time, for example, during the mediation process, and then if mediation failed, until a court date could be arranged.

An arrangement concerning interim spousal support or interim child support could also be used to the detriment of the payor spouse in a later court proceeding. That is, it could be raised in evidence that one party did have sufficient funds to provide support or was willing at one point to provide support, and this might be used as a precedent for a subsequent order.

The important point is that the mediator should not mislead the parties by indicating that interim arrangements are really "without prejudice" in terms of their legal consequences. The mediator should recommend that the parties obtain independent legal advice on the likely effect of their proposed interim arrangements prior to entering into them. Also, any interim agreement should state that the specific terms are intended to be without prejudice to any subsequent agreement and will not be referred to in case of subsequent litigation.

In most cases, an important factor is the amount of time that an arrangement is in effect. For this reason, the mediator should attempt to deal with each mediation case as quickly as possible and should attempt to preserve the status quo on all issues to the extent that this is possible during the mediation process.

The mediator should ask both counsel and both parties to agree that there will be no further court proceedings during the course of mediation with respect to those issues that have been sent to mediation. The mediator in turn should assure counsel that if an urgent situation arises that would ordinarily be dealt with through litigation, the mediator will agree to meet with both parties and, if necessary, the lawyers, immediately, in order to deal with the particular crisis. If the crisis is not resolved through mediation, then the lawyers may have to take legal action. This may mean that mediation will be temporarily suspended or permanently ended.

F. RESPECTIVE RESPONSIBILITIES

With the strong emergence of family mediation as a viable alternative to court-imposed settlement during the past two decades, there has developed some corresponding confusion about the specific roles and responsibilities of the mediator, the lawyer, the clients, and others. The following guidelines clarify the responsibilities of each of the participants in the mediation process:

Participant	Responsibilities
(1) The lawyer will:	(a) Describe the mediation process to the client.
	(b) Obtain consent of client to proceed with mediation preparations.
	(c) Contact the lawyer of the other spouse to suggest mediation.
	(d) Ensure that both spouses are provided with a selection of qualified mediators, if the spouse's lawyer agrees to mediation. (Clients and lawyers both may suggest mediators for consideration.)
	(e) Arrange for the mediator to be contacted by one of the lawyers once a selection has been made. (A three-way meeting of both lawyers and the mediator is usually set up prior to the mediator's contact with the clients.)
	(f) Ensure that an up-to-date *curriculum vitae* is distributed to both lawyers prior to the commencement of mediation.
	(g) Clarify the parameters for mediation, i.e., establish which issues are to be part of the mediation process and which are excluded.
	(h) Agree upon a time limit for the mediation process, as well as the arrangements for the payment of mediator's fee.
	(i) Monitor the progress of mediation with client and mediator.
(2) The court will:	(a) Ensure that both spouses are aware of the option of mediation during pretrial procedures.
	(b) Encourage mediation if it has not been attempted.
	(c) Order open or closed mediation, if the parties agree, with a medi-

ator who is selected on consent of both parties.

(d) Support mediated resolutions as drawn up in minutes of settlement.

(e) Make an order for the payment of fees.

(3) The counsellor will:

(a) Discuss mediation with any client(s) contemplating separation or divorce.

(b) Provide client(s) with a list of qualified mediators to contact.

(c) Assist in the referral process to better ensure that the couple has at least an initial agreed-upon session with the mediator.

(d) Follow up with the couple to check on progress within first month. (If mediation has broken down, the counsellor will attempt a renewed effort with same or alternative mediator.)

(4) The client will:

(a) Commit to a specified mediator (acceptable to both spouses).

(b) Agree upon issues needing mediation and the payment of the mediator's fee.

(c) Work conscientiously to negotiate an agreement within the time period agreed upon.

(d) Attend scheduled mediation sessions.

(e) Remain task oriented.

(f) Avoid angry, disparaging remarks directed at spouse.

(g) Put agreed-upon procedures into operation during the mediation process.

(h) Follow through with spouse on resolutions, once agreement has been signed.

(i) Agree to return to mediation in case of future disputes, rather than initiate litigation.

(5) The mediator will:

(a) Contact both lawyers by telephone and arrange a conjoint meeting with them as soon as his or her selection as mediator is confirmed.

(b) Establish during the meeting the respective responsibilities of all professionals involved, the issues to be mediated, and the time limit agreeable to both parties.

(c) Provide up-to-date copies of *curriculum vitae* for lawyers, with extra copies for both parties.

(d) Contact the clients and commence proceedings for first appointment with mediator.

(e) Meet with both clients (individually or conjointly) to confirm mediation contract, i.e., including all factors previously agreed upon with both lawyers. (Copies of signed contract should be given to both clients and both lawyers.)

(f) Establish regular mediation sessions convenient to both clients.

(g) Inform both lawyers of progress by telephone or letter.

(h) Contact lawyers immediately, should any difficulties develop that interrupt mediation.

(i) Submit copy of mediator's report (of issues resolved and unresolved) to both lawyers and both clients.

(j) Co-operate with both parties to draft minutes of settlement (if requested).

Mediation is an entirely different process from litigation in that the outcome is primarily the responsibility of the two parties rather than that of their respective lawyers or the judge. It is the couple who is in charge of the process as long as mediation is in progress. The following are some of the differences between mediation and litigation:

- Only the two parties themselves can decide to commence mediation and to continue the process until an agreement is reached.
- After the mediator, the lawyers and the court have completed their work, the two parties have the ultimate responsibility for carrying out any agreement made between them and for avoiding future conflict. Therefore, it is essential that both the lawyers and the mediator permit and encourage the clients to take charge of making the decisions that will be affecting their lives and those of their children.
- The parties may have priorities that are not made apparent to the lawyer and that differ from legal entitlements. Therefore, in mediation the parties can reach an agreement that is very different from what a court might otherwise impose.
- The parties are more likely to follow through on settlements they have negotiated directly than on those imposed by the court.

G. RESPECTIVE CONCERNS

The issues of responsibility and power are directly related to a variety of concerns. Some of the more common concerns are listed among the following:

Participant	Concerns
(1) The lawyer(s)	(a) The mediator may fail to keep counsel informed of progress.
	(b) The client may be placed in a vulnerable position vis-à-vis the spouse.
	(c) Agreeing not to litigate issues under mediation could reinforce the status quo.
	(d) The client may be induced to make too many concessions in the effort to reach resolution.
	(e) The time elapsed in mediation may prejudice the client in subsequent litigation.
	(f) The mediator may have unknown biases on issues relevant to the mediation.
(2) The client	(a) The mediation process will not provide the protection provided by legal counsel.

(b) The other spouse may become intimidating in the neutral atmosphere of mediation.

(c) Dealing directly with the spouse may continue conflict and increase personal stress.

(d) Mediating with the spouse may create false hopes about a possible reconciliation.

(3) The mediator

(a) Litigating of other issues may impact negatively on mediation.

(b) Being pressured to achieve a resolution too quickly could result in a less stable agreement.

(c) Worrying about the unilateral withdrawal of a spouse from mediation, which could result in litigation.

(d) Losing the support of one of the lawyers, which would undermine the mediation process.

(e) Encountering parental sensitivities, which may block the effective involvement of the children in the mediative process.

(f) Wondering if the trust and co-operation built up between the parties during mediation will be weakened when they return to their lawyers for resolution of issues other than those in mediation.

(g) Worrying about how well the resolutions will function over the long term.

H. TERMINATION

Mediation can be terminated only by the clients (parties) or the mediator, but not by the lawyers.

- The lawyer may advise the client to terminate mediation, or raise concerns with the mediator. However, the actual decision to terminate rests with the client(s) or the mediator.

- With court-ordered mediation, it would be necessary to return to court to have the original order withdrawn or terminated by the judge. (When mediation is terminated, the judge may decide to order an assessment or family investigation.)

There are a number of reasons why the clients or the mediator may wish to terminate mediation, or the lawyer(s) may advise such termination. Refer to Chapter Nine for a complete development of the termination process.

ANNOTATED BIBLIOGRAPHY

Bartoletti, M., ed. "Family Mediation in Canada." (1985), 11 *Therapy Now Journal* (No. 1). This special issue of the journal was devoted to articles about the most recent developments in family mediation across Canada.

Coogler, O.J. *Structured Mediation and Divorce Settlement: A Handbook for Marital Mediators.* Toronto: Lexington Books, D.C. Heath & Co., 1978. See particularly chapter 3, "How Structured Mediation Works" and chapter 4, "Marital Mediation Procedure," page 23. This is the first major textbook on mediation and outlines the procedure followed in what is known as *structured mediation.*

Fisher, R., and Ury, W. *Getting to Yes: Negotiating Agreement Without Giving In.* Markham, Ontario: Penguin Books, 1981. This is an excellent book outlining a process for arriving at negotiated settlements. It has many useful concepts for the mediator.

Folberg, J., and Taylor, A. *Mediation: A Comprehensive Guide to Resolving Conflicts Without Litigation.* San Francisco: Jossey-Bass Publishers, 1984. See in particular Part Two, "Mediation Stages, Concepts and Skills," page 38. Excellent text covering the theory and practice of mediation.

Haynes, J.M. *Divorce Mediation: A Practical Guide for Therapists and Counsellors.* New York: Springer Publishing Company, 1981. See Part II, "The Mediation Process," and in particular chapter 5 "Implementing the Model," page 47. This is a very helpful book for clinicians practising mediation. It contains a description of the Haynes' model, as well as a number of case studies.

Krantzler, M. *Creative Divorce.* New York: New American Library, 1974. This is a clear, emotionally real book describing the author's own experiences with separation and divorce. This book would be helpful to couples during the transition period following separation.

Lemmon, J.A., ed. "Successful Techniques for Mediating Family Breakup." (1983), 2 *Mediation Quarterly.* This issue of the *Mediation Quarterly* contains a number of excellent articles with respect to the practice of mediation.

McIsaac, H. "Confidentiality: An Exploration of Issues" in "Making Ethical Decisions". (1985), 8 *Mediation Quarterly* 57.

McKie, D.C., Prentice, B., and Reed, P. *Divorce: Law and the Family in Canada.* Ottawa: Minister of Supply and Services, 1983. The authors provide a history of marriage and divorce in Canada, including a penetrating look at the social and legal aspects.

Saposnek, D. *Mediating Child Custody Disputes.* San Francisco: Jossey-Bass Publishers Inc., 1983. See particularly Part II, "Structuring the Mediation Process," page 44. This book would be useful for the mediation practitioner and contains a number of concrete suggestions and case examples of mediation in practice.

Shapiro, J., and Caplan, M. *Parting Sense: A Couple's Guide to Divorce Mediation.* Lutherville: Greenspring Publications, 1983. This book is designed to acquaint separating couples with the process of mediation. Many common questions are answered and a variety of sample agreement forms are described.

Chapter Four

Mediation in Practice: Procedures

While mediators tend to have similar objectives and can usually agree on basic ethical standards, they may use different procedures in their mediation process. Despite differences in the procedure followed, each step should in some way further the overall objectives of mediation, namely:

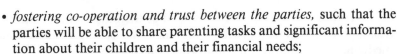

- *fostering co-operation and trust between the parties,* such that the parties will be able to share parenting tasks and significant information about their children and their financial needs;
- *improving the parties' ability to communicate,* such that they can understand each other's feelings about the marriage breakdown and share information and make necessary decisions together;
- *ensuring that all relevant parties have an opportunity to have their views heard,* such that the parties feel they have been dealt with fairly;
- *reducing tension and conflict, particularly when children are involved,* such that the children can continue to have a close relationship with both parents, free from intense conflicts of loyalty;
- *obtaining full disclosure of all relevant facts,* such that decisions are made on the basis of adequate information and after a consideration of alternative proposals for resolving the issues in dispute;
- *encouraging private ordering,* such that the parties arrive at a voluntary resolution of the issues in dispute;
- *arriving at a fair and reasonable settlement,* such that an adversarial court proceeding is avoided.

If an assessment rather than mediation has been requested, either by the court or by the parties or their counsel, many assessors follow a process that is similar to mediation process for the initial stages of the assessment. That is, with the consent of the parties, many assessors first attempt to mediate the issues in dispute in the hope that the parties can arrive at their own resolution, without the need for an adversarial court proceeding.

However, an assessment should be distinguished from mediation in that there is a greater onus on the assessor to form an objective, independent evaluation of the parties in the event that the parties fail to reach an agreement. This is also true of open mediation, where the mediator is required to prepare a report with recommendations.

Whenever the assessor or mediator must make recommendations, a more thorough process of information gathering is generally followed and additional meetings are usually arranged with persons other than the parties themselves, such as with children, nannies or other consistent caretakers, and new partners in the case of custody disputes, or accountants or property evaluators in the case of financial disputes.

Keeping in mind that mediators vary in the specific procedure followed, the following is an outline of some of the major meetings that might take place, their objectives and the procedures followed.

A. MEDIATION MEETINGS

(1) MEETING WITH COUNSEL

(a) Objectives

Where both parties are represented at the outset of mediation, it is desirable to hold a meeting with both counsel present prior to beginning the mediation to accomplish the following objectives:

- *to establish that the mediator will act impartially as between the parties.* One concern that is frequently raised is that the mediator may be biased in favour of the solicitor or client who recommended the mediator. One way of dealing with this spoken or unspoken concern is to have both solicitors meet with the mediator;
- *to build trust between the mediator and counsel.* Counsel may not have worked with a particular mediator previously and may have some questions and concerns about the mediator's experience and competence for dealing with a particular issue;
- *to build confidence in the mediation process as a method for resolving the particular issues in dispute.* Counsel need an opportunity to discuss the process their clients will follow, what will happen if one or more issues are not resolved and how the mediation process will relate to other issues that are not referred to mediation;
- *to clarify for counsel the contract with the clients.* That is, what is expected of the mediator and what the mediator expects of the clients and counsel. For example, there should be clarification about whether the mediation is open or closed, what issues are to be addressed and whether the mediator is being asked for recommendations in the event that the parties fail to reach an agreement on one or more issues;

- *to establish how the mediator's fees are to be paid.* It is usual for the clients to share the mediator's fees equally; however, if this is impossible, it is desirable to have some splitting of fees so that both parties see the mediator as impartial;
- *to obtain from counsel a summary of the history of the case.* Counsel should provide the mediator with any relevant documents, reports or correspondence. Both counsel should have copies of all materials given to the mediator;
- *to establish a co-operative atmosphere with counsel.* This is necessary to encourage counsel to support a non-adversarial approach to resolving the issues in dispute.

(b) Procedure for Meeting with Counsel

The meeting with counsel should be held in the mediator's office if possible, or if not possible, in some other neutral setting (rather than in the office of one or the other lawyer). A face-to-face meeting is preferred, but if this is not possible then a conference call could be used.

The clients are usually not invited to attend this initial meeting, because the lawyers are usually more relaxed, more willing to share information and more direct in stating their concerns if the clients are not present.

During the course of the meeting, the mediator should address the following issues:

- *determine the issues to be resolved* in the mediation process, for example, custody and access, child or spousal support, division of property or exclusive possession of the matrimonial home;
- *clarify what other issues are in dispute and how the lawyers intend to deal with them,* for example, is litigation pending on any other issue such as support at the same time, as custody and access are to be mediated;
- *clarify whether the mediation is to be open or closed;*
- *establish whether the mediator is to make recommendations* in the event that a settlement is not reached on one or more issues;
- *review with the lawyers the experience and qualifications of the mediator* for dealing with the particular issues to be mediated;
- *determine whether there are any concerns or questions with respect to the mediator's qualifications, competence or biases.* Invite discussion openly on these matters, because if they are not dealt with at this point, they could act as a hidden agenda later and result in the lawyers sabotaging any potential settlement;
- *clarify the procedure that is to be followed,* that is, whether the parties are to be seen together or separately for the initial interview;
- *determine whether there are other significant individuals who should be seen during the mediation process.* For example, if the mediation

concerns custody of or access to children, the mediator is strongly encouraged to meet with the children and determine their views, concerns and preferences at some point during the mediation process;

- *determine whether secondary sources should be contacted* (for example, other mental health professionals, such as psychologists, psychiatrists or social workers for information in relation to parenting capacity or the needs of the children, or an accountant with respect to financial status);
- *determine the time frame for the mediation.* For example, are there court dates pending? Is there a concern about the status quo in relation to either children or financial matters?;
- *explain the need for disclosure of all information* that is relevant to the issues in dispute. The mediator should indicate that he or she will determine what is relevant and will need the assistance and co-operation of counsel in ensuring that the parties recognize the need for full disclosure. If financial issues are being mediated, the mediator may ask the lawyers to assist their clients in preparing financial disclosure forms. In cases where custody of or access to children is an issue, counsel should be informed that clients will be asked to sign releases of information for schools, family doctors, mental health professionals and other sources that may have information relevant to the needs of the children or the parenting skills of the parties.

If the mediator intends to have the clients sign a contract for mediation services, then the contract should be shown to the lawyers during this meeting. It may be advisable for the mediator to obtain the signatures of the lawyers on the contract as well as those of the client, particularly if the mediator wishes counsel to guarantee the mediator's fees.

It is also useful to have the lawyers sign the contract specifying whether the mediation is open or closed. Particularly in closed mediation cases, the mediator is advised to obtain the written agreement of the solicitors not to subpoena the mediator to court in the event that mediation fails and the matter proceeds to court.

Having both the lawyers and the clients sign a written contract outlining their expectations of the mediator prevents future disputes about what the mediator is expected to do, what information the mediator will have available and how the mediator will be paid.

The mediator should explain to counsel that he or she may contact the lawyers at various stages of the mediation process in order to give them feedback on progress and if necessary to seek assistance from the lawyers in resolving a conflict. It should be made clear that the mediator will not have a confidential relationship with one solicitor, but rather will have open communication with both solicitors, and if an issue of concern arises, both solicitors will be contacted and given full information.

Note that subsequent contacts can be by telephone, by letter or by face-to-face meeting, if that is necessary. At times, it may be desirable to have a meeting of both counsel with the clients to resolve a particularly difficult issue. During such a meeting, the mediator may spend time with various combinations of persons, for example:

- with the parties alone;
- with the solicitors alone;
- with one solicitor and his or her client and then the other solicitor and his or her client; and/or
- with all of the parties together.

That is, the mediator can use a form of shuttle diplomacy or hold caucuses with various subgroups in order to resolve a particularly difficult matter. It is advisable at the end of such a meeting to draw up a statement of those issues that have been resolved and the nature of the resolution reached. In addition, any issues not resolved should be noted and a statement made as to how those issues are to be dealt with in the future. It is desirable, since both counsel are present, to have the clients sign the written statement. It should be clear that this written statement is a draft and that the clients will have an opportunity to review a more formal statement with their solicitors prior to signing a final agreement. That is, both counsel and the clients will have a further opportunity to consider any changes or refinements that need to be made. Also, any agreement reached may be in the form of an interim agreement or may deal with only one of several issues that have been sent to mediation.

During the course of mediation, the parties may ask the mediator to discuss issues that were not part of the original mediation contract. For example, if the parties have been discussing custody of or access to children, the parties may also wish to discuss exclusive possession of the matrimonial home and possibly support. Usually this occurs in cases where the mediation has been successful in establishing a co-operative atmosphere and in building trust between the parties. The lawyers should be assured that the mediator will not deal with issues that have not been agreed upon without first contacting the lawyers and obtaining their approval. It would be advisable to confirm any changes to the original agreement in a letter sent to both counsel and both clients.

(2) Meeting with the Parties

(a) Objectives

The mediator tries to accomplish the following general objectives in the meeting with the parties:

- *to establish that the mediator will act as an impartial person* as between the parties;

- *to develop trust and co-operation* between the parties;
- *to improve communication* between the parties;
- *to reduce tension* and help the parties develop more constructive ways of dealing with conflict (this is particularly important if children are involved).

In the event that custody of or access to children is an issue, the mediator attempts to fulfill these additional objectives:

- *to help the parties appreciate that their parenting role will continue,* even though their spousal role may end;
- *to help the parents appreciate the importance to the children of co-operating* in their parenting role;
- *to provide the parties with information about the effects of separation and divorce on children;*
- *to obtain a relevant marital history, family history* and a description of the extent to which parenting tasks were shared during the marriage;
- *to educate the parents with respect to options available under the law for resolving custody and access issues* (that is, for sharing parental responsibilities such as sole custody arrangements and joint custody arrangements);
- *to determine other relevant sources of information with respect to the children's needs and the parenting capacity of each parent* (for example, other primary caretakers such as nannies, new partners, members of the extended family, schoolteachers and family doctors). Preference should be given to individuals with direct, frequent and family long-term contact, especially if they have been involved in an impartial capacity with the family.

If financial matters are at issue, the mediator tries to meet the following objectives:

- *to obtain full and complete financial disclosure;*
- *to obtain the names of relevant sources to contact with respect to financial matters,* for example, the family accountant or an experienced real estate appraiser;
- *to educate the parties about the general guidelines provided under the law with respect to support obligations, division of assets, debts, pensions and other financial matters.* If the mediator is not a lawyer, the clients should be referred to their independent counsel for legal information prior to commencing mediation and certainly before signing any agreement. In any event, the mediator should be careful not to give any legal advice to either party regarding the position that he or she ought to take.

(b) Procedure for Meeting with the Parties

In order to achieve these objectives, the mediator will usually need to hold several meetings, during which the parties are seen together and individually. For the first meeting, some mediators prefer to meet with both parties together and others prefer to meet with both parties individually. There are advantages and disadvantages to each approach and, of course, the mediator should take into account the particular circumstances and feelings of the parties before adopting a particular approach.

An initial meeting with both parties together has the following advantages:

- It encourages the parents to see the mediator as an impartial person.
- It decreases the suspicion and mistrust directed at both the mediator and the other party.
- It highlights the importance of communication between the parties.
- It allows the parties to hear each other's views on why the marriage broke down and to deal with unresolved emotional feelings between the parties.
- It sets the stage for dispute resolution directly between the parties.
- It sets the focus on improved communication, particularly with respect to parenting, rather than on individual positions in the conflict.

The advantages of an individual meeting are as follows:

- The parties may be more comfortable meeting the mediator alone, prior to a confrontation with the other party.
- It permits each spouse to tell his or her version of the marriage breakdown without interruption by the other spouse.
- It allows each spouse to develop rapport individually with the mediator in a less stressful environment.
- It offers an opportunity for venting emotional feelings and for obtaining individual support from the mediator prior to beginning negotiations.
- It allows the mediator to evaluate each spouse individually and determine the relative bargaining power, the attitude to reconciliation and any significant concerns or allegations about the other spouse.

Whether the initial meeting is held jointly or with the parties individually, the mediator should ensure that the parties feel relaxed and comfortable. Each party should be reassured that he or she will have an opportunity to be heard without interruption and will have an opportunity to respond to any concerns or allegations raised by the other party. If the parties are particularly anxious, it may be easier to deal with basic demographic information at the outset, rather than highly charged emotional issues.

At this meeting, the mediator should review the mediation contract:

- to ensure that there is agreement on the issues to be resolved;
- to determine whether the mediation is open or closed;
- to determine whether the mediator is expected to make recommendations;
- to establish a basic procedure to be followed;
- to determine who needs to be seen;
- to determine what fees are to be paid.

The mediator should then obtain a history of the marriage and a family and parenting history (this is particularly important if custody of and access to children are an issue). The mediator should also determine the present status of the parties with respect to each of the issues in dispute that are referred to mediation.

If the parties are meeting together, the mediator should ensure that each party has an opportunity to present his or her version of the marital and parenting history and his or her position on each issue, without being interrupted by the other party. It is advisable for the mediator to explain the communication process in advance, so that the parties do not feel personally attacked by the mediator when the mediator intervenes to prevent interruption. It is also advisable for the mediator to explain some basic ground rules such as:

- Make statements about how you personally feel, but do not make statements about how you believe the other person feels.
- Do not refute or criticize how the other person feels. That is, each person can only know how he or she feels and should not make disqualifying or denigrating statements about the other party.
- If a party wishes to disagree with a factual statement or a perception of an event, that spouse must wait for his or her turn and not cut off or interrupt the other party.
- The parties should ask each other questions to determine how the other person felt or perceived an event, rather than presuming how the other person felt and then attacking that feeling or perception.

It is often important to clarify each person's position with respect to the marriage breakdown. Some individuals may still be hoping for a reconciliation, while others may be well along in the process of accepting a divorce. If there is a real imbalance between the parties in their attitude to the marriage breakdown, this could undermine the mediation process, whether the issues relate to children or to finances. If one partner is extremely angry, hurt, depressed or unrealistically expecting a reconciliation, these feelings need to be discussed and resolved to some extent before the actual process of negotiation can begin.

The parties should be encouraged:

- to begin generating options or alternative solutions to each of the issues in dispute;
- to see that a successful settlement is usually one in which each party feels that he or she has made gains on some issues that are particularly important to that individual and has made concessions on other issues that may be more important to the other person;
- to understand that negotiations are rarely successful if one party tries to be a total winner and to humiliate the other party by a total defeat.

The mediator should demonstrate good problem-solving techniques, such as helping the parties generate alternatives and objective criteria for evaluating these alternatives. For example,

- The mediator could ask the parties to consider several different plans for spending time with the children, that is, in addition to the more traditional schemes of one or two days every other weekend with the non-custodial parent.
- The mediator could give the parties blank calendars and ask them to fill in in a different colour ink a variety of options for the children's time with each parent, including time during the week.
- The mediator could ask each parent to indicate the amount of time he or she would want to spend with the children and the amount of time he or she would be prepared to offer to the other parent. This could be done presuming that mother had sole custody and then presuming that father had sole custody.
- The topic of time leads easily into a discussion of sharing parenting responsibilities, such as transporting children to school, team sports, dance classes, swimming lessons, as well as doctor and dentist appointments. Both parties could discuss their willingness to co-operate and share responsibilities in terms of how this would affect sharing time with the children.
- If there is a dispute over the choice of school program or type of day care, both parents could be asked to generate criteria for selecting one program over another, for example, student-teacher ratio, cost, hours, accessibility, nature of program, and so forth. Each program could be given a rating on each criterion or as part of the selection process.

In the first meeting it is important to obtain the parties' agreement to maintain the status quo with respect to the issues in dispute. It may be necessary to develop an interim plan for such matters as interim custody and access, interim support or exclusive possession of the matrimonial home (if these issues are in dispute). To the extent possible, these interim plans should not unduly prejudice either party with respect to his or her legal position. However, both parties should recognize that interim arrangements may have long-term consequences if the parties do end up in court.

The usual mediation process involves a number of joint as well as individual meetings and, depending on the nature of any issues to be resolved, may include meetings with new partners, children and other individuals who are relevant to the issues being mediated.

(3) MEETING WITH PARENTS AND CHILDREN

(a) Objectives

In the case of custody or access issues, it is generally recommended that the mediator meet with the children directly in order to determine their views, concerns and preferences.

If the mediator expects to prepare a report with recommendations, it is particularly important for him or her to see the children and to see the children in conjunction with each parent, in order to form an impression about the parenting arrangements that may best meet the children's needs.

Depending on the issues in dispute, expectations on the mediator and the mediator's preferred method of interviewing, the following types of meetings may be held:

(i) *a meeting of the entire family* (that is, all of the children, with both parents present);

This meeting is recommended particularly in cases where the parties have not as yet separated and in cases where the parties have separated but there is a history of serious conflict involving polarization of the children's feelings about the parents. The primary purpose of such a meeting would be for the parents to explain to the children together that the purpose of mediation is to arrive at a co-operative settlement.

(ii) *a meeting with each parent and all of the children;*

This permits the mediator:

- to observe the parenting style of each parent separately with all of the children;
- to note the capacity of each parent to offer affectionate, supportive behaviour;
- to determine similarities and differences in each parent's ability to set reasonable limits and apply discipline techniques; and
- to assess the parents' respective awareness of the children's needs and their willingness to participate in various aspects of parenting behaviour.

(iii) *a meeting with each parent with the children individually;*

This is particularly recommended where a child has a conflict with one parent. For example, the children are often caught up in a tug of loyalties between the parents and may express a great deal of anger toward one parent. An individual meeting may allow the child and parent to begin resolving their difficulties. Often, the source of the difficulties is that the child feels abandoned or rejected by the parent and is expressing his or her hurt feelings through anger.

(iv) *a meeting with all of the children;*

This is particularly useful when the children are very supportive of each other or in cases where the children have been polarized as a result of the loyalty conflict, with each child supporting a different parent.

(v) *a meeting with each child individually;*

This meeting permits the mediator:

- to determine each child's individual concerns and preferences;
- to assess the emotional impact of the separation on each child;

(vi) *a meeting with each parent individually;*

This gives the mediator an opportunity:

- to obtain relevant family history
- to determine the specific concerns and wishes of each spouse
- to give the parents feedback about the needs, interests and wishes of each child
- to explore alternatives in a less threatening, more supportive atmosphere

(vii) *a follow-up meeting with all of the children and both parents;*

It may be desirable for the mediator to have the children present immediately after the parents reach an agreement, in order to explain the terms of the agreement as they affect the children. The children may be helpful in encouraging the parents to take a more co-operative approach in their future dealings with each other as parents. For example, the children can tell the parents how upsetting it is when they fight and ask the parents to behave in a friendlier, less hostile manner, particularly when they are present. It should be agreed that the children will not be used as message carriers between the parents and that the children can object if either parent makes negative statements about the other.

In cases where the mediator is expected to prepare a report with recommendations, it is preferable for the mediator to observe the children and their parents in a natural setting, such as their home, rather than in the more formal, unfamiliar atmosphere of the mediator's office. Children, particularly children under the age of ten, are far more comfortable in their home setting and are likely to respond more openly and honestly in a familiar setting.

(b) Procedure for Meetings with Parents and Children

In cases where some combination of meetings is being held between the parents and the children, the following procedures should be followed:

- The parents should give the children a clear statement that each child can speak freely and openly with the mediator and not fear any recriminations or pressure to divulge to the parents what they have said to the mediator.
- The parents should explain to the children that the parents will not be hurt or upset by what the children say, but rather that the parents want the children to speak honestly because they are concerned about arriving at a parenting plan that will be in the children's best interests.
- The mediator should explain that he or she may not be able to keep confidential the information told to him or her by the children. However, the mediator should make an effort to tell the children in advance what information is likely to be shared with the parents.
- If the children wish, the children may be present when this feedback is given.
- The mediator should give the children the mediator's office telephone number so that the children can contact the mediator in the case of parental pressure or repercussions for speaking openly. The parents should be told that the mediator has taken this action.
- The mediator should make it clear that the parents will be making the decision for the children, that is, that neither the children nor the mediator will be making the decision, but that it is important for the parents to have input from the children in arriving at a decision.

The children need reassurance that each parent:

- will take care of the children's basic needs, despite the separation and divorce;
- will continue to love the children and that the children will be permitted to love both parents;
- will make an effort not to undermine the relationship between the children and the other parent, for example, by belittling, criticizing or making negative comments about the other parent in the children's presence;
- will not pressure the children to reject the other parent or manipulate the children to choose him or her;
- will support the children's right to respect and love both of their parents and their extended family and to maintain a close and loving relationship with all of these important individuals.

The mediator should ensure that the meeting held with the children individually is held in privacy and in a setting that is as comfortable as possible for the children, that is, preferably in their own home, and usually in the child's bedroom.

During the course of the meeting with each child, the mediator should determine the following types of information:

- feelings about the separation — depression, anger, feelings of rejection or abandonment, feelings of relief;
- reconciliation wishes — how realistic does the child feel these wishes are?;
- the child's basic daily routine with each parent;
- the amount of time spent with each parent;
- how the child feels about the amount of time spent — too little or too much time with a particular parent?;
- how the child feels about the pattern of visits — are they too frequent or too widely spaced — too short or too long — too few or too many overnight visits?;
- the child's attitude to the neighbourhood — friends, school, community activities;
- the parenting responsibilities of each parent during the marriage and subsequent to the marriage (e.g., feeding, bathing, shopping, doctor appointments, after-school activities, wake-up and bedtime routines);
- the attitude of both parents to visits and telephone contact by the other parent — does each parent encourage or obstruct contact by the other parent?;
- whether the parents are prompt in picking up and delivering the children;
- whether parents visit regularly;
- the attitude of the parents to each other at pickup and delivery or during visits;
- the child's feelings about access visits;
- the relationship of the child to each parent;
- the relationship of the parents to each other;
- the relationship of the child with siblings;
- discipline techniques of each parent;
- loyalty conflicts — to what extent do these seem to be fostered by the parents?;
- symptoms of stress or disabilities — school performance, difficulties with peers, nightmares, alcohol or drug abuse, emotional difficulties, physical symptoms;
- strengths and weaknesses of each parent in terms of parenting capacity and any disabilities, such as drug or alcohol abuse, life-threatening illness, emotional difficulties;
- relationship between parent and any new partner and between child and that partner;

- likelihood that parents could act co-operatively in the best interests of the children in future parenting arrangements;
- child's wishes regarding changes in present arrangements or relationships.

(4) Meeting with Significant Others and/or Collecting Information from External Sources

(a) Objectives

Depending on the nature of the issues in dispute and whether any individuals other than the parties are having a significant effect on the negotiations (either facilitating or obstructing the mediation process), the mediator should consider the following meetings or data collection:

(i) *meeting individually with new partners and a joint meeting with both parties and any new partners;*

The purpose of the initial meeting would be to determine the new partner's role with respect to issues of custody of or access to children or with respect to financial matters such as contribution to household expenses and spousal support. It is recommended that an additional meeting be held with new partners and the two parties after an agreement has been reached by the parties, in order to reduce tension and ensure that the new partners will support the settlement.

(ii) *meeting with nannies or other significant caretakers* to obtain information with respect to parenting arrangements, children's care, special needs of children and ability of each parent to meet these needs;

(iii) *telephone call or meeting with schoolteachers* to obtain information with respect to each child's school performance, special academic needs and involvement of parents in meeting these needs;

(iv) *telephone call to family doctor* to obtain health care information on each child and parent;

(v) *telephone call to other mental health professionals* who have been offering counselling assistance to the children and/or the parents to obtain information about their emotional needs, family relationships and other matters relevant to parenting arrangements;

(vi) *telephone call or meeting with property appraisers* to obtain appraisals of all interests in property;

(vii) *telephone call or meeting with the accountant* to obtain information on the financial needs and means of each party and on each party's net family property.

(5) CONTACTS UPON COMPLETION OF MEDIATION

At the point of termination of the mediation, either because an agreement has been reached or because the mediation process has been unsuccessful, both counsel should be contacted by the mediator.

If the parties have succeeded in resolving one or more of the issues in dispute, counsel should be informed that the mediator will be preparing a report or draft agreement that will be forwarded to both parties and their counsel for discussion, prior to signing any agreement.

If the mediation process has broken down, the mediator may suggest a meeting with both counsel to determine whether there is any possibility of breaking the impasse and resuming mediation or achieving a settlement on the outstanding issue(s) through negotiations between the lawyers.

Following the completion of the mediation process, the mediator should prepare a draft memorandum of agreement with respect to the issues that have been resolved. Copies should be sent to the parties and their solicitors, and the parties should be encouraged to obtain independent legal advice prior to signing any agreement.

If the mediator is not a lawyer, then one of the lawyers should redraft the agreement into a legal format with appropriate release clauses and other necessary legal formalities.

If the mediation was *closed mediation* and no issues were resolved:

- the mediator should send a letter to counsel indicating that no agreement was reached, and
- a copy of the letter should be forwarded to each party.

If the mediation was closed mediation and agreement was reached on some issues:

- the mediator should prepare a draft memorandum of agreement with respect to those issues that were resolved,
- the mediator should prepare a covering letter outlining which issues were not resolved,
- the mediator should not comment upon or make recommendations about the issues that were not resolved, and
- the mediator should send a copy of the memorandum of agreement and the covering letter to both counsel and both parties.

If the mediation was *open mediation* and one or more issues were not resolved:

- the mediator should prepare a draft memorandum of agreement with respect to those issues that were resolved;
- in a report or letter, the mediator should indicate those issues that were not resolved. If the mediator was asked to prepare recommendations, then the mediator should submit his or her recommendations for resolving the outstanding issues;

- the mediator should comment on the process followed and each party's position with respect to the unresolved issues; and
- the mediator should indicate that he or she would be willing to assist the parties should there be any difficulties in the implementation of the mediation settlement or should difficulties arise at a later date.

ANNOTATED BIBLIOGRAPHY

Blades, J. *Mediate Your Divorce: A Guide to Co-operative Custody, Property and Support Agreements.* New Jersey: Prentice Hall Inc., 1985. This book contains practical information with respect to mediation of custody, access, support and property issues. It also contains a number of sample brochures and forms, as well as training materials, and is directed at both the mental health professional and the lawyer acting as mediator.

Coogler, O.J. *Structured Mediation and Divorce Settlement: A Handbook for Marital Mediators.* Toronto: Lexington Books, D.C. Heath & Co., 1978. See particularly chapter 3 "How Structured Mediation Works" and chapter 4, "Marital Mediation Procedure," page 23. This is the first major textbook on mediation and outlines the procedure followed in what is known as *structured mediation*.

Evarts, W.R., Greenstone, J.L., Kirkpatrick, G.J., and Leviton, S.C. *Winning Through Accommodation: The Mediator's Handbook.* Iowa, Kendall/Hunt, 1983. This book examines various methods of conflict management and makes practical suggestions for mediating various types of disputes, including landlord-tenant, employer-employee, as well as domestic relations disputes.

Folberg, J., and Taylor, A. *Mediation: A Comprehensive Guide to Resolving Conflicts Without Litigation.* San Francisco: Jossey-Bass Publishers, 1984. See in particular Part Two, "Mediation Stages, Concepts and Skills," page 38. Excellent text covering the theory and practice of mediation.

Grebe, S., Kranitz, M., and Crockett, K. *Starting Your Own Mediation Practice: A Workbook.* Maryland: Casamar Enterprises, 1985. This is a practical guide for those who are establishing a private mediation practice and includes helpful hints for marketing and office management.

Hansen, J.C., ed., and Grebe, S.C., vol. ed. *Divorce and Family Mediation: The Family Therapy Collections.* Aspen Systems Company, 1985. This book contains a number of articles dealing with different aspects of mediation, as well as different models of mediation for both family law and labour disputes. Mediators may be particularly interested in an article entitled "Including Children in Mediation: Considerations for the Mediator" by Karen K. Irvin, at page 94. Her article outlines the arguments for and against including children in the mediation process.

Haynes, J.M. *Divorce Mediation: A Practical Guide for Therapists and Counsellors.* New York: Springer Publishing Company, 1981. See Part II, "The Mediation Process," and in particular chapter 5 "Implementing the Model," page 47. This is a very helpful book for clinicians practising mediation. It contains a description of the Haynes' model, as well as a number of case studies.

Lemmon, J.A., ed. "Successful Techniques for Mediating Family Breakup." (1984), 2 *Mediation Quarterly.* This issue of the *Mediation Quarterly* contains a number of excellent articles with respect to the practice of mediation.

Saposnek, D. *Mediating Child Custody Disputes.* San Francisco: Jossey-Bass Publishers, 1983. See in particular Part II, "Structuring the Mediation Process," page 44. This book would be useful to the mediation practitioner and contains a number of concrete suggestions and case examples of mediation in practice.

Chapter Five

Mediation in Practice: Skills

A. BASIC INFORMATION

(1) THE MEDIATOR AS EDUCATOR: THE EFFECTS ON CHILDREN OF SEPARATION AND DIVORCE

Most parents are so caught up in their own pain, grief and reduced self-esteem that it is difficult for them to focus on the needs of their children. In addition, most parents lack adequate information from which to predict their children's responses or to make decisions that would be in the best interests of their children. This information should be provided in an impartial, constructive manner that avoids laying blame on either parent for the children's responses to the separation.

In the initial meeting with the parents and in subsequent individual and joint meetings, it is important for the mediator to give the parents information about the likely impact of separation and divorce on the children and themselves.

As well, the mediator can assist the parents by discussing some helpful techniques for dealing with their children, so that the parents will feel more in control, less helpless in dealing with their children's reactions and will behave in a more constructive manner than if their energies were spent on self-blame or blaming the other spouse.

The mediator should emphasize that it is important for the parents to share information about the children's responses and to co-operate in their reaction, because this is in the children's best interests. If the parents undermine each other's approaches to discipline and caretaking, the children will quickly learn to play one parent off against the other and are likely to lose respect for both parents.

By emphasizing a co-operative parenting approach, the mediator is helping to divert the parties from their own battle and beginning to model the way in which they must pool their efforts to assist their children, even at a time of high emotional stress. The parents need to learn to focus on the needs of the children, rather than on the fault of the other spouse.

The following information may be helpful:

- *Children are often unaware of conflict in a marriage* or that the conflict is out of the ordinary until one parent is packing his or her bags to leave. Even though parents may see the marriage as intolerable and believe that this has been obvious for some period of time, children tend to accept their family as a "normal family" and do not anticipate a marriage breakdown. Parents need to understand that their children are likely to be shocked by a separation.
- *Children are usually very attached to both parents* and are very upset and depressed at the loss of a parent.
- *Children are often ashamed that their parents are separating and/or divorcing.* They may see this as a failure, as contrary to moral or religious principles, and they may be afraid that this means the family is not "normal". They may be afraid to tell their friends or teachers, particularly if they do not know of other children from separated families.
- *The basic fears of most children at the time of separation relate to their own security.* For example, children worry about:
  Who will take care of me?
  Will I be able to see both my parents?
  Where will I live?
  Who will take care of the parent who is not living with me?
- *Children often feel responsible for the marriage breakdown and may feel equally responsible for returning the family to an intact unit.* That is, children often worry about such things as:
  What did I do that was so terrible that my parent is leaving?
  Was it my fault that the marriage broke down?
  What can I do to save the marriage?
  If I am really good, will the parent who left come back?

Children handle divorce differently at different stages of development, but there are some common themes or psychological tasks that researchers have found associated with reactions to separation and divorce. By way of overview, Dr. Judith Wallerstein (1983) found that children must learn to cope with the following six psychological tasks in dealing with divorce and separation:

- Acknowledging the reality of the marital rupture.
- Disengaging from parental contact and distress and resuming customary pursuits (i.e., age-appropriate tasks, having fun again).
- Resolving the loss (of a parent and an intact family unit).
- Resolving anger and self-blame.
- Accepting the permanence of the divorce.

- Achieving realistic hope regarding (their own) interpersonal relationships (i.e., ability to trust others and conquer fears of betrayal).

Children respond to separation and divorce in different ways at different developmental stages. The following material is based on the work of Dr. Judith Wallerstein and Dr. Joan Kelly. The "Children of Divorce Project" in California is summarized in their book, *Surviving the Breakup: How Children and Parents Cope with Divorce* (1980). Their information is based on follow-up studies of 60 divorcing families with 131 children who were living in California. These families were assessed at the time of separation, one year later, five years and then ten years later. The following is a brief summary of their findings with respect to the reactions of children at different stages of development.

PRESCHOOL CHILDREN — 2 TO 5 YEARS

- *Confusion, anxiety and fear:* Children are confused and unsure about the changes in their family life, because parents rarely explain the basis for the separation or divorce to children this age.
- *Regression:* Children may demonstrate their anxiety and insecurity by lapses in toilet training, increased clinging behaviour, increased fears, for example, of the dark, of changing routines, of being abandoned or hurt by another, or of expressing aggression.
- *Strong reconciliation fantasies.*
- *Feelings of guilt:* Children may experience feelings of self-blame for the marriage breakdown.
- *Increased aggression:* Children may display a greater irritability with siblings, parents, peers, or in school. This anger may stem from the child's feeling of loss or rejection. The child may have lost the psychological parent, that is the one the child feels closest to. Also, both parents may be so preoccupied with their own feelings of hurt and depression that they are emotionally unavailable to the child.

SCHOOL AGE — 5 TO 7 YEARS

- *Pervasive sadness and grieving:* This is sometimes related to the intensity of turmoil in the home, but some children are intensely sad even when the parents are not demonstrating great upset.
- *Preoccupation with their own bitterness, humiliation and plan for revenge.*
- *Yearning for the departed parent:* This is similar to grief for a dead parent.
- *Feelings of rejection, abandonment and fear.*
- *Fantasy of responsibility for marriage breakdown.*
- *Reconciliation fantasies.*

- *Anger:* The child often directs anger at the custodial parent or whichever parent the child believes is responsible for the marriage breakdown. Anger is also directed at teachers, friends and siblings, in many cases.
- *Conflicts of loyalty:* The child feels caught in a tug of war between both parents; that is having to accept one parent and reject the other.
- *Changes in academic and social behaviour.*

School age — 9 to 12 years

Children at this stage are more aware of parental conflict and the causes and consequences of divorce.

- *Profound feelings of loss, rejection, helplessness and loneliness.*
- *Feelings of shame, moral indignation and outrage at the parents' behaviour.*
- *Extreme anger, temper tantrums and demanding behaviour.*
- *Fears, phobias and use of denial.*
- *Fears with respect to the absent parent.*
- *Increased somatic complaints:* Children may experience more headaches, stomach aches, and sleep disorders at this age.
- *Loyalty conflicts:* The child identifies one parent as the good parent and one as the bad parent.
- *Low self-esteem:* The child may have increased problems in school and with peers and become involved in delinquent activities.

Adolescence — 13 years and older

Adolescents often express anger at the parents because:

- They feel burdened by the increased responsibility for younger siblings and emotionally weak parents.
- They have to share visits with new partners.
- They have to act as a messenger between parents in conflict.
- They are ashamed of the parents' childish behaviour, particularly if the conflict continues over a considerable time period.
- They feel torn between wanting to be with their friends and wanting to go on an access visit.
- They are anxious about their own future marriage.
- They have fears about forming long-term relationships.
- They worry about money, that is, whether the custodial parent will be able to provide for them.
- They experience loyalty conflicts.
- They have a heightened awareness of their parents' sexual behaviour. As a result, adolescents often display increased promiscuous behaviour and tend to withdraw from parental contact and control.

(2) THE MEDIATOR AS FACT GATHERER

Depending on the issues being mediated, the mediator must collect basic information from the parties and other relevant sources. In cases of open mediation or an assessment, the mediator should collect more background information than would be necessary for closed mediation. This is because the mediator may be asked for recommendations and should have a good factual basis for the recommendations. In cases of closed mediation, the mediator should use his or her discretion about what information might be desirable in order to understand the nature of the conflict and to facilitate a settlement.

For *custody and access* issues, the mediator should collect information with respect to the following:

- childhood history of each parent;
- courtship and marital history;
- involvement in child care during the marriage and following separation;
- employment history;
- future plans (remarriage, residence and employment).

If the mediation involves *financial issues,* then the mediator will need the following information:

- educational and employment history;
- past and present financial status;
- future plans (education or retraining, employment, remarriage).

The following are examples of the type of information to be collected. Remember that detailed historical information may not be necessary for closed mediation.

(a) Childhood History of Each Parent

The childhood history of each parent gives valuable clues about the character development and personality of the parent. Also the type of treatment received by a parent significantly affects his or her approach to parenting.

Information should be collected with respect to such matters as:

- birth history — normal or complications;
- relationship between the parent and each of his or her parents;
- relationship of the parents to each other. Was there a marriage breakdown? If so, what were the circumstances and how did each family member react?;
- atmosphere in the home, that is, was it a happy home? Was there a great deal of conflict? Was it a comfortable or tense atmosphere?;
- the personality of each parent, particularly with respect to his or her parenting. That is, was each parent warm and able to show affection

or cold and undemonstrative, patient or impatient, easygoing or demanding, interested and involved or preoccupied with matters outside the family?;

- feelings of acceptance in the family, that is, did the parent praise their child? Did the child feel that he or she had met each of the parent's expectations? Were the parents proud of him or her or did the child feel inadequate in the parents' eyes?;
- the nature of discipline used; that is, what type of discipline, how frequent and was the discipline seen as arbitrary or predictable? Was the punishment fair and reasonable or excessive?;
- the amount of time that was spent with each parent and as a family unit. Was the time spent enjoyable or filled with tension and conflict?;
- whether the parents were good providers. Did they carry out their other parenting responsibilities in a way that met the child's needs?
- the siblings, including their personalities and the relationship between the siblings and between each sibling and the parents;
- academic history and parents' involvement in school activities;
- parents' attitude to religion and the role of religion or other moral values in the household;
- history of significant problems with respect to alcohol, drugs, mental illness or criminal activities;
- other significant events or perceptions in relation to the childhood history.

It is important to determine whether the parent had a loving, secure, stable home environment or whether the parent grew up in an abusive, deprived or neglectful environment. Of particular importance is the nature of discipline, the role that each parent played in the family and the degree to which the child felt accepted and loved as opposed to unwanted and inadequate.

The type of family background and parenting experienced by the mother and father have a considerable influence on how each of them will parent and their expectations about how their partner should participate in parenting. The mediator should ask the parents how their own childhood history has affected their parenting and how they think that the childhood history of their partner has affected their partner's parenting.

(b) Courtship and Marital History

It is important to determine the history of the relationship between the parents in order to find out:

- whether the relationship was satisfactory at any time;
- whether the parents loved and respected each other at any point during the relationship;

- at what point and for what reasons one or both parents changed their feelings about the relationship;
- whether the parties have similar feelings about the relationship at present or whether one party is hoping for a reconciliation and is unable to separate emotionally from the relationship;
- whether the parents were able to co-operate with each other in the past and the present level of trust and co-operation, particularly with respect to the children;

At this point there should be some consideration of the possibility of reconciliation. That is, the mediator should clarify with both parties whether either or both feel that there is some possibility of saving the marriage. The fact that the parties would like to consider reconciliation does not mean that mediation would necessarily terminate. The parties might find it helpful to have a clear, impartial and fair agreement worked out through mediation, so that they can then consider reconciliation free of anxiety about adversarial legal proceedings during this time period. In the event that the parties have separated or are considering a period of separation, such an agreement would help to preserve the parties' rights while they consider their future relationship.

If the parties have decided to separate permanently and if custody and access are issues, then the mediator should obtain a history of the courtship and marriage. This is particularly important for open mediation or for situations where the mediator has been asked to prepare an assessment report in the event that mediation does not resolve all of the issues in dispute. The following types of information should be gathered:

- a history of the relationship from the time of meeting until the time of the marriage, including what each parent found attractive and unattractive about the other, the interests they had in common, as well as separate interests, and whether the relationship was a stable relationship during the courtship period;
- who decided to marry and how did the other partner feel about the marriage?;
- what was the attitude of the extended family to the marriage?;
- were there major religious or cultural differences between the families and how did these affect their relationship?;
- how satisfying was their sexual relationship in the early stages of the relationship, before and after child bearing and at the present time? Did the parties have different opinions about whether the sexual relationship was satisfying?;
- when did they decide to have children? Who decided and how did the other partner react?;
- the history of the pregnancy, including the involvement of both parties throughout the pregnancy, as well as during labour and delivery;

- how were parental responsibilities shared after the birth of the children, and how did each parent feel about the other parent's involvement?

If the parents had a strong marriage at one point and did love and respect each other, it is important for the mediator to help the parties recall the strengths of the marriage at a time when the parties may only be able to see the weakness and feel the disappointed expectations. If there was some evidence of parental co-operation during the lifetime of the children, the couple should reflect on how beneficial the co-operation was, not only for the parents, but particularly for the children. The mediator should emphasize that it is important for parents to continue to act co-operatively as parents, even though the spousal role may be at an end. By reliving what is good in the relationship and bringing this to the couple's attention, the mediator can sometimes begin to dissolve the present feelings of anger and hurt.

The review of the marital history is also useful for deterring the couple from blaming the marriage breakdown on one or the other parent. The couple can be helped to reframe the reasons for the marriage breakdown so as to remove allegations of fault and feelings of guilt. For example, the couple may discover that the marriage broke down primarily because of differences in culture, values or interests, or because they had very different expectations about marriage and family life to begin with.

By reducing blame, the mediator can often begin the process of developing a more co-operative relationship. In addition, if the parties no longer feel they are personally to blame for the marriage failure, they will be less likely to feel the need to justify their behaviour to the children. This could help to reduce loyalty conflicts, where each parent blames and criticizes the other and encourages the children to take sides. Loyalty conflicts and a lack of co-operation create a tremendous emotional strain on children and are significantly related to poor adjustment to the separation and divorce.

An important reason for collecting the marital history, particularly with the couple present together, is to test the emotional climate between the parties and to help the mediator predict the likelihood that the parties will be able to co-operate in the future.

(c) Parental Involvement in Child Care

It is suggested that the mediator obtain information about each parent's involvement with the children and sharing of parental responsibilities within the context of the marital history. At this time, the mediator should deal with each parent's perception of his or her own and the other parent's:

- *affection for the children* and concern for the safety and welfare of the children;

- *method of discipline* used by each parent and each parent's views on his or her own and the other parent's discipline techniques. Do the parents approve of each other's methods? Do they feel these methods are appropriate and effective for meeting the needs of the child?
- *sharing of parenting tasks and responsibilities* from the birth of the child to the present time. Did one parent take primary responsibility for the care of the child? Attitude to each other's involvement and opinion of each other's competence to do parenting tasks, both in the past and in the future;
- *competence in providing direct parenting,* and interest and involvement in significant aspects of the child's life, for example, school, extra-curricular activities, medical and health care needs.

It is preferable to obtain this information when the discussion is not centred on the question of custody, but rather more informally during a discussion of the marital history. It is also recommended that this discussion occur with the parties together, so that each party can respond to the other party's perception of his or her parenting role.

If information emerges that suggests abuse or neglect with respect the children, the mediator should pursue these topics in more depth with each parent individually and, in addition, should check any external sources, such as doctors, hospital records, the Children's Aid Society, police records and other relevant sources, to determine the extent of any harm done.

The mediator should avoid any prolonged discussion of these allegations with both parties present because:

- The parent who is making the allegations is likely to make them in a more dramatic, forceful and abusive manner when the other parent is present.
- The accused parent is likely to feel defensive and demoralized and is therefore likely to minimize the incidents and their effects. In addition, the accused parent may feel the need to rebut any allegations, because of a desire not to lose face in front of the other parent, particularly with the mediator present.
- It may be easier for the mediator to get a more truthful, balanced account of any abusive incidents if the parties are seen individually.
- One parent may be afraid to make serious allegations in an open and honest manner in front of the other parent for fear of a reprisal.
- The joint discussion of serious allegations is likely to make subsequent communication and co-operation between the parties more difficult.

For these reasons, the mediator should deal with serious allegations on an individual basis and in a constructive and supportive manner. Any recommendations made as a result of such discussions could then be reviewed with both parties present together.

If there are allegations of abuse or neglect, the mediator has a statutory obligation to report this information to the appropriate child welfare authorities. For example, in Ontario the statutory duty is set out in s. 68 of the *Child and Family Services Act, 1984,* S.O. 1984, c. 55. The mediator should tell the parents that this is his or her legal duty and should explain to each parent the essence of what he or she will say. If the mediator prepares a written report, a copy should be given to the parents so that they are fully informed about any allegations.

If the mediator feels that one or both of the parents need some assistance in parenting skills or mental health counselling, in relation to parenting ability, the mediator should make a referral to an appropriate professional or agency. The mediator should not become involved in an individual counselling relationship with one of the parents, as this would violate his or her impartial role.

(d) Employment History

This information is necessary for both financial mediation and for the mediation of custody and access disputes. The employment history gives some indication of the motivation of the parents, their stability, goals, lifestyle and ability to relate to individuals outside the home. The work history also assists in predicting which parent will be able to provide best for the financial needs of the child. In addition, if one spouse has not been employed outside the home, it is important to determine when that spouse can become self-supporting and at what financial level.

If either or both parents anticipate a change in employment at the present time, it is important to determine the impact of that change on the family, that is, on the family's financial status, the caretaking arrangements for the children and the ability of each parent to spend time with the children.

If a parent, usually a woman, is anticipating entering the work-force, the mediator should determine whether that individual will need career counselling with respect to career selection and job skills. In addition, women who have been out of the work-force for some time often feel inadequate, insecure and frightened at the prospect of re-entering the work-force. These concerns should be addressed, because they will have an impact on how quickly the individual will become self-supporting. If necessary, these individuals should be referred for professional counselling or work-adjustment training.

(e) Future Plans

The mediator should discuss the parents' work schedule, the likelihood that a parent will move some distance away, any plans for remarriage and other issues that may necessitate a change in the parenting arrangements. It would be important to take these factors into account in working out a plan for the present and in designing a procedure for changing the parenting arrangements, should the need arise in the future.

(3) THE MEDIATOR AS COMMUNICATOR

One of the primary reasons given for marriage failure is difficulties in communication between the parties. That is, spouses will often state that one or both of them are unable to understand:

- each other's feelings — often spouses give ambivalent messages to each other about their satisfaction with the marriage,
- each other's motives for leaving the marriage or for wanting it to continue,
- why one or both were unhappy during the marriage,
- what was expected of them by the other spouse to save the marriage.

The spouses often report that they never clarified or discussed feelings of anger, disappointment or resentment, and as a result, important issues in the marriage were unresolved. Such couples generally have a long history of distrust and suspiciouness about the other partner's motives and behaviour.

Mediation is a technique that depends on effective communication in order to reach an agreement. The task is made difficult because the mediator is faced with two people who by this time usually dislike each other, are very poor communicators, are highly distrustful and are fearful of being hurt again. It is essential that the mediator help the parties to develop more effective communication techniques from the very beginning or the mediation will likely fail.

Because the mediation sessions, particularly the initial sessions, are likely to be highly emotionally charged, it is important for the mediator to explain certain basic communication skills or rules of procedure prior to beginning the content of the discussion. There are several reasons for establishing basic communication skills in the initial meeting, namely:

- The parties can begin to communicate more effectively right from the beginning of mediation.
- The parties are more likely to absorb information about communication techniques when they are not in the midst of discussing emotionally charged information.
- The parties are likely to present their information more effectively and more constructively, that is, with less conflict and assignment of blame, if they have discussed appropriate methods of communication.

By developing more effective communication skills from the beginning, the mediator is improving the chances of the parties listening to each other, reducing their tension and beginning the process of talking constructively about the issues in dispute.

Examples of listening and communication techniques that should be taught to the parties are:

- *speaking in the first person* — that is, if a party has a concern, the party should state that concern as his or her concern, not as a general concern or as a concern of some other person. For example, "I am concerned about the fact that you make hostile comments about me in front of the children", rather than "It is not a good idea for children to hear parents badmouthing each other";
- *making eye contact with each other* when they are speaking, that is, they should look at each other when they are making statements;
- *directing comments about the other spouse to that spouse* rather than to the mediator;
- *speaking one at a time* and not interrupting the other;
- *making direct statements about how they feel rather than asking questions,* particularly questions directed at the mediator. For example, "I think that you should pick up the children for an access visit at the time that you agreed. It is very disappointing to the children when you are late", rather than a question addressed to the mediator, "Don't you think that it is psychologically damaging to children when parents are late for access visits?";
- *stating specifically the behaviour that is upsetting* rather than attacking the other spouse in more general terms. In addition, each spouse should state the behaviour that he or she would prefer, so that the discussion can become focused on what behaviour is upsetting and what changes are needed, rather than defending against personal attacks. For example, "It is upsetting to me when you change access arrangements at the last minute. I would appreciate it if you would notify me of changes at least two days in advance" (statement of the problem); "I would be much more willing to co-operate if you would ask me if it was convenient to change the access arrangements rather than just telling me that you are changing them, without any concern for alternative plans that I may have made" (specifying the preferred behaviour);
- *paraphrasing what he or she heard the other spouse saying.* This ensures that both spouses are listening to each other, and it also helps to clarify any confusion or misinterpretation;
- *asking for clarification rather than attacking the other spouse.* That is, they should be sure that they have correctly understood any communication, before they become upset. Too often, couples who are already upset and distrustful of each other misinterpret both the intent and the actual content of the communication. A great deal of hostility can be eliminated if they learn to ask for clarification. For example, "I am not sure that I understood what you just said, could you explain that again please", or, "Could you give me some more

information about that?" rather than, "You are a liar and you have always tried to undermine me and there you are doing it again — I knew I could not trust you!";

- *using direct versus indirect statements,* for example, "I was upset when you telephoned last night and did not tell me about the parent-teacher interviews to be held next week", rather than, "You never communicate with me about how the children are doing in school";
- *identifying feelings, that is, the person's own feelings and his or her perception of the feelings expressed by the other person.* For example, "It made me feel hurt when you said that I was not a good mother." Or, "I guess it must have made you feel angry when I refused to share the transportation of the children for access visits";
- *talking about feelings rather than acting them out through aggressive retaliatory behaviour.* For example, one spouse might say, "It makes me feel that you do not really care about your children when you refuse to pay child support", rather than cutting off access to the non-paying spouse. An even better approach would be for the spouse to ask for clarification, for example, "Is there some reason why you are not paying child support?" This permits the other spouse to give some explanation for his or her behaviour, such as, "I am now unemployed" or "I feel that you are interfering with my relationship with the children so that I did not feel like paying child support." By asking for clarification, important issues that need to be dealt with in mediation can be identified. These issues would not be resolved if the parties resorted to acting-out behaviour;
- *accepting the fact that each person is entitled to his or her own perception of a situation.* That is, rather than putting the mediator in the position of judging who is right or wrong, who is lying or truthful, both parties need to accept that they may perceive situations differently and therefore may feel and act differently.

Once the mediator has taught the parties basic communication techniques, the next step is to help the parties orient toward their future relationship rather than dwelling on events and feelings of the past. The mediator should emphasize that:

- What has happened in the past cannot be changed. While these events will certainly colour the parties' perceptions, nevertheless it is important for them to make a commitment to be different today. The focus of mediation should be on determining what it is that the parties would like their relationship to be like in the future.
- The parties should not expect that the relationship will change overnight or that there will not be setbacks. The important thing is to recognize and encourage each other when positive steps are made and not to become overly upset or discouraged when difficulties

arise. The parties should use the communication techniques explained above in order to avoid undue hostility.

- Each spouse should tell the other spouse when he or she has done something right. For example, "I really appreciated it when you called to ask whether it would be convenient for me to change the access arrangements this weekend. I felt that you were giving me a choice and that you were concerned about disrupting my plans. It felt good to co-operate." So often in cases of marriage breakdown, the parties get no positive reinforcement, but only hear about the things that they did wrong. This is particularly true of cases that go to litigation. In order to orient the parties toward more co-operative behaviour in the future, the parties must learn to give each other positive reinforcement for improved behaviour in the present.

In addition to improving the parties' ability to communicate, the mediator needs to focus the discussion on the particular issues in dispute. If the mediator has been successful in establishing some level of trust, a willingness to co-operate and an improvement in communication skills, then the next step is to help the parties identify some objective criterion or a governing principle for resolving those issues that are in dispute. For example, if one issue is custody of or access to children, then the mediator might determine whether the parents agree that the best interests of the children ought to be the primary criteria for evaluating a solution, as opposed to whether one parent wins or loses. The mediator could spend some time with the parents identifying what is meant by "best interests of the children". For example, the parties might agree that:

- It is desirable for children to have a close, loving relationship with both parents.
- Children should feel comfortable expressing feelings of love and respect for one parent in the other parent's presence.
- Parents should not criticize or demean the other parent in the children's presence.
- Children should spend considerable time with both parents, in keeping with the children's needs, stage of development and wishes and with the ability and willingness of the parents to spend time with the children.

It is important for the mediator to establish these general principles or criteria before dealing with the specific questions of where the children will live and at what specific times the children will see each parent. The aim is to help the parents deal with these issues in terms of the children's needs rather than their own bargaining position.

As a further example, if the mediation is with respect to spousal or child support, the parties could be asked to come to some agreement on the basic principles to apply in resolving this dispute. An example might be that the level of support should be fair and reasonable given each spouse's ability to earn income and each spouse's financial needs. The parties could then be asked to identify specific criteria or factors to be taken into consideration in determining:

- who should pay support?;
- what amount of support?; and
- for how long or until what conditions occur?

The parties might agree that the following types of criteria would be important, for example:

- the present level of income of both spouses;
- the educational history;
- work experience;
- the length of time out of the work-force;
- the need for retraining;
- the financial responsibilities of both spouses;
- the age and health of the spouses;
- the age and health of the children;
- the standard of living enjoyed by the spouses prior to separation;
- the level of income required for both spouses to be self-sufficient; and
- a realistic time frame for achieving financial independence. For some spouses it may be unrealistic ever to achieve full financial independence, but perhaps some partial goal could be reached.

It is important to focus the parties on realistic, objective criteria, rather than each party's position, which may be based on emotional factors, such as a desire for revenge for a matrimonial fault.

The previous discussion centred on improving communication techniques and changing behaviour patterns, which should in turn increase the chances of reaching a settlement. While many couples will successfully resolve all of the issues in dispute, some couples will not settle some or all of the issues because:

- One or both do not wish to end the spousal relationship.
- One spouse wants to punish the other spouse for feelings of hurt or humiliation suffered in the marriage breakdown.
- Delaying a settlement is to the spouse's advantage in the courts.
- There is not sufficient trust by one or both spouses to reach a full settlement.
- One spouse has strong feelings of guilt about settling. That is, a spouse may not be able to settle the issue of custody because of a concern that the children will later blame him or her for abandoning them. This type of parent often needs a court order or at least a professional's recommendation before he or she can agree to the other spouse having primary residence or sole custody of the children.

These are important factors for the mediator to recognize when they arise in the mediation process. The mediator needs to be prepared with some special techniques for dealing with each of these potential obstacles to mediation.

In addition, there are circumstances in which the parties reach agreement that should cause the mediator some concern. For example, situations where one party is too eager to settle, particularly where the settlement may not be in the best interests of the children or may be an unfair or unreasonable financial settlement. This often occurs when:

- One spouse feels totally responsible for the marriage breakdown and wants to atone for his or her guilt by giving up everything to the other spouse;
- one spouse feels completely dominated by the other spouse or is under physical or emotional duress to reach a settlement (whether the duress is real or just perceived). In this situation a spouse may submit to the other spouse's demands to avoid conflict or prevent some feared retaliation;
- one spouse is so anxious to end the marriage and not have to deal face to face with the other spouse that he or she is prepared to concede everything in the mediation. A variation of this type of individual is a spouse who is so angry at the other spouse that he or she cannot accept anything from that spouse, even if it would be reasonable to do so;
- the spouses are of such unequal bargaining power, for example, in verbal skills, self-confidence or control of important resources, that one spouse gives up immediately in defeat;
- one spouse may be prepared to accept an unreasonable settlement on one issue in order to win on the issue that is most important to him or her. For example, in a custody battle, a spouse may forgo reasonable support or a reasonable division of property in order to gain custody.

Both the failure to settle and an unreasonable settlement should be of concern to the mediator, particularly when it affects the welfare of children. Three examples will be given of situations described above in order to give the mediator a better appreciation of the problem and of the techniques for resolving or dealing with these situations.

(a) The Stonewalling Parent

The mediator should be alert to the fact that it may be in one party's interest to delay a settlement. This can arise in cases involving custody and access and in financial disputes. For example, in custody cases, the party who has *de facto* custody of the children is at a considerable advantage in that a court usually awards custody to the parent who has had the primary care and control of the children from the date of the separation. The reason for this is that the court considers the stability of the children to be a very significant factor in determining custody. As a result the parent who has the care and control of the children at the time of mediation will have less motivation to settle than the party who does not have *de facto* custody. If the mediation is delayed or prolonged and no resolution is reached, the party with *de facto* custody will have gained a considerable advantage over the other party by the time the matter reaches trial.

A stonewalling or delaying tactic can also be used in financial mediation to the advantage of one party over the other. For example, in determining the level of spousal or child support to award, the court will take into consideration the level of support and the length of time the interim arrangement has been in effect. If one party has managed to survive financially for some period of time on a low level of support, the court will take this level of support into account. It is therefore to the advantage of the payor spouse to delay matters in mediation and to agree to a low level of support in any interim agreement.

The reasons for stonewalling set out above are related to improving a spouse's position in court. In some cases a spouse may stonewall for very different reasons, such as:

- not wanting to end the spousal relationship;
- not wanting to lose face by making concessions to the other spouse;
- not wanting to lose face in the eyes of a third party (for example, a new partner or the spouse's lawyer).

When a mediator suspects that one party is not negotiating in good faith, the mediator should take the following steps:

- *discuss with the parties the mediator's concerns about possible stonewalling.* Perhaps a better of way of dealing with this issue is to discuss the significance of a time delay in the first meeting, that is, before either party has shown any evidence of stonewalling. By raising the issue the mediator may prevent this problem from arising;
- *encourage the parties to come to an interim agreement* that would be the least prejudicial to both parties during the course of mediation;
- *help the parties to agree on an early termination date,* or at least a date by which progress will be reviewed, at the outset of the mediation in order to prevent one side from prolonging matters unnecessarily.

These are preventive steps that it is hoped will avoid or minimize the effects of stonewalling. If the problem continues, then the mediator could use some of the following techniques to resolve the impasse:

- *breaking the issues in dispute into subparts,* so that the parties can deal with each issue in smaller pieces, rather than an all-or-nothing approach. For example, if access is in dispute, rather than dealing with each spouse's entire access plan, the discussions could focus on:

whether access should be supervised or unsupervised;

whether access should be daytime only or should include overnight visits;

whether access should include midweek visits; and

whether telephone access should be specified.

Once agreement has been reached on these types of parameters, then the discussion can focus on such things as how many weekends and for what length of time on a weekend or on what special days during the year, such as Mother's Day, Father's Day, Christmas Day or the child's birthday.

In the event that the parties reach agreement on some of the sub-issues, they should be praised and encouraged by the mediator for making progress toward a settlement. It is often easier to reach agreement on smaller issues and gradually build toward resolving the entire issue.

- *meeting individually with each spouse.* This is often called an *individual caucus.* The individual caucus can be held on a separate day or can be part of a joint session. That is, the mediator can ask one spouse to leave the room so that the mediator can spend some time with each spouse individually before returning to a joint session. During the individual sessions, the mediator can determine what the road blocks are to agreement and can encourage each of the parties to generate some realistic alternatives that may lead to a settlement. It may be easier for the mediator to arrive at compromise proposals in an individual session rather than in a joint meeting, because the parties may be concerned about losing face in each other's presence.

- *helping the parties refocus their attention on the principles they have agreed upon as the basis for a settlement.* For example, the best interests of the child or a fair and reasonable financial settlement could be discussed in the context of a time delay. The parties could be asked:

    whether it is in the best interests of the children to have a long period of uncertainty with respect to a parenting plan;

    whether it is fair and reasonable for the children to suffer unnecessary hardship as a result of a delay in determining child support.

If the parties fail to respond to these techniques and if the delay is significantly prejudicing one spouse, then the mediator should state his or her concerns to the parties and their counsel and should terminate the mediation. This would allow the disadvantaged spouse to make an immediate application to court for resolution of the dispute.

(b) The Rejected Parent

A parent who is rejected will respond in one of several ways, namely:

- *intense anger* at the other partner, often in proportion to the feelings of lowered self-esteem, humiliation or rejection;

- *depression,* that is, the parent may be immobilized from taking any constructive action because of strong feelings of inadequacy resulting from the rejection;
- *cautious hope,* that is, the parent may believe that the rejection is temporary or that if he or she makes a change in behaviour a reconciliation will be possible.

It is extremely important to deal with each of these feelings at an early stage for the following reasons:

- The spouses will not be able to deal with the practical issues in dispute until their feelings have been addressed. Therefore, dealing with feelings actually facilitates mediation and removes a primary obstacle to settlement, namely, the client's self-esteem and feelings about the other partner.
- It is important for the parties to stop blaming each other so that they can be mobilized to take more constructive action. This is in their own interests as well as in the interests of their children.

(i) The Angry Parent

There are a number of techniques that can be used to deal with an intensely angry parent:

- Arrange individual sessions in the early stages of mediation. The client needs an opportunity to ventilate in a supportive atmosphere; however, it could be extremely destructive to the mediation process if the client were permitted to ventilate in the other partner's presence.
- Help the spouse to identify the source of the anger. That is, "I am angry because [for example] I feel humiliated because my partner left me for someone else." Encourage the spouse to talk through what it is that he or she is specifically concerned about and to share the fears and frustrations that are behind the anger.
- Determine whether the reasons for the anger are in the past or are continuing in the present. Ask the spouse to determine in what way the anger will affect the spouses' future relationship.
- Ask the spouse to consider ways in which the anger could be reduced. For example, is it important that the partner recognize the cause of the anger and apologize for the humiliation? Does the spouse need to rebuild his or her self-confidence independent of the previous relationship (for example, through a new more satisfying relationship or through psychotherapy)?
- Help the spouse to develop techniques for controlling the anger or expressing it more constructively.

- Help the spouse to appreciate the effects on the other partner, and in particular on the children, of hanging on to the anger, rather than learning more constructive techniques for dissipating or controlling the anger.

Parents are often motivated to change their behaviour when they recognize the destructive impact on them and in particular on their children. These spouses often need some concrete suggestions for changing their behaviour and some positive feedback to rebuild their self-confidence.

(ii) The Depressed Parent

If the mediator believes that a parent is very depressed and overcome by feelings of inadequacy as a result of the marriage breakdown, the mediator should recommend that the individual obtain appropriate professional assistance such as:

- individual psychotherapy or counselling;
- group therapy, that is, a support group of individuals with similar problems;
- vocational counselling; or
- assistance with budgeting or financial management.

The mediator should discuss the client's emotional state with him or her in an individual session before making a recommendation for additional assistance. In the event that the client is too depressed to reasonably negotiate the issues in dispute, the mediator should consider:

- delaying the mediation for some period of time until the individual has the appropriate counselling. This should not be done without discussions with both the clients and their counsel. It would be important to discuss the implications of a time delay as opposed to the implications of attempting to mediate when one party was not emotionally able to negotiate on equal terms;
- continuing the mediation once the supportive assistance has been initiated. In cases where the individual is still functioning at a fairly reasonable level, this might be a desirable alternative;
- terminating the mediation. Mediation is not an appropriate technique when the client is extremely depressed.

(iii) The Hopeful Parent

It is important to clarify whether the parties intend to separate or reconcile at an early stage of the mediation. If one party is hoping for a reconciliation and the other is determined to separate, then this information must be clarified so that the parties are not bargaining under a false impression.

It is often the case that one party is unrealistic in his or her hopes for reconciliation. This party may offer to give up virtually everything in order to please the other party, in the hope that the party will return to the marriage. Once the party is disillusioned, he or she is often angry at the mediator as well as himself or herself for permitting an unfair bargain. While the parties are in a joint session, the mediator should ask each party to clarify his or her position on reconciliation versus separation.

It is recommended that the mediator discuss this issue further in an individual session to determine whether the hopeful parent is acting out of love for the other partner or out of an anxiety about being left alone. If the spouse is concerned about how he or she will cope with loneliness or new responsibilities, these specific issues should be dealt with. The mediator may feel that, as with the depressed person, the individual needs some counselling, and should make an early referral for appropriate assistance. For example, if the spouse is anxious about managing financially on his or her own, he or she should be referred for career counselling and budgeting assistance. Such specific information may increase self-confidence and help the spouse to accept being single again.

If the mediator believes that one party is making an unreasonable settlement because of unrealistic hopes, the mediator should encourage the parties to reach an interim, time-limited agreement that can be reviewed at some point in the future when the party may be more realistic.

(c) The Guilty Parent

In this case, the parent who feels responsible for the marriage break-down may make concessions to the other parent out of guilt, rather than out of a firm belief that a particular plan is fair, reasonable or in the children's best interests. For example, a parent who has committed adultery may agree to give up all of his or her assets, pay an unreasonably high level of support or give custody of the children to the other parent in order to atone for his or her behaviour. For this reason the mediator should:

- be sensitive to non-verbal as well as verbal cues to indicate that a parent is feeling extremely guilty (for example, excessive crying or little eye contact);
- determine whether one parent is behaving out of guilt and the other parent is behaving out of a need for revenge. Once the mediator has identified the problem, he or she should encourage the parties to talk about this issue both together and separately;
- help both of the spouses refocus away from the assignment of blame and onto the particular issues in dispute. That is, even though a party may have caused the marriage breakdown, that does not necessarily mean that that person is not needed by the children and does not have good parenting skills. Both spouses should be made aware of the fact that in many provinces the legislation specifically states that

marital misconduct is not a factor in determining custody of or access to children unless that conduct is relevant to parenting. The *Divorce Act, 1985,* S.C. 1986, c. 4, which applies to all provinces and territories, also takes this position. If the spouses understand that the court will not use matrimonial fault as a factor in determining custody, this should help to refocus the mediation onto the best interests of the children;

- explain to spouses who are mediating financial issues that most provinces specifically exclude marital misconduct as a factor to be considered in determining eligibility for support or the quantum of support. This is the same type of approach as with custody and should be discussed because spouses often believe that they will be entitled to a higher level of support if they are the innocent party in the marriage breakdown. It is particularly important to clarify this matter, because previous legislation in most provinces did award support on the basis of matrimonial fault. Matrimonial fault is specifically eliminated as a criterion in the *Divorce Act, 1985* which applies across all provinces and territories.

If the mediator is unable to resolve successfully the issue of guilt and if this guilt is interfering with the ability to mediate a reasonable solution, then the mediator should discuss this matter with the spouse individually and should suggest delaying the mediation until that spouse receives individual counselling. If the spouse agrees to a delay, this should be discussed with both spouses and both counsel. Following the discussion with the mediator, if the parent who is feeling guilty wishes to continue the mediation, the mediator should encourage the spouses to reach an interim settlement that is time limited, so that the spouse can review his or her decision at a later date.

If the guilty spouse wishes to proceed to a final settlement, the mediator should document the advice given to the client and should give the client a copy of the memorandum outlining the mediator's concerns. As long as the settlement reached does not jeopardize the health or safety of the children, the mediator may decide not to terminate the mediation. For example, if the mediator feels that the bargain reached in a financial mediation is unreasonable because of the party's feelings of guilt, the mediator may decide not to interfere with the agreement, provided that there has been full financial disclosure and the mediator has indicated his or her concerns both to the client and to counsel for the client.

B. DEALING WITH IMPASSES

The mediator may find that the parties get stuck or reach an impasse at several points during the mediation. Often the reason for the impasse has to do with how the parties are feeling about each other rather than with the substance of the issues in dispute. In order to resolve impasses successfully, the mediator has to avoid being caught up in the conflict between the spouses, and has to skillfully redirect the spouses to the practical task of arriving at a mediated settlement. There are a number of techniques for dealing with impasses, some of which were mentioned previously under the discussion of communication techniques. Examples of approaches that could be used by the mediator are:

- *reframing the issue,* for example, "I wonder whether the issue is that the children must be returned home by 5:00 p.m. on Sunday, or whether the issue is really that you feel it is important for the children to have time to unwind and readjust before going to bed following an access visit. If it is the latter, let's discuss how long it takes your children to readjust before their bedtime";
- *identifying the underlying feelings or problem,* for example, "I get the feeling that you are very angry about having to do all the transporting of the children for access visits. Is that a factor in your refusal to agree to more frequent visits?";
- *recognizing the impasse,* for example, "We seem to be stuck on this point";
- *identifying the criteria that can be used to evaluate different alternatives,* for example, if the issue is the choice of a doctor for the children, the parents might suggest such criteria as:
  location
  office hours
  specialization (paediatrician versus general practitioner)
  access to a particular hospital
Or if the issue is division of particular assets, the criteria might include:
  the appraised value of the property; or
  a particular mechanism for selection, such as one spouse draws up two lists of items and the other spouse selects the list he or she wants;
- *having each of the clients take responsibility for the impasse,* that is, "We seem to be stuck, what can you do about this?";
- *providing information to the clients to break the impasse,* for example, information about the effects of parental conflict upon the children;
- *suggesting alternatives,* particularly face-saving options. For example, if one party wants to spend every weekend with the children and the other party wants to offer every other weekend, the mediator might consider alternatives for a compromise, such as in those months where there are five weekends, possibly one party could have three of the weekends and the other party two weekends. Another

option would be to offer a greater number of long weekends that occur on statutory holidays or professional development days;

- *holding an individual caucus with each spouse* and then bringing them together after considering separately the options;
- *letting the parties think about the session and coming back with a proposal the next time.* The mediator could give the spouses homework to complete, such as listing the advantages and disadvantages of each of the options that have been considered;
- *asking the spouses to write out the advantages and disadvantages of the proposals from the other spouse's point of view.* This technique attempts to get each spouse to stand in the other spouse's shoes; that is, it encourages both spouses to consider the other's point of view;
- *having the spouses submit a written final offer to the mediator.* The mediator picks the best proposal and uses it as the basis for discussion. This technique is moving somewhat closer to arbitration, although the mediator does not make the final decision. The final decision is still left to the parties.

C. POWER IMBALANCES

The mediation process presumes that the parties are able to negotiate with each other on relatively equal terms. If there is a significant imbalance in power between the two spouses, this may undermine the mediation process.

The following are some reasons for an imbalance of power between the parties:

- lack of information;
- difference in education;
- difference in intellectual ability;
- difference in verbal ability;
- difference in culture or language;
- difference in age;
- difference in socioeconomic status;
- difference in personality, for example, dominant versus submissive;
- difference in the availability of a support system for each spouse, for example, extended family, close friends or organizations (such as the church); or
- difference in attitude to the marriage breakdown; that is, one spouse may feel responsible for the marriage breakdown and very guilty about the effects on the family.

The following are methods that the mediator might use for dealing with the power imbalance:

- ensure that the spouses make full disclosure to each other of all relevant information;

- ensure that the spouses obtain independent legal advice before signing any agreement;
- refer the spouses for appropriate outside assistance, such as to an accountant, mental health professional or vocational counsellor;
- ensure that only one individual speaks at a time;
- prevent the spouses from interrupting each other;
- prevent one spouse from attacking the other personally;
- restate the position of the weaker spouse. That is, if the weaker spouse is not as articulate as the stronger spouse, the mediator can help to state the spouse's position more clearly;
- help the clients to make more direct statements about their wishes. The mediator can assist the weaker spouse to say, "I want you to assist with the transportation of children to and from access visits", rather than other spouse continuing to carry all the responsibility and resenting the more dominant spouse;
- point out certain process aspects of the communication that the spouses may not be conscious of. For example, one spouse may always look at the mediator when he or she wants assistance rather than make demands directly to the other spouse, or one spouse may always precede a request for co-operation with a criticism. The mediator should draw attention to the process and to the response of the other spouse to this behaviour;
- request an individual session with one spouse or recommend an individual caucus during a joint session in order to assist a weaker spouse;
- give positive reinforcement and support during the session whenever the weaker spouse demonstrates more assertive behaviour;
- give positive reinforcement to the more dominant spouse whenever he or she demonstrates co-operative behaviour.

If the imbalance of power is so great as to jeopardize the possibility of a fair outcome, then the mediator should discuss this directly with both clients and also with their counsel.

D. REFERRAL TO OUTSIDE PROFESSIONALS

There are some problems that arise during mediation that require the expertise of another professional. In some situations, mediation can continue concurrently with the involvement of the other professional. In other instances, mediation may have to be suspended or even terminated. This would depend on the reason for referral. The mediator should discuss both the reason for referral and its effect on the mediation process with both clients before the referral is made.

The following list includes examples of professionals who may have special skills to offer:

- *accountants* — for information about tax implications, understanding corporate financial statements, business valuations, and so forth;
- *property appraisers* — for appraisals of commercial, residential and personal property;
- *investment analysts and pension experts* — to determine the present value of pensions, RRSP's and annuities and to obtain information regarding returns on investments;
- *mental health professionals* — for example, psychologists, psychiatrists and social workers, for emotional support and counselling;
- *vocational counsellors* — for information on career alternatives and retraining;
- *budget counsellors* — for assistance in money management, particularly with respect to managing household expenses.

This chapter has discussed the role of:

- *the mediator as educator,* informing the spouses about the effects on them and their children of separation and divorce;
- *the mediator as fact gatherer,* collecting relevant information with respect to the parties' history, present behaviour and future plans; and
- *the mediator as communicator,* helping the parties to communicate more effectively.

If the mediator successfully fulfills these three roles, the clients are likely to reach and maintain a settlement and to relate to each other more constructively in the future.

ANNOTATED BIBLIOGRAPHY

Bach, G., and Wyden, P. *The Intimate Enemy: How to Fight Fair in Love and Marriage.* New York: Avon Books, 1968. This is a very readable book dealing with communication problems in marriage. It is a useful guide to clients for effective conflict resolution and uses examples with which all of us can identify.

Barsky, M. "Emotional Needs and Functional Communication as Blocks to Mediation." In "Successful Techniques for Mediating Family Break-ups." (1983), 2 *Mediation Quarterly* 55. This article explores techniques for improving communication during the mediation process.

Bienenfeld, F. *My Mom and Dad Are Getting a Divorce.* EMC Corporation, 1980. This is a book for children to read to help children deal with their feelings with respect to separation and divorce.

Bowman, M.E., and Ahrons, C.R. "Impact of Legal Custody Status of Fathers' Parenting Post-Divorce." (1985), *Journal of Marriage and the Family* 481. This study examines 28 joint-custodial fathers and 54 non-custodial fathers with respect to (a) contact and activities with the children and (b) shared responsibility and decision making. The results demonstrated that joint-custodial fathers were more involved with their children than non-custodial fathers one year after divorce.

Fisher, R., and Ury, W. *Getting to Yes: Negotiating Agreement Without Giving In.* New York: Penguin Books, 1981. This book contains a number of very useful strategies for helping clients focus on their needs, rather than taking fixed positions.

Folberg, J., and Taylor, A. *Mediation: A Comprehensive Guide to Resolving Conflicts Without Litigation.* San Francisco: Jossey-Bass Inc., Publishers, 1984. For Section (2), "The Mediator as Fact Gatherer," see Part Two, "Mediation Stages, Concepts and Skills", particularly chapter 3, "Stages in the Mediation Process," page 38. For Section (3), "The Mediator as Communicator," see also Part Two, especially chapter 4, "Counselling Concepts for Developing Mediation Skills," page 73. Chapter 4 outlines a number of the techniques for resolving impasses and in general for dealing with the conflict between the parties while mediating matrimonial disputes. See also chapter 5, "Methods of Enhancing Communications," page 100. This chapter contains some useful communication techniques for the mediation process.

Francke, L.B. *Growing Up Divorced: How to Help Your Child Cope with Every Stage — From Infancy Through the Teens.* New York: Fawcett Crest Books, 1983. This is a book written by a parent who experienced divorce. She has combined her own perceptions with a review of major research in the field.

Francke, L.B. "The Sons of Divorce." May 1983. *New York Times Magazine.* This article examines the research demonstrating that boys have a more difficult period of adjustment than girls, on average, following separation and divorce.

Gardner, R. *Family Evaluation in Child Custody Litigation.* New Jersey: Creative Therapeutics, 1982. This book contains specific suggestions for information to collect in interviews with children and their parents in custody disputes.

Gardner, R. *The Boys and Girls Book About Divorce.* New York: Bantam Books, 1970.

and

Gardner, R. *The Parent's Book About Divorce.* New York: Bantam Books, 1979. These two books are written by an experienced clinician who offers many insights about the impact of divorce and separation on children and their parents. The children's book can be read with children or by an adolescent and can be used as the basis for their discussions during a counselling process.

Goldstein, S. *Divorce Parenting: How To Make It Work.* Toronto: McGraw-Hill Ryerson Limited, 1982. This is a practical book to assist parents and professionals to deal with the impact of divorce and separation, particularly on children. It is a helpful, practical guide for dealing sensitively with children's fears and concerns.

Haynes, J. M. *Divorce Mediation: A Practical Guide for Therapists and Counsellors.* New York: Springer Publishing Company, 1981. See Part I, "Professional Intervention in Divorce Situations," in particular, chapter 2, "The Emotional Aspects of Divorce," and chapter 3, "The Special Problems of Children," page 15. These two chapters help the mediator focus on the unique problems faced by families who are separating and divorcing and on the role of children in the mediation process.

Hess, R.D., and Camara, K.A. "Post-Divorce Family Relationships as Mediating Factors in the Consequences of Divorce for Children." (1979), 35 *Journal of Social Issues* 39.

Hetherington, E.M., Cox, M. and Cox, R. "The Aftermath of Divorce." In *Mother-Child, Father-Child Relations,* edited by I.J.P. Stevens, Jr., and M. Mathews. Washington, D.C.: National Association for the Education of Young Children, 1979.

Hetherington, E.M., Cox, M., and Cox, R. "Play and Social Interaction in Children Following Divorce." (1979), 35 *Journal of Social Issues* 26. This article presents the results of a longitudinal study on the effects of divorce on play and social interaction in 48 middle-class white preschool children from divorced families. These children were compared to 48 children from non-divorced families and were studied at intervals of two months, one year and two years after divorce. This study found that the adjustment to divorce appeared to be more difficult for boys than girls.

Ives, S.B., Fassler, B., and Lash, M. *The Divorce Workbook: A Guide for Kids and Families.* Vermont: Waterfront Books, 1985. This is a practical workbook for use by therapists to help children express their feelings about separation and divorce. The book combines both statements of feelings and children's art and can be incorporated into therapy sessions with children who are experiencing separation and divorce.

Kelly, J., and Wallerstein, J.S. "The Effects of Parental Divorce: Experiences of the Child in Early Latency." (1976), 46 *American Journal of Orthopsychiatry* 20. See entry for Wallerstein and Kelly, below.

Kulka, R.A., and Weingarten, H. "The Long Term Effects of Parental Divorce in Childhood on Adult Adjustment." (1979), 35 *Journal of Social Issues* 50. This article examines data from two national cross-sectional surveys conducted nearly 20 years apart and draws certain conclusions about the long-term effects of parental divorce on the children's later adjustment.

Levitan, T.E. "Children of Divorce: An Introduction." (1979), 35 *Journal of Social Issues* 1. This article contains an overview of research methodology with respect to the subject of children and divorce and a brief study of each article in this special issue of the *Journal of Social Issues.*

Ricci, I. *Mom's House, Dad's House.* New York: Macmillan, 1981. This is an excellent book for mental health professionals as well as other family members and the solicitor. This book contains many helpful, clear ideas for dealing with hostile spouses who need to learn more appropriate ways to communicate with each other.

Roman, M., and Haddad, W. *The Disposable Parent.* New York: Holt Rinehart & Winston, 1978. This book explores the impact on fathers, in particular, and on children of sole custody awards. The book makes a case for a shared parenting approach.

Santrock, J.W., and Warshak, R.A. "Father Custody and Social Development in Boys and Girls." (1979), 35 *Journal of Social Issues* 112. This study examined 33 boys and 27 girls from 60 white middle-class families ranging in age from 6 to 11 years. One-third of the children came from families in which the father was awarded custody, one-third from families in which the mother was awarded custody and one-third from parentally intact families. Videotaped observations were used to evaluate the children's social development in the three research groups.

Saposnek, D. "Strategies in Child Custody Mediation: A Family Systems Approach." In "Successful Techniques for Mediating Family Break-ups." (1983), 2 *Mediation Quarterly* 29.

Saposnek, D. *Mediating Child Custody Disputes.* San Francisco: Jossey-Bass Publishers, 1983. For Section (1), "The Mediator as Educator," see particularly Part III, "Strategies Used by Children, Parents and Mediators," page 118, and especially chapter 6, "How Children Contribute to Custody Disputes," page 118. For section (2), "The Mediator as Fact Gatherer," see particularly Part II, "Structuring the Mediation Process," particularly chapter 4, "Phases of Mediation: From Gathering Information to Reaching Agreements," page 71. For section (3), "The Mediator as Communicator," see in particular Part III, "Strategies Used by Children, Parents and Mediators," particularly chapter 8, "Strategies for Eliciting Co-operation Between Parents," page 106, and chapter 9, "Skills and Techniques for Managing Conflict," page 176. This book contains many useful clinical techniques for resolving disputes during mediation.

Statistics Canada. "Divorce: Law and the Family in Canada." (February 1983). This book chronicles the changes in Canada to the structure of the family, the divorce rate, the outcome of divorce and family laws from 1800 to the present date.

Wallerstein, J.S. "Children of Divorce: The Psychological Tasks of the Child." (1983), 53 *American Journal of Orthopsychiatry* 230. This paper attempts to conceptualize the major coping tasks faced by children who are experiencing separation and divorce.

Wallerstein, J.S. "The Long Over-burdened Child: Some Long-term Consequences of Divorce." (1985), *Social Work* 116. This article looks at the needs of children under circumstances where their parents' capacity to parent has been diminished by the effects of separation and divorce.

Wallerstein, J.S. "Women After Divorce: Preliminary Report from a Ten Year Follow-Up." (1986), 56 *American Journal of Orthopsychiatry* 65. This article contains the findings from a ten-year longitudinal study of 60 divorcing families from a middle-class California population.

Wallerstein, J.S., and Kelly, J.B. "The Effects of Parental Divorce: The Adolescent Experience." In *The Child and His Family — Children At a Psychiatric Risk,* edited by E.J. Anthony and C. Koupernik. New York: John Wiley, 1974.

and

Wallerstein, J.S., and Kelly, J.B. "The Effects of Parental Divorce: Experiences of the Child in Later Latency." (1976), 46 *American Journal of Orthopsychiatry* 256. These two articles, plus the article by Kelly and

Wallerstein, cited above, are based on data collected from the "Children of Divorce Project," carried out by Wallerstein and Kelly. These papers discuss the impact of divorce on children from 60 divorcing families who have a total of 131 children. The study began in 1970 and the longitudinal research is still continuing. These articles formed part of the material for the book *Surviving the Breakup: How Children and Parents Cope with Divorce,* written by the same authors, cited below.

Wallerstein, J.S., and Kelly, J.B. "Effects of Divorce on the Visiting Child Relationship." (1980), 137 *American Journal of Psychiatry* 1534. This article reports on the changes in relationship between the child and father in the five years following divorce. The data collected were derived from the "Children of Divorce Project."

Wallerstein, J.S. and Kelly, J.B. *Surviving the Breakup: How Children and Parents Cope with Divorce.* New York: Basic Books Inc., 1980. This is the best-known report of research on the effects of separation and divorce on children and parents. It is a longitudinal project and at the time the book was published, children and parents were studied at various intervals up to five years following separation or divorce. This is an extremely readable, enlightening book that can be used by the mediator to assist parents in understanding the possible consequences for themselves and their children and to help parents plan a strategy for dealing with the consequences of separation and divorce.

Ware, C. *Sharing Parenthood After Divorce: An Enlightened Custody Guide for Mothers, Fathers and Children.* Toronto: Bantam Books, 1984. This is a book written by a parent who attempted mediation as a method of resolving a contested custody dispute. She reports on her own experience and the experience of many other couples with respect to sharing parenthood after divorce. She is a strong advocate for both the mediation process and for a shared approach to parenting.

Weiss, R.S. "Growing Up a Little Faster: The Experience of Growing Up in a Single-Parent Household." (1979), 35 *Journal of Social Issues* 97. This article examines the change in expectations for children in single-parent households. The author concludes that there may be some positive benefits for children in terms of increased self-esteem, independence and a sense of competence as a result of being given increased responsibility.

Chapter Six

Major Issues: Custody and Access

A. CUSTODY AND ACCESS

Often the most significant issue in dispute between parents is who will have custody of the children. On a psychological level, this is often a competition for control, affection, continuity of lifestyle and acceptance as a parent. Feelings of anger, a desire for revenge, fears of loneliness and guilt compete with feelings of genuine concern about the welfare of the children and the knowledge that children need both parents and usually show better psychological adjustment if the conflict between the parents is kept to a minimum.

Often the party who is successful in winning custody succeeds in other aspects of the dispute, such as obtaining exclusive possession of the matrimonial home, support and familiar family possessions. The party who loses custody of the children faces the most radical change in lifestyle, and even if that parent chooses to leave the marriage, he or she often experiences strong feelings of loneliness, depression, a sense of failure, guilt or rejection.

The more adversarial the process for determining custody and the more the law establishes one parent as a winner and the other as a loser in custody matters, the more devastating the psychological effect on both parents and children. Within this psychological context, the following is a discussion of the law of custody, both at a provincial and a federal level, including alternative orders that can be made by the court.

(1) WHAT IS CUSTODY?

In the context of parental disputes over children, custody refers to the totality of rights and duties in relation to the child. That is, it encompasses both control of the physical person of the child and the right to make decisions about the child's upbringing.

Custody essentially includes the following rights:

- the right to control the child;
- the right to make decisions regarding the child's education, religion and lifestyle; and
- the right to grant or withhold consent to the marriage of an underage child.

Custody also includes such responsibilities as:

- providing for the child's physical, mental and moral care and development; and
- providing for the child's basic needs, such as food, clothing and housing.

Custody is often used interchangeably with *guardianship;* however, *guardianship* is really a broader term that applies in situations other than "legal custody" in the sense described above.

(2) What Is Access?

Access is defined as the right of non-custodial parents to visit with the child. An order for access does not include the legal right to make decisions with respect to the child's upbringing, nor does it include the legal responsibility for the child's care and control. The purpose of access is to encourage the continuation of a parent-child relationship following a marriage breakdown. A non-custodial parent who has access rights no longer has a legal right to participate as a parent in many significant areas of the child's life, such as determining the child's residence, education or religion.

The non-custodial parent would have the same responsibilities for the care of the child as any adult acting in a caretaking capacity. That is, the non-custodial parent is responsible for emergency health care, informing the custodial parent of any delay in returning the child at the agreed-upon time, and requesting in advance any changes in the visitation schedule.

In some provinces, such as Ontario, and in the federal *Divorce Act, 1985,* S.C. 1986, c. 4, anyone who has access to the child has a legal right to make inquiries and receive information about the health, education and welfare of the child.

(3) Custody Disputes: The Historical Context

Under the English common law, children were considered to be the property of their fathers and custody awards were routinely made to fathers.

During the 19th century, the industrial revolution resulted in many fathers working away from the home and mothers remaining in the home as the primary caretakers of children. In addition, society began to place a higher value on children as more children survived the high risk of infant mortality. Legally, the courts shifted from a preference for fathers as custodians to mothers as custodians. This was particularly true of young children.

During the early 1900s, the "tender years" doctrine was applied as the principal rule for determining custody disputes. That is, custody was routinely awarded to mothers, particularly for children under the age of seven, unless the mother was found to be unfit.

In the mid-1970s a further cultural change took place that had an effect on the criteria for awarding custody. The child's needs and interests became a more important factor, and custody was awarded on the basis of "the best interests of the child". Custody awards were not supposed to be contingent on the sex of the parent, but rather were to reflect the best interests of the child. In fact, the courts still demonstrated a considerable preference for maternal custody, unless the mother was demonstrated to be unfit.

In the 1980s, a number of social factors have had an impact on custody awards; for example, such changes as:

- more women are in the work-force and out of the home;
- more men are participating in child rearing and household tasks; and
- a greater concern about discrimination on the basis of sex, both as it applies to women and to men.

In keeping with the movement toward greater sharing of parental rights and responsibilities during the marriage, there has been an increased trend toward continued sharing of the parental role even after marriage breakdown. This trend is responsible for the movement away from a determination of sole custody to one parent, that is, exclusive parental rights to one parent, toward a concept of continued parental co-operation and sharing after the marriage has ended. This trend has led to a number of variations in the traditional award of custody to one parent and access to the other.

(4) Custody Arrangements

(a) Sole Custody

Sole custody refers to an order whereby one custodial parent is awarded the totality of rights and duties in relation to the child. Custody can be determined by the courts, or it can be determined by the parties through their own agreement.

(b) Split Custody

This type of custody has been applied in many cases in England and consists of an arrangement or order whereby "physical custody" of the child is granted to one parent and "legal custody" is granted to the other parent. That is, the custodial parent does not have the actual physical control of the child, but does have the exclusive right to make all important decisions with respect to the child's upbringing. Physical custody is granted to the parent who has "care and control" of the child.

This type of arrangement has some obvious difficulties, in that the parent who is physically responsible for the child is excluded from making significant decisions with respect to the child's education, religion and upbringing. If a parent has the ability to offer the child adequate care and control, it would seem to be both reasonable and desirable that the parent participate in important decisions with respect to the child.

(c) Alternating Custody

Alternating custody means that one parent has full custody, including care and control of the child for a specified time period and then the other parent has full custody, including care and control for a specified time period (not to be confused with alternating or rotating residence, which is described in subsection (d)).

While the child is residing with one parent, that parent is entirely responsible for all decisions with respect to the child's upbringing, although the non-custodial parent usually has the right to access. This custody arrangement divides, rather than shares, the custodial responsibilities between the parents. This is to be distinguished from joint custody, which will be discussed next.

(d) Joint Custody

In contrast to split or alternating custody, joint custody preserves, at all times, both parents' joint legal responsibility for the upbringing of the child. That is, even following separation, both parents maintain their legal rights and responsibilities for significant decisions affecting the child.

Joint legal custody does not necessarily mean that the child spends an equal amount of time physically living with each parent. There is no requirement that the child spend any particular amount of time with each parent, although both parents retain their legal status as parents.

In California, and in some other jurisdictions in the United States, courts distinguish between joint legal custody and joint physical custody.

- *Joint legal custody* means that both parents retain the right to make decisions with respect to the child.
- *Joint physical custody* means that the child spends approximately equal amounts of time living with each parent.
- *Sole legal custody* means that one parent has the legal right to make all decisions with respect to the child's upbringing.
- *Sole physical custody* means that the child primarily resides with one parent and has access visits with the other parent.

In California, any combination of the above-mentioned aspects of custody is possible. That is, a family can have joint legal and joint physical custody or joint legal but sole physical custody or sole legal and sole physical custody or sole legal but joint physical custody.

In Canada, couples who have joint custody of their children generally share decisions with respect to upbringing, but have an arrangement whereby the child has a primary residence with one parent. However, there are a growing number of cases in which parents share both decision making and physical care and control on an approximately equal-time basis.

Under both provincial and federal legislation, it is possible for a court to order joint custody, particularly in cases where the parties consent to such an order. However, the Northwest Territories is the only jurisdiction in Canada to specifically include the term joint custody as an option available to the judge under its custody provisions. The legislation does not contain either a presumption or a preference for joint custody, but rather permits the judge, in appropriate cases, to make such an order.

In practice, Canadian courts usually do not make joint custody orders in cases where the parties do not request it, particularly if there is evidence that the parties cannot co-operate with each other in the interests of their children. There are some recent exceptions to this general rule, particularly at the stage of an interim custody order. At this point, the court may make a joint custody or alternating custody award to preserve the status quo as between the parties until the date of trial.

Many couples who mediate rather than litigate the issues of custody and access decide on a shared parenting arrangement, which is, in effect, joint custody. According to the research data collected by Howard Irving on a sample of 201 Ontario couples, joint custody appears to have many benefits for both the parents and children. Particularly where these arrangements were arrived at voluntarily, the parents reported a higher level of satisfaction; it was found that coparental relationships were likely to have been less litigious than sole custody arrangements: the children tended to be happier when they maintained frequent, reliable and ongoing contact with both their parents and this arrangement encouraged joint fiscal responsibility, with a far higher percentage of joint custodial fathers paying support.

(5) THE CRITERIA FOR AWARDING CUSTODY AS DETERMINED BY PROVINCIAL AND FEDERAL STATUTE

Custody decisions are made by both the provincial government and the federal government. In the usual case, custody decisions made prior to divorce are made pursuant to a provincial statute, although interim orders can be made under the federal *Divorce Act, 1985*.

At the time of divorce, custody and access decisions are considered a part of corollary relief, that is, relief that the courts can grant in conjunction with their power to grant a divorce. It is also possible to apply for a custody order under a provincial statute at the time of divorce.

When an action for divorce is commenced under the *Divorce Act, 1985,* any application for custody under a provincial statute that has not as yet been determined by the court is stayed, except by leave of the court. This is because the decision under the federal Act would be constitutionally paramount to a decision under a provincial Act. Therefore, there would be no reason for competing claims under the two Acts to proceed at the same time.

Provincial statutes and the federal *Divorce Act, 1985* vary in the way in which custody is described and also vary in the criteria that are stated in determining custody. Some statutes refer only to the best interests of children, whereas other statutes set out specific criteria for the judges to consider in making a custody award.

For example, the Ontario *Children's Law Reform Act,* R.S.O. 1980, c. 68, sets out very specifically the criteria to be applied by a judge in making an order of custody. These criteria reflect the common law position on custody awards. As a result, even in those provinces that do not set out elaborate criteria for determining custody, most jurisdictions would apply the same or similar criteria on the basis of common law.

The Ontario *Children's Law Reform Act* deals with custody as follows:

24(1) The merits of an application under this Part in respect of custody of or access to a child shall be determined on the basis of the best interests of the child.

(2) In determining the best interests of the child for the purposes of an application under this Part in respect of custody of or access to a child, a court shall consider all the needs and circumstances of the child including,

    (*a*) the love, affection and emotional ties between the child and,

        (i) each person entitled to or claiming custody of or access to the child,

        (ii) other members of the child's family who reside with the child, and

        (iii) persons involved in the care and upbringing of the child;

    (*b*) the views and preferences of the child, where such views and preferences can reasonably be ascertained;

    (*c*) the length of time the child has lived in a stable home environment;

    (*d*) the ability and willingness of each person applying for custody of the child to provide the child with guidance and education, the necessaries of life and any special needs of the child;

    (*e*) any plans proposed for the care and upbringing of the child;

    (*f*) the permanence and stability of the family unit with which it is proposed that the child will live; and

    (*g*) the relationship by blood or through an adoption order between the child and each person who is a party to the application.

(3) The past conduct of a person is not relevant to a determination of an application under this Part in respect of custody of or access to a child unless the conduct is relevant to the ability of the person to act as a parent of a child. [en. 1982, c. 20, s. 1]

It is important to note that this statute apparently does not establish a preference for biological parents over psychological parents, and in addition it specifically excludes matrimonial fault or other aspects of past conduct if they are not relevant to parenting ability. It is often necessary for the mediator in discussions of custody, as well as in discussions of support, to point out to the parties that the court does not make awards of custody or support on the basis of matrimonial fault.

By way of contrast, the federal *Divorce Act, 1985* does not set out the criteria for evaluating the child's best interests, although it does adopt "best interests" as the sole test for determining custody awards. One unique feature of the federal Act is that it places a heavy emphasis on ensuring that the child has an opportunity to spend considerable time with both parents. In fact, to preserve the child's relationship with both parents, the Act directs the court to give consideration, when determining custody awards, to the parent who is most likely to encourage the involvement of the non-custodial parent. This Act is similar to the Ontario Act in that matrimonial fault is expressly excluded as a factor in awarding custody or access, unless the conduct is relevant to parenting. The custody provisions of the Divorce Act are set out below:

16(8) In making an order under this section, the court shall take into consideration only the best interests of the child of the marriage as determined by reference to the condition, means, needs and other circumstances of the child.

(9) In making an order under this section, the court shall not take into consideration the past conduct of any person unless the conduct is relevant to the ability of that person to act as a parent of a child.

(10) In making an order under this section, the court shall give effect to the principle that a child of the marriage should have as much contact with each spouse as is consistent with the best interests of the child and, for that purpose, shall take into consideration the willingness of the person for whom custody is sought to facilitate such contact.

The federal and provincial statutes also differ in the way in which entitlement to custody is described and in the way in which the rights and privileges of the custodial and the non-custodial parent are specified. For example, the Ontario *Children's Law Reform Act* deals with these issues in the following way:

20(1) Except as otherwise provided in this Part, the father and the mother of a child are equally entitled to custody of the child.

(2) A person entitled to custody of a child has the rights and responsibilities of a parent in respect of the person of the child and must exercise those rights and responsibilities in the best interests of the child.

(3) Where more than one person is entitled to custody of a child, any one of them may exercise the rights and accept the responsibilities of a parent on behalf of them in respect of the child.

(4) Where the parents of a child live separate and apart and the child lives with one of them with the consent, implied consent or acquiescence of the other of them, the right of the other to exercise the entitlement to custody and the incidents of custody, but not the entitlement to access, is suspended until a separation agreement or order otherwise provides.

(5) The entitlement to access to a child includes the right to visit with and be visited by the child and the same right as a parent to make inquiries and to be given information as to the health, education and welfare of the child. [en. 1982, c. 20, s. 1]

It is clear that this Act sets up an equal statutory entitlement on the part of fathers and mothers to custody of their children. In addition, while the Act does not prevent an order of joint custody, it is written from the perspective of a sole custody award. It does not at any time specifically mention joint custody or split or alternating custody.

This Act does give some of the rights of a parent to the non-custodial parent. That is, it does give the non-custodial parent a right to make inquiries and be given information with respect to the child's health, education and welfare. However, it should be noted that this is a right to information and not a right to participate in decision making.

Under the federal *Divorce Act, 1985* the entitlement to custody and the allocation of rights and privileges between the custodial and non-custodial parent are as follows:

> 16(1) A court of competent jurisdiction may, on application by either or both spouses or by any other person, make an order respecting the custody of or the access to, or the custody of and access to, any or all children of the marriage.
>
> (2) Where an application is made under subsection (1), the court may, on application by either or both spouses or by any other person, make an interim order respecting the custody of or the access to, or the custody of and access to, any or all children of the marriage pending determination of the application under subsection (1).
>
> (3) A person, other than a spouse, may not make an application under subsection (1) or (2) without leave of the court.
>
> (4) The court may make an order under this section granting custody of, or access to, any or all children of the marriage to any one or more persons.
>
> (5) Unless the court orders otherwise, a spouse who is granted access to a child of the marriage has the right to make inquiries, and to be given information, as to the health, education and welfare of the child.
>
> (6) The court may make an order under this section for a definite or indefinite period or until the happening of a specified event and may impose such other terms, conditions or restrictions in connection therewith as it thinks fit and just.
>
> (7) Without limiting the generality of subsection (6), the court may include in an order under this section a term requiring any person who has custody of a child of the marriage and who intends to change the place of residence of that child to notify, at least thirty days before the change or within such other period before the change as the court may specify, any person who is granted access to that child of the change, the time at which the change will be made and the new place of residence of the child.

This statute does not presume that the parents have an equal entitlement to custody. There is no reference to joint custody in the legislation (only in a marginal note, which has no statutory significance); however, the *Divorce Act, 1985* does establish a right to information by the non-custodial parent, including the right upon application to be notified of a change of address if the custodial parent decides to move to a new location.

This chapter has examined different types of custodial arrangements. It is important to understand the recognized options for custody, because the parties may be unaware of the alternatives, and this information could facilitate a settlement.

ANNOTATED BIBLIOGRAPHY

Fineberg, A. "Joint Custody of Infants: Breakthrough or Fad?" (1979), 2 *Canadian Journal of Family Law* 417. The author clarifies the difference between sole custody, split custody, alternating custody and joint custody. She then explores the present status of joint custody in Canadian law. The author examines psychological research with respect to the impact on the children and parents and arrives at a positive view of joint custody, when the parents meet certain specific criteria.

Folberg, J., ed. *Joint Custody and Shared Parenting.* Washington, D.C.: The Bureau of National Affairs Inc. and the Association of Family and Conciliation Courts, 1984. This book contains an excellent collection of articles examining the issue of joint custody from a variety of viewpoints. Folberg has included a range of conflicting views about the desirability of joint custody. In addition, the book contains articles on different parenting arrangements, factors influencing joint custody, research findings with respect to joint custody and the law of joint custody. It is an excellent and exhaustive summary of the literature at the time it was published.

Irving, Dr. H.H., and Benjamin, Dr. M. "Shared Parenting in Canada; Questions, Answers and Implications." (1986), 1(1) *Canadian Family Law Quarterly* 79. This article reports on the results of the Shared Parenting Project a research study comparing the experience of 201 shared parents with that of 194 (maternal) sole custody parents. This is a very informative article that explodes some of the myths about joint custody.

Joyal-Poupart, R. "Joint Custody." In *Family Law in Canada: New Directions,* edited by E. Sloss, p. 107. Ottawa: Canadian Advisory Council on the Status of Women, 1985. This author examines custody legislation and jurisprudence in a number of jurisdictions. Arguing from the feminist point of view, he takes the position that joint custody should be granted in cases where parents expressly request it.

Mills, B.G. (Judge), and Belzer, S. "Joint Custody As a Parenting Alternative." (1982), 9 *Pepperdine Law Review* 53. The authors present the legislative history of the California Joint Custody Statute and summarize a variety of viewpoints with respect to joint custody. This article contains a discussion of the legislative intent behind the statute and the issue of whether the current law is the most effective means of protecting the best interests of the child and of assuring children a frequent and continuing contact with both parents following a marriage breakdown.

Ryan, J. "Joint Custody in Canada: Time for a Second Look." 49 R.F.L. (2d) 119 and published in *Children's Rights in the Practice of Family*

Law, edited by B. Landau. Toronto: Carswell Publishing Co., 1986. This is an excellent article reviewing the literature on joint custody. The author concludes that joint custody appears to be a preferred approach to parenting following divorce, for a variety of reasons.

Ryan, J.P. "The Overlapping Custody Jurisdiction: Co-existence or Chaos?" (1980), 3 *Canadian Journal of Family Law* 95. This article examines the overlap between provincial and federal jurisdiction with respect to custody legislation. The author also discusses the potential for conflict and confusion between the superior courts and inferior courts with respect to their custody jurisdiction. The author concludes by advocating reform of custody legislation and the establishment of a Unified Family Court system.

Chapter 7

Major Issues: Support and Property

A. SUPPORT FOR SPOUSE

Financial provision for a spouse or former spouse is often called alimony, maintenance or support, often interchangeably. For the purposes here, we will use the term *support* to include financial provision for either a spouse or former spouse. Support is designed to provide financial assistance to a dependent spouse. Support can be provided to a spouse during separation, but prior to divorce, or after a divorce. Provincial statutes have the jurisdiction to deal with spousal support prior to divorce. After a divorce, and during divorce proceedings themselves, the federal government has exclusive jurisdiction to deal with support under the *Divorce Act, 1985*, S.C. 1986, c. 4. The definition of who qualifies for spousal support under the provincial and federal statutes is very different in some instances. However, the criteria for awarding support are generally very similar, regardless of whether the provincial or federal legislation is being applied.

(1) THE DIVORCE ACT, 1985

(a) Who Qualifies?

Under the *Divorce Act, 1985* only spouses who have married each other can obtain support. The jurisdiction to award support under the *Divorce Act, 1985* depends on a judgment for divorce being granted. Of course, a judgment for divorce may only be granted to dissolve the marriage of a man and a woman who are married to each other.

(b) Criteria

The *Divorce Act, 1985* sets out in s. 15(2) that a court may make whatever order it deems "reasonable" for the support of a spouse. The major criteria, or factors, which a court is to consider are set out in s. 15(5), which reads as follows:

> 15(5) In making an order under this section, the court shall take into consideration the condition, means, needs and other circumstances of each spouse and of any child of the marriage for whom support is sought, including
>> (a)   the length of time the spouses cohabited;
>> (b)   the functions performed by the spouse during cohabitation; and
>> (c)   any order, agreement or arrangement relating to support of the spouse or child.

In addition to these factors, the Act sets out specific objectives of an order for support in s. 15(7), which reads as follows:

> 15(7) An order made under this section that provides for the support of a spouse should
>> (a)   recognize any economic advantages or disadvantages to the spouses arising from the marriage or its breakdown;
>> (b)   apportion between the spouses any financial consequences arising from the care of any child of the marriage over and above the obligation apportioned between the spouses pursuant to subsection (8);
>> (c)   relieve any economic hardship of the spouses arising from the breakdown of the marriage; and
>> (d)   in so far as practicable, promote the economic self-sufficiency of each spouse within a reasonable period of time.

At the time of writing (June 1986) the Act has just been proclaimed in force, so it will be impossible to state with any degree of authority what the various subsections actually mean until there has been judicial comment on them. However, as in the prior statute, *Divorce Act,* R.S.C. 1970, c. D-8, the main factors are the means, needs and other circumstances of the parties. Means and needs emerge as the major factors: What means does each party have? Are they sufficient to meet his or her needs? And if they are not, to what extent does the other spouse have means to contribute?

The old legislation included a reference to the conduct of the parties as a factor to be considered by the court in making an order for support. Now, by virtue of s. 15(6) any misconduct of a spouse is not to be taken into account in making an order for spousal support.

New factors added by the new legislation are the specific references to the length of cohabitation, the functions each spouse performed during cohabitation, and any other order or agreement relating to support. These factors suggest (although certainly not clearly) that a divorce court may award less support in the case of a marriage of short duration, and conversely may order more if the marriage has been a lengthy one; similarly, if one spouse has performed all household functions and has been out of the work-force, this may warrant a greater or lengthier support order.

The objectives of an order for support of a spouse are interesting. For the first time, federal legislation squarely addresses the issue of a dependent spouse becoming self-sufficient, and an enumerated objective of an order is to promote economic self-sufficiency within a reasonable period of time.

This suggests that time-limited support orders geared to realistic retraining programs of spouses will become more prevalent in the future.

Another new feature of support is that it is to relieve economic hardship resulting from the breakdown of the marriage. A typical example of this might be the situation of a wife who has postponed her own career plans in order to stay at home and raise a family. If the marriage breaks down before she has been able to establish herself in the work-force, it can be said that she suffers economic hardship as a result of the breakdown of the marriage. Marriage breakdown has occurred at a time when she has lost years of productivity and when she is not able to support herself.

Practically speaking, notwithstanding the enumerated criteria in the *Divorce Act, 1985,* it is suggested that the primary analysis of the support obligation will be a practical rather than a philosophical one. While it may be an enumerated goal of a support order to promote economic self-sufficiency, in most situations, there is simply not enough money to support two households, and the promoting of economic self-sufficiency is a practical imperative, rather than a philosophical or legal one. Accordingly, the prime considerations will always be the degree of dependency, the extent to which the dependency can be decreased by the dependent spouse's own efforts to become self-sufficient, and the extent to which the other spouse has the means to contribute to the dependant's needs, and still meet his or her own needs.

(2) PROVINCIAL STATUTES

(a) Who Qualifies?

In many provinces, the provincial legislation relating to spousal support applies not only to spouses who have married one another, but in some circumstances extends the right to be supported to common law partners as well. The qualifications from province to province may vary, but generally speaking, the legislation is designed to recognize situations of economic dependency, and to provide for support when these types of economic units break down, notwithstanding that there may be no marital relationship between the parties. An example of this type of extension of support rights is found in the Ontario *Family Law Act, 1986,* S.O. 1986, c. 4. Part III of the Act deals with support obligations, and extends the definition of *spouse* to include not only spouses who are married to one another, but in addition, includes:

> 29. . . . either of a man and woman who are not married to each other and have cohabited,
>> (*a*) continuously for a period of not less than three years, or
>> (*b*) in a relationship of some permanence, if they are the natural or adoptive parents of a child.

These two categories of "common law" spouses have the same rights and obligations relating to support as do married spouses.

(b) Criteria

In Ontario, the general rule is that each spouse has an obligation to provide support for him or herself, and also to support his or her spouse in accordance with need, to the extent that he or she is capable of doing so. Accordingly, the primary obligation is to be self-supporting and to provide support in accordance with means and in accordance with the need of the other spouse. The twin criteria of "means" and "needs" are therefore the paramount criteria for support under provincial legislation, as they are under the *Divorce Act, 1985*. In each case "needs" will reflect the lifestyle of the parties while they were together, so reasonable needs will vary from couple to couple.

Like the federal legislation, the Ontario legislation, for example, sets out the purposes of an order for support of a spouse. This is done in s. 33(8), which reads as follows:

> 33(8) An order for the support of a spouse should,
> (a) recognize the spouse's contribution to the relationship and the economic consequences of the relationship for the spouse;
> (b) share the economic burden of child support equitably;
> (c) make fair provision to assist the spouse to become able to contribute to his or her own support; and
> (d) relieve financial hardship, if this has not been done by orders under Parts I (Family Property) and II (Matrimonial Home).

The court is to consider all the circumstances of the parties in determining the amount of support, including the following criteria, which are set out in s. 33(9):

> 33(9) In determining the amount and duration, if any, of support in relation to need, the court shall consider all the circumstances of the parties, including,
> (a) the dependant's and respondent's current assets and means;
> (b) the assets and means that the dependant and respondent are likely to have in the future;
> (c) the dependant's capacity to contribute to his or her own support;
> (d) the respondent's capacity to provide support;
> (e) the dependant's and respondent's age and physical and mental health;
> (f) the dependant's needs, in determining which the court shall have regard to the accustomed standard of living while the parties resided together;
> (g) the measures available for the dependant to become able to provide for his or her own support and the length of time and cost involved to enable the dependant to take those measures;
> (h) any legal obligation of the respondent or dependant to provide support for another person;
> (i) the desirability of the dependant or respondent remaining at home to care for a child;
> (j) a contribution by the dependant to the realization of the respondent's career potential;
> (k) if the dependant is a child,
>   (i) the child's aptitude for and reasonable prospects of obtaining an education, and
>   (ii) the child's need for a stable environment;

(*l*)   if the dependant is a spouse,
>> (i) the length of time the dependant and respondent cohabited,
>> (ii) the effect on the spouse's earning capacity of the responsibilities assumed during cohabitation,
>> (iii) whether the spouse has undertaken the care of a child who is of the age of eighteen years or over and unable by reason of illness, disability or other cause to withdraw from the charge of his or her parents,
>> (iv) whether the spouse has undertaken to assist in the continuation of a program of education for a child eighteen years of age or over who is unable for that reason to withdraw from the charge of his or her parents,
>> (v) any housekeeping, child care or other domestic service performed by the spouse for the family, as if the spouse were devoting the time spent in performing that service in remunerative employment and were contributing the earnings to the family's support,
>> (vi) the effect on the spouse's earnings and career development of the responsibility of caring for a child; and

(*m*)   any other legal right of the dependant to support, other than out of public money.

As under the *Divorce Act, 1985,* conduct does not affect the obligation to provide support.

As can be seen from the Ontario legislation, the focus is very similar to that under the *Divorce Act, 1985.* The criteria can be viewed as essentially the same, the only difference between the two pieces of legislation, in general terms, being who qualifies for an order for support.

B. SUPPORT FOR CHILDREN

(1) THE DIVORCE ACT, 1985

(a) Who Qualifies?

To be supported pursuant to the provisions of the *Divorce Act, 1985,* a child must fall within the definition of the term *child of the marriage* in the legislation. This means a child who is either under the age of 16 years, or 16 years of age or over and under the charge of the parents but unable, by reason of illness, disability or other cause to withdraw from their charge or to obtain the necessaries of life. This definition includes children who are completing their education (including post-secondary education) and who are unable by this reason to support themselves. Generally speaking, when considering the issue of child support under divorce legislation, children are considered to be entitled to support until they complete their first post-secondary diploma or degree, as long as they remain in full-time attendance at school.

(b) Criteria

Again, under the *Divorce Act, 1985,* when dealing with an order for support of a child, the court may make such order as it thinks reasonable.

The same factors as are relevant in determining an order for support of a spouse are also to be taken into account in determining an order for support for a child, namely, the conditions, means, needs and other circumstances of each spouse and any child of the marriage for whom support is sought, including the length of time the spouses cohabited, the functions performed by the spouse during cohabitation, and any order, agreement, or arrangement relating to support of the spouse or child.

As was the case with spousal support, objectives of an order for support of the child are also set out, in s. 15(8), which reads as follows:

15(8) An order made under this section that provides for the support of a child of the marriage should
    (a) recognize that the spouses have a joint financial obligation to maintain the child;
    and
    (b) apportion that obligation between the spouses according to their relative abilities to contribute to the performance of the obligation.

This section is really a codification of the law as it has developed since 1968, namely, that child support is the joint obligation of the parents, and that the obligation should be apportioned between the parties in accordance with their ability to pay.

More and more, child support is being examined more closely, and parties are being asked to direct their minds very carefully to the issue of the necessary items to support their children. These include not only the obvious, such as clothing and babysitting, but also all of or a portion of the following types of expenses:

- day care expenses;
- housing expenses, including mortgage, taxes, utilities;
- transportation expenses, including necessity of a family car, public transit, and the like;
- entertainment, including such items as birthday parties;
- recreation, including such things as club memberships, Cubs, Beavers, Brownies, Girl Guides, music lessons, skating lessons, art, drama, and so forth;
- allowances;
- special education or tutoring;
- costs incidental to religious education, confirmation and the like;
- university tuition, if children are of that age;
- diapers, formula, related sundries;
- medical expenses, including drugs, eye glasses;
- dental expenses, including orthodonture;
- summer vacation, including holidays, trips, summer camp.

This list is designed as an initial guide to isolating the children's expenses. Once this is done, it becomes easier to apportion the load between the parents in accordance with their ability to pay, taking into account income tax consequences that will flow from certain types of payments, which are dealt with more thoroughly in Section E of this chapter.

(2) PROVINCIAL STATUTES

(a) Who Qualifies?

Under provincial statutes, support for a child is generally required as long as that child is a minor. Definitions of *minority* will vary from province to province. In Ontario, the obligation of a parent to support a child extends to any unmarried child who is a minor, or is enrolled in a full-time program of education. The obligation to support a child does not extend to a child who is 16 years or over and has withdrawn from parental control. As is the case under the *Divorce Act, 1985,* generally, under provincial legislation, support obligations apply to children who are still at school.

(b) Criteria

The *Family Law Act, 1986* of Ontario sets out specifically the purposes of an order for support of a child. These are found in s. 33(7), which reads as follows:

33(7) An order for the support of a child should,
    (*a*) recognize that each parent has an obligation to provide support for the child;
    (*b*) recognize that the obligation of a natural or adoptive parent outweighs the obligation of a parent who is not a natural or adoptive parent; and
    (*c*) apportion the obligation according to the capacities of the parents to provide support.

This is very similar to the provision under the *Divorce Act, 1985.*

Subparagraph (*b*) is interesting in that it focuses, for the first time, attention on the fact that a child may have several "parents". Under the *Family Law Act, 1986* of Ontario, a parent includes a person who has demonstrated a settled intention to treat a child as a child of his or her family. Accordingly, in a combined family situation, a stepparent may well be recognized as a "parent" for the purposes of the legislation. What this subsection makes clear is that a stepparent's obligation to support a stepchild is not as great as the obligation of that stepchild's natural or adoptive parent to support him or her. The legislation thus recognizes that blood is, indeed, thicker than water.

In determining the amount of support, the same criteria are relevant, including the child's aptitude for and reasonable prospects of obtaining an education and the child's need for a stable environment.

Notwithstanding all of these enumerated criteria, the basic issue will still be what the child realistically needs by way of support, having regard to the lifestyle the parties enjoyed while they were living together, and the extent to which this level of lifestyle can be maintained by the parents now that they are living apart.

C. FINANCIAL DISCLOSURE

(1) LEGAL OBLIGATION TO DISCLOSE

Financial disclosure is a necessary precondition for working out resolutions of both property and support issues. There are both practical and legal reasons for this.

Practically speaking, it is impossible to agree on a reasonable level of support without having a clear idea of the income and needs of each of the parties. Similarly, you cannot approach the question of property division without knowing what property there is to be divided and what the value of the property is, for often the property will not be divided in kind, but property that each party has will be set off against property that the other one has, and equalization payments will be made to ensure that each spouse ends up with an equal value of whatever property or assets provincial legislation decrees should be shared.

Legally speaking, financial disclosure is crucial. Agreements can be set aside if the parties failed to disclose to each other their significant assets, income and liabilities existing at the time an agreement was made. For example, in the Ontario legislation the relevant section of the *Family Law Act, 1986* is s. 56(4)(*a*) which reads as follows:

> 56(4) A court may, on application, set aside a domestic contract or a provision in it,
>
>   (*a*)   if a party failed to disclose to the other significant assets, or significant debts or other liabilities, existing when the domestic contract was made.

The reason this is so is clear. For example, if a husband fails to disclose to his wife an asset worth $100,000 that yields annual income of $10,000, and the wife accepts a level of support that she believes is all the husband can afford, she has been misled and has relied on misleading information to reach her decision about settlement. Similarly, if the asset hidden by the husband is one that provincial legislation says should be shared, she has been cheated out of $50,000 of her settlement. All decisions should be informed ones; if the wife in either case had known the true state of affairs, she would not have accepted either the level of support she did or the property settlement she did. Because she did not have a complete picture, she would be able to attack the agreement in the future. Since the goal of mediation is to reach not only an agreement, but one that will be legally binding and that the parties can live with comfortably in the future, there is no point in mediating financial issues without complete financial disclosure; to do so is to invite an attack on whatever agreement is reached, and makes the mediation process a waste of time, money and energy.

(a) What Constitutes Full Disclosure?

To make full disclosure, *all* income, assets and liabilities must be disclosed. Even though a party might object, he or she must still disclose:

- property acquired after separation,
- property the other knows nothing about,
- income the other party knows nothing about,
- property owned prior to the marriage,
- property acquired by inheritance or gift,
- property that provincial law exempts from sharing, and
- property that will be shared pursuant to provincial legislation.

(b) Valuation of Assets, Debts, etc.

Disclosure of assets has two elements:

- the asset itself, and
- the value of the asset.

Identifying the asset itself is usually quite simple. Valuing the asset may be extremely complicated. Valuators can differ wildly in their estimates of the value of any particular asset, and valuation in itself has been the subject of numerous and lengthy articles. Generally speaking, the value of any particular asset will be its fair market value; the price a willing buyer will pay a willing seller on the open market. It is not book value, or replacement value, or cost. In complex situations, it will often be necessary to obtain professional opinions on the valuation of various assets such as real estate, shares in private companies, family businesses, professional practices and things of that nature.

Debts and liabilities must be disclosed also. These may include contingent liabilities, for example, notional costs of disposition that would be attracted on the sale of the asset. For example, when valuing the matrimonial home, it is customary to take the estimated sale price of the matrimonial home and deduct from it any

- outstanding mortgages, liens, or encumbrances;
- real estate commission that would be paid; and
- legal fees and other costs of sale.

The value then remaining is the net value that would be subject to division.

Most provinces have regimes of property or asset sharing that provide for calculating the net value of assets in order to determine what should be shared.

(2) SUPPORTING DOCUMENTATION

Most jurisdictions have specific court forms that are used to make financial disclosure. There is usually a section to list income from all sources, a budget section to list monthly expenses, and assets sections (often broken down by categories, such as land, bank accounts, stocks and bonds and the like) and a section for debts and liabilities. The financial statement that is used in the District and Supreme Courts of Ontario, pursuant to the *Family Law Act, 1986* of Ontario, is found in Section F of this chapter and is an example of this type of financial form.

Although the form is designed for court use, it is not limited that way. The form is usually used as the method of complying with the initial requirements of financial disclosure in negotiation situations, and should be used that way in mediation also. It is customary to exchange sworn financial statements and then to produce whatever additional documentation is required in order to substantiate the figures set out in the form.

The statements in the financial form should be verified as much as possible by requesting additional supporting documentation to corroborate the figures set out in the statement.

Examples might include some or all of the following:

- income tax returns to substantiate income;
- financial statements to substantiate corporate value;
- bank statements to substantiate values in bank accounts;
- RRSP statements to substantiate total value of RRSPS;
- real estate appraisals to substantiate the value of land, buildings, homes, and so forth;
- pension statements to substantiate pension values;
- benefits package statements to disclose the total benefits available to an employee and their value;
- corporate valuation to substantiate the value of an interest in a closely held corporation;
- partnership agreements to show any particular rights the partners have against one another, and to give some indication of the value of a partnership interest;
- shareholder's agreements to show a potential value of a shareholder's interest;
- insurance policies to confirm the extent of insurance and benefits payable;
- copies of leases, telephone bills, VISA and department store accounts, utility bills, tax bills and the like to corroborate estimated expenses.

This list is not meant to be exhaustive, but to indicate some areas where supporting documentation could and often should be obtained.

D. INCOME TAX IMPLICATIONS: Property

All the provinces have slightly different regimes for property sharing, ranging from deferred community for certain assets only, to more complete deferred property sharing. A "deferred" regime is one in which the actual sharing of the property or its value is postponed until a triggering event happens, usually something like separation, divorce or death. Until one of the triggering events happens, the parties remain "separate as to property", which means that each can deal with his or her own property as he or she see fits.

Special treatment of the family home: Most provinces treat the family home in a special way, both in terms of eventual sharing and its treatment during cohabitation. For example, in Ontario the general rule is that the value of the matrimonial home will be shared equally regardless of any special circumstances relating to its acquisition; and during cohabitation of the parties neither spouse may sell or mortgage the family home without the other spouse's consent.

Whatever the scheme, the mediator must know and understand it fully before attempting to mediate these issues, and must be aware of certain tax consequences to certain property transfers. Property is an extraordinarily complex and difficult area of family law. It is usually important to have the help of outside experts, such as chartered accountants, valuators and so on, to help with the resolution of property issues.

(1) PROPERTY TRANSFERS BETWEEN SPOUSES

The *Income Tax Act,* R.S.C. 1952, c. 148, is quite old fashioned in terms of its treatment of married couples when dealing with transfers of property between spouses. When looking at property transfers between spouses, the Act essentially treats husband and wife as one person. For example, if the wife has an income-producing asset, like shares paying high dividends, and wishes to transfer some or all of the shares to her husband in order to split the income on the shares betwen them and save some income tax, the *Income Tax Act* will not permit this to happen. Even if the wife transfers the shares to her husband, the *Income Tax Act* will treat all the income on all the shares as being the wife's, and will tax it all in her hands. She must pay all the tax, but the husband will get to keep the dividend income. This result is not so terrible when couples are together, but when this rule (called "attribution") is applied to separating couples who are making a property settlement, it is most unfair.

(2) THE ATTRIBUTION RULES

(a) The General Rule

As can be seen, an attribution rule is one that disallows the split of income between spouses, and attributes it all to the donor spouse who had the asset in the first place. Attribution applies in two separate situations:

- income, and
- capital gains.

Income attribution is of the type mentioned in the example above, where the property transferred is income producing. If, however, in the example above, the husband sold the shares for more than the wife had bought them for, this would trigger a capital gain: an increase in value of capital property from the date it is acquired to the date it is sold. Again, the general rule is that the capital gain would be attributed back to the wife, who would have to pay tax on one-half of it (the taxable portion), subject to the new lifetime capital gains exemption rules. This is how attribution generally works between spouses. As mentioned before, this is quite unfair when applied to separating spouses who are attempting to resolve financial issues between them.

(b) Special Rules for Separated Spouses

Because the general attribution rules caused a great deal of hardship to separated spouses, and property transfers often would have to be delayed until after a divorce (when the parties are no longer husband and wife) special rules were enacted to avoid the hardship. There are two kinds of special rules relating to attribution:

- automatic, and
- by election.

Automatic: If a couple has separated pursuant to a written separation agreement or court order, and there are transfers of income property between them, there is no longer any attribution of income between them. This occurs automatically.

By election: If the separated couple (living apart pursuant to a written separation agreement or court order) does not wish to have attribution of capital gains between them, they must jointly choose this option. To make this choice, they must sign a joint written election not to have the capital gains attribution provisions of the *Income Tax Act* apply to them.

(3) PRINCIPAL RESIDENCE EXEMPTION

The family home is given special treatment not only by provincial family law legislation in terms of how it is to be shared and how each spouse's right to live in it is to be protected, but also by the federal *Income Tax Act* in terms of its tax treatment. The *Income Tax Act* gives a taxpayer's "principal residence" special tax treatment, and if certain conditions are met, when the principal residence is sold any capital gain realized on the sale of the property will be tax free. Each family unit may have only one principal residence, which may be designated as such if and only if:

- the property is solely or jointly owned;
- the taxpayer, his or her spouse or former spouse, or dependent child ordinarily inhabits the property after 1981;
- no other property is designated in this way by the taxpayer or his or her spouse (except for a spouse who has been living separate and apart from his or her spouse throughout the year); and
- the taxpayer is a resident of Canada.

If the spouses separate, and one of them owns the home and the other spouse lives in it, it will still remain the principal residence of the spouse who owns it.

In the year that the parties separate, the spouses will continue to be viewed by the *Income Tax Act* as a single family unit until the end of the year, and during that time they can only have one principal residence. If they remain living separate and apart, in the following years each can have his or her own principal residence with the special tax treatment.

The principal residence provisions of the *Income Tax Act* are very complex. This is a very general overview of what they are and cannot be relied on as a statement of the law. This description is designed to alert the mediator to the issues and potential problems of the family home, and to suggest that expert advice be obtained to deal with this issue.

(4) Registered Retirement Savings Plans

Registered Retirement Savings Plans (RRSPS) provide a popular way to amass savings and create a tax deferral at the same time. A yearly contribution to an RRSP to the statutory maximum is fully tax deductible, creating an immediate tax saving, and all interest earned on all contributions to the RRSP (whether these have been fully deductible or not) are completely tax sheltered as long as the money remains in the plan.

As soon as funds are withdrawn from the plan, they are fully taxable in the hands of the recipient. This is why the plans create only a deferral of tax. Payment of income tax is postponed until the funds are withdrawn. It is generally expected that the funds will be accumulated until the taxpayer's retirement years, when he or she has no other income, and that the funds will therefore be able to be withdrawn gradually when the taxpayer has a low taxable income and will be taxed at a lower rate than they would have been were the funds taxed when they went into the plan.

If, as part of a property settlement, it is necessary to use the funds in a RRSP and withdraw the funds in the recipient's prime earning years, a huge tax liability would result if the general rules were applied.

Again, there are special rules for a separated spouses that allow for a less onerous result. All or part of one spouse's RRSP can be transferred completely tax free to the other spouse's RRSP if the following conditions are met:

- the transfer is made on or after marriage breakdown,
- the transfer is made pursuant to a written separation agreement or court order,
- the order or agreement must require the transfer in settlement of rights that arise out of the marriage,
- the funds must go directly from one plan into another,
- Revenue Canada must receive a copy of the order or agreement and a special form within 30 days of the transfer.

While it will be advantageous from a tax point of view for the original owner of the RRSP to make use of these special rules, it may not be to the advantage of the recipient spouse to receive the funds this way. As has been mentioned, the funds must go directly into an RRSP of the recipient spouse. If he or she needs the funds immediately to purchase a home or meet living expenses, the collapse of his or her plan or the withdrawal of any funds from it will trigger an immediate income tax liability in the hands of the recipient. What this means is that if a lump sum payment is funded by an RRSP transfer, the recipient spouse will end up with less cash in hand than he or she would receive if a simple lump sum cash payment were made.

As is the case with all matters relating to income tax, issues are complicated and expert advice should always be obtained.

E. INCOME TAX IMPLICATIONS: Support

There are income tax implications not only for property transfers, but also for support payments.

(1) LUMP SUM VERSUS PERIODIC PAYMENTS

A support payment can be a single, once-and-for-all payment designed to sever all ties between the spouses (a lump sum) or may be a series of payments over either a fixed period of time, or continuing until the happening of certain events (periodic payments). Each type of payment has certain advantages and disadvantages.

Lump sums have the advantage of being once and for all, and of severing ongoing ties between the parties. Once paid, the recipient spouse need not worry about default in the future and difficulties in collection. Their disadvantages are that they are not tax deductible to the payer, may carry the risk of being varied in the future to provide for more money if the other spouse has used up the lump sum, and cannot be gotten back if the other spouse immediately gets married or lives in a common law relationship, two situations that would normally terminate an ongoing support obligation.

Periodic payments have the advantage of being tax deductible to the payer, and are terminable if certain conditions are met (such as remarriage or cohabitation) and are usually variable if either spouse suffers a change in circumstances. Their disadvantages are that they continue an ongoing and often lengthy financial relationship between the spouses, carry the risk of default and the related cost and aggravation of attempts to collect, and provide a fertile ground for continued conflict and resentment between the spouses.

Periodic payments are far more common than lump sums, because generally ongoing funds are required by a dependent spouse to meet day-to-day expenses, and there is usually not enough capital to fund an adequate lump sum payment.

(2) DEDUCTIBILITY OF SUPPORT PAYMENTS

As we have already seen, the general income tax rules disallow attempts to split income between spouses. However, where spouses separate, special rules come into play that allow this kind of division. The separated family unit usually still has only the same amount of family income, which must now support two households rather than only one. The deductibility of support payments operates as a method of splitting income between the two households and generally reducing the overall amount of tax paid by the family as a whole, thus creating slightly more family income. A simple example helps to illustrate this point. Assume a working husband earning $50,000 per year and paying support on a non-deductible basis of $1,500 per month to his wife. The husband's after-tax position can be calculated as follows:

Gross Income		$50,000.00
Deduct:		
Personal Deduction	$ 4,180.00	$ 4,180.00
Creating taxable income of		$45,820.00
Federal Tax payable (1986)	$10,483.00	
Provincial Tax (Ontario)	$ 5,241.50	
Ontario surtax	$ 7.25	
TOTAL TAX	$15,731.75	
Paid to wife	$18,000.00	
TOTAL PAYMENTS	$33,731.75	$33,731.75
Net to husband		$16,268.25

If, however, the payments are deductible to the husband, the following result will occur:

Gross Income		$50,000.00
Deduct:		
Personal Deduction	$ 4,180.00	
Support Payments	$18,000.00	
TOTAL DEDUCTIONS	$22,180.00	$22,180.00
Creating taxable income of		$27,820.00
Federal Tax (1986)	$ 5,519.00	
Provincial Tax (Ontario)	$ 2,759.50	
Surtax	nil	
TOTAL TAX	$ 8,278.50	
Paid to Wife	$18,000.00	
Net to husband		$23,721.50

As can be seen from the above examples, the effect of making the support payments tax deductible to the payer are incredible. However, the *Income Tax Act* has very stringent requirements that must be met in order to make support payments deductible. The requirements are as follows:

- the parties are living separate and apart and remain living separate and apart during the remainder of the taxation year;
- the payments are made pursuant to a written separation agreement signed by the parties or pursuant to a court order;
- the payments are for the maintenance of the recipient;
- the payments must be a pre-determined amount of money payable on a periodic basis, that is, at fixed, recurring intervals;
- once paid, the funds must be at the sole discretion of the recipient.

It used to be that to be deductible, the payments had to occur after the signing of an agreement or a granting of a court order, which meant that if the payer had made any voluntary payments before, or had paid in anticipation of an agreement being signed or an order being granted, the payments would not be deductible. These stringent rules have been somewhat relaxed, and payments made prior to the signing of an agreement may still be deductible if:

- the payment is made in the year of or the year immediately preceding the signing of the agreement,
- all other criteria regarding deductibility have been met,
- the agreement refers to the prior payments specifically and states that they are to be deductible to the payer and includable in the income of the recipient.

If a payer has been making voluntary payments, and wishes to claim a deduction for them, a negotiated agreement that allows this deduction will often provide for the payer to pay the tax attracted to these earlier payments. The reason for this is that the recipient will likely not have planned for the eventual tax deductibility of these payments, not knowing that this would be the case, and often the money will have already been spent. The making of prior payments deductible confers a very great benefit on the payer, and even if he or she pays the tax attracted by the payments in the hands of the other spouse, there is usually still a significant benefit to be gained.

Where the payment is deductible in the hands of the payer, the receipt of the support will be included in the income of the recipient. Taking the prior example from the wife's point of view, and assuming that the wife has no other income, if the payments are not taxable in her hands, her net disposable income will of course be $18,000, the full amount of the payments received from the husband. If, however, the payments are included in her income, the following will result:

Gross income		$18,000.00
Deduct:		
Personal deduction	$4,180.00	$ 4,180.00
TAXABLE INCOME		$13,820.00
Federal Tax (1986)	$2,346.20	
Provincial Tax (Ontario)	$1,173.10	
Surtax	nil	
TOTAL TAX	$3,519.30	$ 3,519.30
Wife's net income		$14,480.70

In this last example, if the husband were to deduct the support payments and pay the wife's tax in addition, his total tax burden, including the wife's taxes, would be $11,797.80, a saving of $3,933.95 in total taxes were the payments not to be deductible at all.

As can be seen from these very simple examples, the effect of the deductibility of support payments on the after-tax position of the spouses is considerable.

(3) OTHER RELEVANT TAX PROVISIONS FOR MARRIAGE BREAKDOWN

When dealing with the issue of support in the context of separation, it is not enough to consider only the questions of the deductibility or includability of the proposed support payments. Two additional areas that should be reviewed are the tax deductions available to each spouse and the potential use and tax effect of third party payments.

(a) Income Tax Deduction

Personal deduction:

Every taxpayer may claim a basic personal deduction that is subtracted from his or her gross income before calculating income tax. In 1986, this amount is $4,180.

Married exemption: In addition, a spouse may deduct the sum of $3,660 as a married exemption if he or she wholly supported his or her spouse during the taxation year. Where there is a separation, the supporting spouse must choose whether to claim the married exemption or the support payments. Generally, since the support payments are greater than the deduction, the support payments are claimed rather than the married exemption.

Even where there is a separation, the married exemption is not lost completely if there are dependent children. The spouse who maintains the children, either wholly with his or her own income, or with that income plus support payments, may claim an "equivalent to married" exemption for one of the children.

Dependent children deductions: Deductions may be claimed for all dependent children; the deduction is $710 for each child who is under the age of 18, and $1,420 for each dependent child who is 18 years of age or older. Usually, the spouse with custody of the children receives support payments for them, and the paying spouse deducts the payments, while the recipient spouse claims the deduction for the children. Effectively, the use of the equivalent-to-married deduction means that the first $3,660 of child support paid to a spouse will be tax free. There are some reductions that will be made to the deductions where the dependant earns some income. The *Income Tax Act* should of course be consulted, and as is the case with all tax matters, expert advice should be obtained to explore fully the most advantageous tax position for the parties.

Child care exemption: Often, even where there are young children, it is necessary for both spouses to work outside the home. Young children require child care, whether in day care centres, private homes, or with nannies. Some of the expense incurred by parents for providing day care for their children is tax deductible. Currently, the parents may deduct up to $2,000 per child of their actual child care expenses, to a family maximum of $8,000. Where the spouses are still living together, it is the spouse with the lower taxable income who is entitled to deduct the child care expenses. Where the parties are separated, it is the parent who claims the child as a dependant who claims the child care expenses. A payer spouse cannot claim both support payments and the deduction for the children. Child support is paid to the spouse who has custody of the children, and usually, the amount paid in the year (including the year of separation) is greater than the deduction for the children. Therefore, the payer spouse usually claims the support payments as his or her deduction and the recipient spouse (who also has custody) claims the children as dependants, and the child care exemption.

Family allowance payments: Family allowance payments are also taxed in the hands of the parent who claims the child as a dependant. Generally, this will be the parent with custody.

Child tax credit: A child tax credit may be available to the spouse who receives the family allowance payments. This is usually the mother. Where the spouses are together, their joint income is taken into account to determine if a child tax credit is available to reduce the total tax payable or to generate a refund. If the spouses are living apart, only the income of the spouse claiming the child tax credit is taken into account.

(b) Third Party Payments

Often, for many different kinds of reasons, a payer spouse may wish to make certain payments for the benefit of the other spouse and children directly to a third party. These types of payments include:

- medical and dental insurance
- medical and dental costs
- school fees
- university tuition
- camp fees
- mortgage and utilities.

Because the requirements to make a support payment tax deductible are so very stringent, it has been very difficult to make this type of payment fall within the defined criteria, and complex wording has been necessary in agreements or court orders to make this type of third party payment deductible.

However, changes in the law since 1983 have made the task much easier. These types of payments will be tax deductible if the following criteria are met:

- the parties are living separate and apart both when the expense is incurred and when it is paid;
- there is a written separation agreement or court order that specifically describes the obligation to pay (for example, "the husband will pay all camp fees");
- both parties must agree specifically that the payments are to be tax deductible to the payer;
- the agreement or court order must refer specifically to the application of ss. 60.1(2) (en. 1984, c. 45, s. 20(1)) and 56.1(2) (en. 1984, c. 45, s. 17(1)) of the *Income Tax Act;*
- the payments must be for the maintenance of a spouse or former spouse.

Note that payments relating to the family home, that is, mortgage payments, utilities, and the like, will *not* be deductible if the payer owns the home, or an interest in it in any way.

F. EXAMPLE OF FINANCIAL DISCLOSURE FORM

The following is the financial disclosure form that is used in the Province of Ontario in the District and Supreme Courts for the purposes of both the *Family Law Act, 1986* and the *Divorce Act, 1985*.

FINANCIAL STATEMENT—S.C.O
(Form 70K under the Rules)
AMENDED JUNE 1, 1986

DYE & DURHAM CO. LIMITED—Form No. 904

Court file no.

SUPREME COURT OF ONTARIO

(Parties in title of proceeding) **BETWEEN:**

and

FINANCIAL STATEMENT

I, ...
(Full name of deponent)

of the .... of .... in the
(City, Town, etc.)

.... of .... MAKE OATH AND SAY:
(County, Regional Municipality, etc.) / AFFIRM:

1.   Particulars of my financial situation and of all my property are accurately set out below, to the best of my knowledge, information and belief.

ALL INCOME AND MONEY RECEIVED

(Include all income and other money received from all sources, whether taxable or not. Show gross amount here and show deductions on pages 2, 3, 4 & 5. Give current actual amount where known or ascertainable. Where amount cannot be ascertained, give your best estimate. Use weekly, monthly or yearly column as appropriate.)

Category	Weekly	Monthly	Yearly
1. Salary or wages			
2. Bonuses			
3. Fees			
4. Commissions			
5. Family allowance			
6. Unemployment insurance			
7. Workers' compensation			
8. Public assistance			
9. Pension			
10. Dividends			
11. Interest			
12. Rental income			
13. Allowances and support from others			
14. Other (Specify)			
TOTAL	$	**(A)**$	$

Weekly total $_____ × 4.33 = **(B)** $_____ monthly

Yearly total $_____ ÷ 12 = **(C)** $_____ monthly

GROSS MONTHLY INCOME **(A)** + **(B)** + **(C)** = **(D)** $_____

Page 2—FINANCIAL STATEMENT—S.C.O.
(Form 70K under the Rules)
AMENDED JUNE 1, 1986

DYE & DURHAM CO. LIMITED
Form No. 904

OTHER BENEFITS

(Show all non-monetary benefits from all sources, such as use of a vehicle or room and board, and include such items as insurance or dental plans or other expenses paid on your behalf. Give your best estimate where you cannot ascertain the actual value.)

Item	Particulars	Monthly Market Value

TOTAL (E) $_____

GROSS MONTHLY INCOME AND BENEFITS **(D)** + **(E)**=$_____

ACTUAL AND PROPOSED BUDGETS

	ACTUAL BUDGET *for twelve month period from* _____, 19____ to_____, 19____ *Show actual expenses, or your best estimate where you cannot ascertain actual amount.*			PROPOSED BUDGET *Show your proposed budget, giving your best estimate where you cannot ascertain actual amount.*		
CATEGORY	Weekly	Monthly	Yearly	Weekly	Monthly	Yearly
Housing						
1. Rent				1.		
2. Real property taxes				2.		
3. Mortgage				3.		
4. Common expense charges				4.		
5. Water				5.		
6. Electricity				6.		
7. Natural gas				7.		
8. Fuel oil				8.		
9. Telephone				9.		
10. Cable T.V.				10.		
11. Home insurance				11.		
12. Repairs and maintenance				12.		
13. Gardening and snow removal				13.		
14. Other (Specify)				14.		
Food, Toiletries and Sundries						
15. Groceries				15.		
16. Meals outside home				16.		
17. Toiletries and sundries				17.		
18. Grooming				18.		

Page 3—FINANCIAL STATEMENT—S.C.O.
(Form 70K under the Rules)
AMENDED JUNE 1, 1986

DYE & DURHAM CO. LIMITED
Form No. 904

CATEGORY	ACTUAL BUDGET			PROPOSED BUDGET		
Food Toiletries and Sundries—cont'd.	Weekly	Monthly	Yearly	Weekly	Monthly	Yearly
19. General household supplies				19.		
20. Laundry, dry cleaning				20.		
21. Other (Specify)				21.		
Clothing						
22. Children				22.		
23. Self				23.		
Transportation						
24. Public transit				24.		
25. Taxis, car pools				25.		
26. Car insurance				26.		
27. Licence				27.		
28. Car maintenance				28.		
29. Gasoline, oil				29.		
30. Parking				30.		
31. Other (Specify)				31.		
Health and Medical						
32. Doctors, chiropractors				32.		
33. Dentist (regular care)				33.		
34. Orthodontist or special dental care				34.		
35. Insurance premiums				35.		
36. Drugs				36.		
37. Other (Specify)				37.		
Deductions from Income						
38. Income tax				38.		
39. Canada Pension Plan				39.		
40. Unemployment insurance				40.		
41. Employer pension				41.		
42. Union or other dues				42.		

Page 4—FINANCIAL STATEMENT—S.C.O.
(Form 70K under the Rules)
AMENDED JUNE 1, 1986

DYE & DURHAM CO. LIMITED
Form No. 904

CATEGORY	ACTUAL BUDGET			PROPOSED BUDGET		
Deductions from income—cont'd.	Weekly	Monthly	Yearly	Weekly	Monthly	Yearly
43. Group insurance				43.		
44. Credit union loan				44.		
45. Credit union savings				45.		
46. Other (Specify)				46.		
Miscellaneous						
47. Life insurance premiums				47.		
48. Tuition fees, books, etc.				48.		
49. Entertainment				49.		
50. Recreation				50.		
51. Vacation				51.		
52. Gifts				52.		
53. Babysitting, day care				53.		
54. Children's allowances				54.		
55. Children's activities				55.		
56. Support payments				56.		
57. Newspapers, periodicals				57.		
58. Alcohol, tobacco				58.		
59. Charities				59.		
60. Income tax (not deducted at source)				60.		
61. Other (Specify)				61.		
Loan Payments						
62. Banks				62.		
63. Finance companies				63.		
64. Credit unions				64.		
65. Department stores				65.		
66. Other (Specify)				66.		

Page 5—FINANCIAL STATEMENT—S.C.O.
(Form 70K under the Rules)
AMENDED JUNE 1, 1986

DYE & DURHAM CO. LIMITED
Form No. 904

	ACTUAL BUDGET			PROPOSED BUDGET		
CATEGORY	Weekly	Monthly	Yearly	Weekly	Monthly	Yearly
Savings						
67. R.R.S.P.				67.		
68. Other (Specify)				68.		
	$	$	$	$	$	$

TOTALS OF ACTUAL BUDGET

Monthly Total $_____

Weekly Total $_____ × 4.33 = $_____

Yearly Total $_____ ÷ 12   = $_____

MONTHLY ACTUAL BUDGET   = (F) $_____

TOTALS OF PROPOSED BUDGET

Monthly Total $_____

Weekly Total $_____ × 4.33 = $_____

Yearly Total $_____ ÷ 12   = $_____

MONTHLY PROPOSED BUDGET   = (G) $_____

SUMMARY OF INCOME AND EXPENSES

Actual

Gross monthly income
(Amount D from page 1) $_____

Subtract Monthly actual budget
(Amount F from page 5)   — $_____

ACTUAL MONTHLY SURPLUS / DEFICIT $_____

Proposed

Gross monthly income
(Amount D from page 1) $_____

Subtract Proposed monthly budget
(Amount G from page 5)   — $_____

PROPOSED MONTHLY SURPLUS / DEFICIT $_____

Page 6—FINANCIAL STATEMENT—S.C.O.
(Form 70K under the Rules)
AMENDED JUNE 1, 1986

DYE & DURHAM CO. LIMITED
Form No. 904

LAND

(Include any interest in land owned on the valuation date, including leasehold interests and mortgages, whether or not you are registered as owner. Include claims to an interest in land, but do not include claims that you are making against your spouse in this or a related proceeding. Show estimated market value of your interest without deducting encumbrances or costs of disposition, and show encumbrances and costs of disposition under Debts and Other Liabilities on page 9.)

Nature and Type of Ownership State percentage interest where relevant.	Nature and Address of Property	Estimated Market Value of Your Interest as of: See instructions above.		
		Date of Marriage	Valuation Date	Date of Statement
	TOTAL $		(H)	

GENERAL HOUSEHOLD ITEMS AND VEHICLES

(Show estimated market value, not cost of replacement for these items owned on the valuation date. Do not deduct encumbrances here, but show encumbrances under Debts and Other Liabilities on page 9.)

Item	Particulars	Estimated Market Value of Your Interest as of: See instructions above.		
		Date of Marriage	Valuation Date	Date of Statement
General household contents excluding special items (a) at matrimonial home(s)				
(b) elsewhere				
Jewellery				
Works of art				
Vehicles and boats				
Other special items				
	TOTAL $		(I)	

Page 7—FINANCIAL STATEMENT—S.C.O
(Form 70K under the Rules)
AMENDED JUNE 1, 1986

DYE & DURHAM CO. LIMITED
Form No. 904

SAVINGS AND SAVINGS PLANS

(Show items owned on the valuation date by category. Include cash, accounts in financial institutions, registered retirement or other savings plans, deposit receipts, pensions and any other savings.)

| Category | Institution | Account Number | Amount as of: | | |
			Date of Marriage	Valuation Date	Date of Statement
		TOTAL $		(J)	

SECURITIES

(Show items owned on the valuation date by category. Include shares, bonds, warrants, options, debentures, notes and any other securities. Give your best estimate of market value if the items were to be sold on an open market.)

| Category | Number | Description | Estimated Market Value as of: | | |
			Date of Marriage	Valuation Date	Date of Statement
		TOTAL $		(K)	

LIFE AND DISABILITY INSURANCE

(List all policies owned on the valuation date.)

| Company and Policy No. | Kind of Policy | Owner | Beneficiary | Face Amount | Cash Surrender Value as of: | | |
					Date of Marriage	Valuation Date	Date of Statement
				TOTAL $		(L)	

Page 8—FINANCIAL STATEMENT—S.C.O.
(Form 70K under the Rules)
AMENDED JUNE 1, 1986

DYE & DURHAM CO. LIMITED
Form No. 904

ACCOUNTS RECEIVABLE

(Give particulars of all debts owing to you on the valuation date, whether arising from business or from personal dealings.)

Particulars	Amount as of:		
	Date of Marriage	Valuation Date	Date of Statement
TOTAL $		(M)	

BUSINESS INTERESTS

(Show any interest in an unincorporated business owned on the valuation date. A controlling interest in an incorporated business may be shown here or under Securities on page 7. Give your best estimate of market value if the business were to be sold on an open market.)

Name of Firm or Company	Interest	Estimated Market Value as of:		
		Date of Marriage	Valuation Date	Date of Statement
	TOTAL $		(N)	

OTHER PROPERTY

(Show other property owned on the valuation date by categories. Include property of any kind not shown above. Give your best estimate of market value.)

Category	Particulars	Estimated Market Value as of:		
		Date of Marriage	Valuation Date	Date of Statement
	TOTAL $		(O)	

Page 9—FINANCIAL STATEMENT—S.C.O.
(Form 70K under the Rules)
AMENDED JUNE 1, 1986

DYE & DURHAM CO. LIMITED
Form No. 904

DEBTS AND OTHER LIABILITIES

(Show your debts and other liabilities on the valuation date, whether arising from personal or business dealings, by category such as mortgages, charges, liens, notes, credit cards and accounts payable. Include contingent liabilities such as guarantees and indicate that they are contingent.)

Category	Particulars	Amount as of: Date of Marriage	Amount as of: Valuation Date	Amount as of: Date of Statement
	TOTAL $		(P)	

PROPERTY, DEBTS AND OTHER LIABILITIES ON DATE OF MARRIAGE

(Show by category the value of your property and your debts and other liabilities calculated as of the date of your marriage. Do not include the value of a matrimonial home that you owned at the date of marriage.)

Category	Particulars	Value as of date of marriage Assets	Value as of date of marriage Liabilities
	TOTAL $	(Q) $	(R) $

NET VALUE OF PROPERTY OWNED ON DATE OF MARRIAGE (Amount Q Subtract Amount R) = **(S)** $_____

Page 10—FINANCIAL STATEMENT—S.C.O.
(Form 70K under the Rules)
AMENDED JUNE 1, 1986

DYE & DURHAM CO. LIMITED
Form No. 904

EXCLUDED PROPERTY

(Show the value by category of property owned on the valuation date that is excluded from the definition of "net family property".)

Category	Particulars	Value on Valuation Date
	TOTAL	(T) $

DISPOSAL OF PROPERTY

(Show the value by category of all property that you disposed of during the two years immediately preceding the making of this statement, or during the marriage, whichever period is shorter.)

Category	Particulars	Value
	TOTAL	(U) $

Page 11—FINANCIAL STATEMENT—S.C.O.
(Form 70K under the Rules)
AMENDED JUNE 1, 1986

DYE & DURHAM CO. LIMITED
Form No. 904

CALCULATION OF NET FAMILY PROPERTY

Value of all property owned on valuation date (Amounts H,I,J,K,L,M,N and O from pages 6 to 8) $_____

Subtract value of all deductions (Amounts P and S from page 9)   — $_____

Subtract value of all excluded property (Amount T from page 10)   — $_____

NET FAMILY PROPERTY $_____

2. The name(s) and address(es) of my employer(s) are:

3. Attached to this affidavit are a copy of my income tax return filed with the Department of National Revenue for the last taxation year, together with all material filed with it, and a copy of any notice of assessment or reassessment that I have received from the Department for that year.

4. I do not anticipate any material changes in the information set out above.

(Delete inapplicable paragraph 4)

4. I anticipate the following material changes in the information set out above:

(Give particulars:)

Sworn before me at the
Affirmed

in the

on   19   }

_____
Signature of deponent

Commissioner for Taking Affidavits, etc.

Court file no.

SUPREME COURT OF ONTARIO

Proceeding commenced at

FINANCIAL STATEMENT

(Form 70K under the Rules)

DYE & DURHAM CO. LIMITED—Form No. 904

SOLICITOR(S) FOR THE

Address

Tel. No:

and

(Short title of proceeding)

Chapter Eight

Mediation in Practice: Professional Conduct

A. STANDARDS OF PRACTICE

(1) ETHICAL CONSIDERATIONS

Mediation is a relatively new field in professional practice, particularly the area of divorce mediation. While there have been court-connected mediation services for over 25 years in some jurisdictions in the United States, such as California, and in some parts of Canada for almost 15 years, namely, Alberta and Ontario, nevertheless the real impetus for developing mediation as a profession dates back to approximately 1980. Today, increasing numbers of mental health professionals, lawyers and judges are endorsing mediation as a preferred approach for resolving family law disputes, and as a result mediation is gaining recognition as a distinct mode of professional practice. As its use becomes more widespread, there is considerable agreement among mediators themselves, as well as among legislators, lawyers, judges and potential clients, that the following issues require clarification, namely:

- What is mediation?
- What are the standards of practice that define responsible, competent professional practice as a mediator?
- Is there a mechanism for supervision and discipline of mediators? That is, does a member of the public or another profession have a mechanism for complaining about conduct by a mediator that is inept, unprofessional or unethical?
- If there is a governing body, what are its powers and procedures for decision making?
- What are the qualifications, that is, the training and experience, necessary to be a mediator?
- Are there guidelines for appropriate procedures to follow, a fee

structure and other rules of practice that distinguish a good mediator from a poor one?

- Are there or should there be special rules of practice for lawyers acting as mediators?
- Are there potential conflicts between the lawyer's role as counsel and the lawyer's role as mediator?
- Similarly, are there possible conflicts between the role of the mental health professional as clinician and the mental health professional as mediator?

These basic questions deal with the issues of standards of practice, ethical conduct for professional mediators and the qualifications necessary to become a mediator. It is important to address these issues for several reasons, namely:

- Mediation is a practice that crosses professional boundary lines. That is, at present there is no single profession that governs mediation and monitors the standards of practice within the profession.
- Mediators come from a variety of disciplines, namely, law, psychology, social work, psychiatry, counselling and other disciplines whose standards of professional conduct may be in conflict with the standards that are considered desirable for mediators.
- In cases of lawsuits against mediators, the liability insurance that is usually held by professionals may not cover the practice of mediation. That is, if a lawyer is acting as a mediator, the lawyer's malpractice insurance may not cover actions against that lawyer in his or her capacity as a mediator. This would probably be true of mediators from other professional disciplines.
- One of the distinct advantages of mediation is the fact that parties can arrange their own settlement of issues in dispute in an atmosphere of confidentiality. The key elements of mediation are private ordering of dispute resolution and confidentiality. However, these elements also create the greatest risk if the parties are unequal in bargaining power, if the mediator is incompetent or unethical or if the parties fail to disclose adequate information for reaching an appropriate solution. Because litigation tends to be conducted in public, while mediation tends to be conducted in a private setting, protection of the public can only be achieved by the enforcement of standards of practice, codes of professional conduct and, eventually, procedures for certification and licensing.

Definition: Most definitions of *mediation* incorporate the following elements:

Family mediation is:

- a process,
- in which a qualified and impartial third party (the mediator),

- helps the family resolve their disputes by agreement,
- the agreement is to be reached voluntarily,
- should be based on sufficient information, and
- should include independent legal advice for each participant.

The above definition is taken from the Code of Conduct of the Ontario Association for Family Mediation and Family Mediation Canada.

Most definitions of mediation emphasize the fact that the mediator must act in an impartial role:

The mediator must:

- ensure that the parties reach a consensual agreement, that is, without duress;
- ensure that the parties are properly informed, that is, that all relevant information has been exchanged;
- ensure that the agreement reached is fair and reasonable, particularly where children are involved.
- ensure that the parties are not under a disability (such as emotional disturbance, intellectual impairment or fear of physical abuse) during the negotiations;
- clarify with the clients his or her professional role, that is, that the mediator is acting as a mediator and not as a lawyer or psychologist or other professional. For example, the mediator (if a lawyer) should clarify with the clients that he or she cannot be the solicitor for either client if he or she has been their mediator. Similarly, the mediator should explain that he or she cannot be the individual clinician for either party after he or she has acted in the impartial role of mediator.

(2) CODES OF PROFESSIONAL CONDUCT

Codes of professional conduct contain both standards of practice and a code of ethical conduct. These terms can be described as follows:

- Standards of practice refer to the minimally acceptable, commonly understood practices of a profession. These standards are designed to protect the public and ensure a reasonable level of competence among practitioners. If followed, the standards of practice should protect a mediator from liability, because the standards establish the reasonable level of care to be exercised by a person practising mediation.
- Guidelines for the qualifications for mediators, their licensing and certification are still in the early stages of development in both Canada and the United States.
- An ethical code is usually thought of as the moral and social obligations of the professional that are imposed by the governing body on members of the profession. Adherence to an ethical code is usually

required as a prerequisite to certification or licensing. Ethical codes have been described as the "do nots" of each profession. There are a number of conflicts still to be resolved between the ethical code of mediators and the ethical code of some other disciplines, such as law or certain mental health professions. In addition, guidelines for the qualifications for mediators, their licensing and certification are still in the early stages.

- Codes of professional conduct are intended to govern the behaviour of professionals when they are acting in their capacity as mediators. These codes are not intended to replace or in any way compete with the codes of conduct of the mediator's basic profession, that is, law, psychology, social work or other. The major elements that are present in most codes of professional conduct for mediators are set out below.

(a) Competence

It is recognized that mediators may be trained in different professional disciplines; however, it is essential that:

- The individual have specific training in the skills, knowledge and techniques necessary to be an effective mediator.
- The mediator should only agree to mediate those issues for which he or she has adequate training and experience. That is, lawyers should not mediate custody and access issues unless they have specific training and knowledge with respect to such matters as child development, family dynamics, the effects on children and adults of separation and divorce, appropriate parenting techniques, and stages of physical, emotional and social development of children. Similarly, a mental health professional should not agree to mediate such issues as property division, support or complex financial arrangements unless he or she has adequate training in family law, income tax, and in some cases accounting.
- Mediators should co-operate with other professionals who are assisting the clients, such as lawyers, accountants or business evaluators and, in fact, should suggest that relevant professionals be retained to assist with specific issues in the mediation. For example, if the mediation is dealing with the issue of division of property, specialists such as business evaluators, accountants or real estate appraisers may be needed to provide the necessary background information for mediating the issues in dispute.
- The mediator should attend continuing education programs and read recent literature with respect to mediation to ensure that his or her mediation skills are up to date.

(b) Duty to Describe the Mediation Process and Its Cost at the Outset

The mediator should discuss the following information with the clients by telephone prior to the first session and/or during the first session:

- The process to be followed during mediation, including whether the meetings will be conjoint, individual or a combination of conjoint and individual. Also, who will be included in these meetings and the location of the meetings should be defined.
- A definition of mediation should be given and an explanation made about the difference between mediation and other forms of conflict resolution that would be available to the parties (such as litigation, arbitration or marital counselling).
- The issues to be discussed in mediation.
- Whether the mediation is to be open or closed, that is, the issues of privilege and confidentiality.
- The requirement to make full disclosure of all relevant information with respect to the issues being mediated.
- The advisability of both parties having independent legal advice throughout the mediation process and certainly prior to signing any mediated agreement.
- The process for terminating the mediation by either the
  the clients
  the mediators
  the lawyers
  the court.
- The mediator's fees and billing practices should be fully explained, including the hourly rate, the activities for which the clients will be charged, the method of billing, whether a retainer is required, cancellation policy, and expert witness fees if required in court.

During the process of explaining the mediation process to the clients, the mediator should also be assessing the suitability of the clients for mediation. That is:

- Whether the clients show significant signs of emotional disturbance, or whether it appears that one party is under duress by the other party to the point where mediation would not be possible.
- If for some other reason related to the client's personality or the ability of the mediator to relate to the clients, the mediator believes that the mediation is unlikely to be successful, then the mediator should share this information with the clients and either terminate the mediation or refer the clients to some other mediator who might be more successful.
- If the mediator does not have the special knowledge or expertise to deal with the particular issues in dispute in the case, then he or she

should terminate the mediation and assist the clients in finding a mediator with the requisite background.

(c) Impartiality

One of the primary features of mediation is the private ordering of dispute resolution. The role of the mediator in this process is to facilitate communication, offer educational input and ensure that the parties are fully informed. All of these roles must be fulfilled in an impartial manner. That is, the mediator must:

- Disclose to the clients any biases the mediator may hold that are relevant to the issues in dispute. For example, if the mediator has strong beliefs that the custodial spouse should not be employed outside of the home, or that young children should be in the primary care of a mother, or that it is important for children to have a strong religious upbringing, or that it is important for children to be raised in a home setting with mother and father figures, then these biases or beliefs should be communicated to the parties if custody of and access to children is being discussed.
- The mediator should discuss these beliefs or biases during the orientation session, that is, before the mediation process is under way. If relevant biases or beliefs do not become apparent until later, then they should be raised at the first opportunity.
- The mediator should not mediate those cases where he or she has had a significant *prior* involvement, that is, if the mediator or a partner or an associate of the mediator has conducted individual therapy or counselling with either of the parties previously, or if the mediator has acted as legal counsel for either of the parties.
- In a number of cases the mediator may have offered marital counselling to the couple, and this may create some problems with respect to ethical standards. This is less of a problem if the clients initially contracted with the mediator to provide marital counselling but, if the counselling should fail or the couple decide to separate, then to mediate some or all of the terms of a separation agreement. That is, the contract contemplated from the beginning that mediation would be tried in the event that the couple decided to separate.
- In any event, it would be essential as a minimum for the mediator to discuss fully with the clients the nature of the prior involvement and would require the express consent of both participants prior to continuing with mediation. The mediator should clarify the differences between his or her prior involvement and the specific tasks to be performed in mediation.
- Some codes of conduct expressly prohibit mediators from acting when there has been any form of significant prior involvement, either as a mental health professional or as a lawyer. Other codes of

conduct are more flexible, but in every case, it is essential that the mediator make full disclosure of prior involvement and obtain the consent of both parties in writing.

Another area that needs consideration is whether the mediator can change from the role of mediator into the role of counsellor for one or both parties *following* the mediation process. It is probably inappropriate for the mediator, once he or she has taken on an impartial role, subsequently to take on any form of *partial role* in dealing with the parties. There are several issues that should be considered, namely:

- It is important for the client and for the general public to maintain a distinction between the role of the mediator and the role of the therapist. By changing from one role to another, the mediator may create a confusion of roles and give the clients contradictory messages about the mediation process.
- In the event that the clients need the assistance of the mediator to deal with subsequent disputes, the mediator would be unable to assist if he or she had subsequently offered services to one of the parties.
- It may be appropriate for the mediator to continue assisting the couple in an impartial capacity following the mediation. For example, if the parties wish further assistance in developing communication skills so as to carry out effectively the mediation agreement, the mediator is probably in a very good position, given his or her knowledge of the parties and their communication problems, to assist in this matter. This is unlikely to be any form of long-term therapy, but rather is directed at implementing effectively a mediation plan. This could also be seen as preventing a breakdown of the mediation agreement because the parties lack the essential skills to carry it out.
- It may also be appropriate for the mediator to assist in monitoring how the parents are carrying out their agreement and its impact on the children from time to time. Again this is an impartial role, and if the mediator did not carry out this function, then the parties would have to go to a totally new professional at considerable expense and further emotional turmoil for them and the children. Also, it would take some time to develop a sufficient relationship with the new professional so that that individual could monitor their progress. The key test is whether the mediator is maintaining an impartial role and whether the purpose of the assistance is to implement and stabilize the plan developed in mediation.

It is not appropriate for the mediator to represent either party as a lawyer, either prior to or subsequent to the mediation process. Some codes of conduct permit the mediator to act as a lawyer for one or both parties in uncontested matters or in matters that are totally unrelated to the divorce proceedings. Other codes of conduct prohibit not only the mediator, but also any partners or associates in the law firm, from acting on behalf of either party, either in contested or possibly even in uncontested matters in the future. It is probable that all codes of conduct would prohibit as a minimum acting on behalf of either party in a contested legal matter arising out of any of the issues discussed during the mediation. This would prohibit any representation of a party in a matter related to the divorce or separation and would probably prohibit a lawyer who had mediated financial and property issues from acting as the lawyer in real estate matters arising out of the divorce, such as the sale of the matrimonial home.

It is important for lawyers who are mediators to check not only the code of conduct for mediators in their jurisdiction, but also the code of conduct for their law society. The broadest rule is a prohibition against representing either spouse on any matter at any point in the future, but as a minimum it is essential:

- that the lawyer disclose any prior involvement to the clients, either legal involvement or as a mediator, and
- that both clients consent, preferably in writing, to any subsequent involvement.

It would be unwise and probably unethical for a lawyer to act in any contested family law matter once the lawyer has acted as a mediator.

The mediator should take constructive steps to ensure that the agreement will be fair and reasonable to both parties and the children.

- The mediator should encourage both parties to have independent legal representation from the outset so that both parties are aware of their legal entitlements.
- The mediator should ensure that both parties have full disclosure of all relevant information prior to reaching an agreement on any issue in dispute. This may mean referring one or both clients to an accountant, real estate appraiser, business evaluator, for special information about the children's health, educational progress or emotional adjustment.
- The mediator can raise concerns about the fairness of settlement proposals directly with both parties together, as well as in individual caucuses. The purpose would be to ensure that each individual understood his or her rights and was acting without duress.

On the one hand, mediation is a voluntary process whereby parties reach an agreement that they have engineered. Mediation encourages private ordering, but on the other hand there is an obligation on the part of the mediator to prevent a grossly unfair result, particularly where children are involved. While the mediator should not interfere with most settlements arrived at by the parties, nevertheless the mediator may need to intervene in the following types of circumstances:

- if the mediator realizes that there is a great inequality of bargaining power between the spouses, such that one spouse appears to be under duress by the other spouse to reach a particular agreement;
- one party is seriously emotionally disturbed and therefore unable to negotiate as an equal;
- one party is withholding significant relevant information from the other and refuses to disclose this;
- one party is feeling so guilty about the marriage breakdown or is so anxious to reconcile that he or she is unable to protect his or her own interests, and
- one party is being coerced to give up certain rights in return for other benefits. For example, one spouse may be pressured into giving up the right to support in exchange for custody of the children.

In all of these circumstances, it is important for the mediator to discuss these issues with the clients and, if necessary, with their solicitors. If the mediator feels that the issue can be resolved by referring one or both clients out for additional assistance, from a therapist or an accountant, for example, then this should be done, and the mediation may need to be delayed until this occurs. If the situation cannot be remedied, then the mediator may have to withdraw from the mediation and should write a letter to the clients and their lawyers explaining the reason for this action.

(d) Duty of Confidentiality

In both open mediation and closed mediation, the mediator should clarify from the outset that he or she will not voluntarily disclose to any third party information that is obtained during the mediation process except:

- if both parties consent to the release of information in writing to a particular individual or organization;
- if the mediator is ordered to disclose information by an appropriate judicial authority or is required to disclose information by law;
- if the mediator has reasonable cause to believe that there may be an actual or potential threat to human life or safety;
- non-identifying information for research or educational purposes. If the clients are the subject of research, they should each have given their consent to participate.

The mediator should explain to the clients that even though the mediator will not voluntarily disclose information, he or she may be obligated to do so, for example, if the mediator learns information that creates a concern about physical or sexual abuse of children. In this case, the mediator would be under a statutory or ethical duty to inform the child welfare authorities about this information. In addition, even if the parties agree in writing that the mediator will not be called as an expert witness to testify in court, the court may decide that the mediator's testimony is essential to the issues in dispute and may require that the mediator testify.

It is important for the mediator to determine whether there are individuals whom the mediator should speak to with respect to the issues in dispute. For example, in a child custody dispute, the mediator may consider it essential to speak to the schoolteacher and the family doctor. In financial mediation, the mediator may wish to speak to the accountant or a property appraiser. The mediator should ask the spouses to sign a consent form permitting the mediator to receive and, if necessary, exchange information with specific individuals or agencies. In addition, the mediator will want permission to speak to the lawyers, new spouses and significant caretakers for the children. In each case, it is important that both parents consent to these discussions.

(e) Independent Legal Advice

It is the duty of every mediator to advise clients to obtain independent legal advice prior to commencing mediation and certainly before signing any agreement. The purpose of independent legal advice is to ensure:

- that both clients understand their legal rights and entitlements;
- that both clients understand the effect of alternative proposals for resolving the issues in dispute;
- that both clients understand the consequences of an agreement under the law. For example, the clients must understand that the agreement will be binding unless the agreement was made under duress or without full disclosure of relevant information.

(f) Duty to Ensure No Harm or Prejudice to Participants

The mediator is under a duty to suspend or terminate mediation whenever he or she believes that the process may be harmful or prejudicial to one or more of the participants. That is:

- The mediator should suspend or terminate the mediation when the mediator suspects that one or both parties are either unwilling or unable to participate effectively in the mediation process. For example, one party may be suffering from a serious emotional disorder and be unable to bargain in a reasonable manner.
- The mediator should end mediation when he or she believes that the mediation is no longer useful, in order to avoid unnecessary expenses for the clients.

If the mediation process is suspended or terminated, the mediator should suggest additional professional services to the parties, if they are appropriate. For example, the mediator may recommend that one or both parties obtain individual counselling or that one or both parties have the assistance of an accountant or tax lawyer prior to resuming mediation.

The mediator has a duty to ensure that both clients are reaching agreement freely, voluntarily and without undue duress. Despite the mediator's obligation to ensure that participants are not harmed or prejudiced by their participation in mediation, it is also a fundamental principle of mediation that the participants can design their own agreement, voluntarily, without being bound by statutes or common law. The mediator must walk a fine line between permitting the clients to design their own agreement and permitting an unreasonable agreement to occur. At a minimum, the mediator needs to draw the client's attention to possible areas of unfairness and may need to discuss these with the client's counsel.

These are the principal issues that are generally addressed in professional codes of conduct. By way of illustration the code of conduct that has been adopted by the Ontario Association for Family Mediation is set out in Appendix 9B. This is the first code of conduct for family mediators in Canada. Family Mediation Canada has recently adopted a federal code, and several provinces are developing their own provincial code.

(3) THE ROLE OF THE LAWYER

The role of the lawyer in the practice of family law has changed considerably during the past two decades. According to the traditional role, each spouse selected a lawyer who would represent his or her interests against the other spouse. That often precipitated the entry of spouses into a system that made them adversaries even when there may have been no particular issue in conflict.

Conversely, the expanding use of family mediation has created at least three possible role options. In each of the following roles described for the lawyer, the spouses are assumed to be in mediation to effect a resolution of the issues between them due to a decision to separate or divorce.

Role	Functions
(1) Independent legal advocate	(a) Is familiar with the practice of law and supportive of family mediation.
	(b) Represents one of the spouses in conflict.
	(c) Consults on the terms of mediation with the mediator and other lawyer and is committed to same.

(2) Impartial legal consultant

This option is not accepted at present in Canada but is accepted in some jurisdictions in the United States.

(a) Contracts carefully with both spouses to ensure that his/her functions preclude representing either in any capacity during or after mediation.

(b) Functions as an impartial consultant on legal issues and points of law to the couple.

(c) Provides neutral input to both spouses about their rights and responsibilities before the law.

(d) Consults with the mediator as required, to remain informed on the progress of the couple and the issues resolved.

(3) Lawyer as mediator

(a) Functions within the non-traditional role as developed and practised by Coogler.

(b) Places herself/himself in a non-adversarial position impartially between the two spouses.

(c) Contracts carefully with both spouses to ensure their understanding that she/he is not functioning as a legal advocate for either spouse.

(d) Encourages each spouse to obtain separate legal counsel. (Some lawyers as mediators will refuse to mediate unless separate legal counsel is arranged.)

(e) Establishes collaboration with both lawyers consistent with the professional practice of family mediation.

(f) Submits a report of resolutions reached to both clients and their lawyers when mediation is concluded.

The roles and functions now possible for lawyers specializing in family law are expanding. Training programs for lawyers should include specific reference to the knowledge and skills required by such roles.

(4) Areas of Conflict for Lawyers Acting as Mediators

There is some concern that there may be conflicts between the requirements for lawyers when they are acting in a legal capacity and when they are acting as mediators. The most important concern is whether lawyers are violating their code of professional conduct as lawyers by acting on behalf of parties who are in a conflict of interest. Virtually all codes of conduct for lawyers require that they act in a partisan fashion and clearly advocate their client's position. There are usually strong rules prohibiting or limiting any situations in which lawyers may be acting for parties who are adverse in interests.

Those jurisdictions that have addressed the issue of the lawyer as mediator generally have set out special rules in order to protect the public and preserve the traditional role of the lawyer. That is, most codes of professional conduct require that the lawyer acting as mediator must make the clients aware of the following:

- that the lawyer has acted in some capacity for one or both parties. This matter must be disclosed to the other party and fully discussed. If the lawyer has acted in a legal capacity for one or both parties, the lawyer probably should not act as a mediator for the case;
- that the mediator will strongly recommend that both parties obtain independent legal advice throughout the mediation process and certainly before signing any agreement;
- that the lawyer who is acting as a mediator will not give independent legal advice to either party;
- that the mediator can give legal information, but cannot explain the implications of the law with respect to each party's specific position;
- that the mediator will require full disclosure of all relevant information prior to negotiating a settlement on any issue;
- that the mediator will not act on behalf of either or both clients in a legal capacity following the mediation. This is particularly true of any contested legal matters, especially if they arise out of issues referred to mediation;
- that the mediator will not deal with issues that are beyond the mediator's special training as a lawyer. For example, if the lawyer who is acting as a mediator does not have special training in dealing with issues related to custody of and access to children, then these issues will not be included in the mediation process.

In Ontario, the Law Society of Upper Canada is considering whether special rules are necessary for lawyers who are acting as mediators. At present, a special committee of the family law section of the Canadian Bar Association has recommended that the Law Society not formulate special rules to govern lawyers who also practice as mediators. The committee took the position that the Law Society should not attempt to govern the behavior of lawyers who act in professional capacities outside of the practice of law.

The committee did recommend one amendment to the existing Code of Professional Conduct for Lawyers Practising in Ontario and that is that Rule 5, Commentary 10 be expanded to include a specific reference to mediation. Rule 5, Commentary 10 now provides as follows:

> C10: The rule will not prevent a lawyer from arbitrating or settling, or attempting to arbitrate or settle, a dispute between two or more clients or former clients who are sui juris and who wish to submit the dispute to him.

Commentary 10 could be amended to include a reference to mediation. For example:

> The rule will not prevent a lawyer from arbitrating, *mediating,* or settling, or attempting to arbitrate, *mediate,* or settle a dispute between two or more clients or former clients who are sui juris and who wish to submit the dispute to him.

The committee did take the position that the Law Society should provide guidelines to those lawyers who wish to practise family law mediation. They suggested the following guidelines:*

- A lawyer acting as a family law mediator should not provide legal advice, but rather should encourage the parties to obtain independent legal advice.
- The lawyer acting as mediator and any member of his law firm should not accept legal work arising from the mediation. The purpose of this guideline is to avoid a possible conflict of interest.
- The Law Society should encourage mediators to obtain additional academic and professional training in mediation.
- The lawyer acting as mediator should be aware and should make the parties aware that the mediator may not be able to keep the contents of any communication from one of the parties confidential or privileged. In addition, the lawyer acting as mediator should explain to the parties that the communications he or she receives as a mediator are not protected by the solicitor-client privilege and there is a possibility that the mediator could be forced to reveal all or part of a communication if ordered by a court of law to do so.

---

* See Appendix 9A, "Communique Plus, Number 13, Family Law Mediation", Law Society of Upper Canada.

- The Law Society should inform lawyers acting as mediators that professional liability insurance through the Law Society would not cover a lawyer acting as a mediator. Lawyers acting as mediators should be encouraged to obtain separate insurance coverage as mediators.

(5) QUALIFICATIONS FOR MEDIATORS

This is an issue that is being discussed currently by a number of mediation associations. Most associations have not reached a consensus on the qualifications for practising as a mediator, the nature of training required, the requirements for being licensed or certified and the mechanism for disciplining individuals who violate the code of conduct. However, a number of associations, such as the Academy of Family Mediators, the Ontario Association for Family Mediation and the Alberta Family Mediation Society have made considerable progress in dealing with these issues. All of these Associations have developed standards for practising mediators and the Academy of Family Mediators and the Ontario Association for Family Mediation have adopted guidelines and training requirements for mediators. Set out in Appendix 9B are the Standards for Practising Mediators adopted by the Board of Directors of the Ontario Association for Family Mediation in 1986. These Standards include the following:

AREAS OF COMPETENCE

In order to qualify for and maintain membership in the Ontario Association for Family Mediation (hereinafter referred to as O.A.F.M.) as a "Practising Member", an applicant/member must satisfy the Association that he or she possesses the areas of competence set out below:

1. PROFESSIONAL EDUCATION: A graduate or law degree.
    A.   To be a member in good standing in one's own professional organization is preferable, but not essential, because:
        (i) Some mediators may not wish to practise their own profession(s);
        (ii) Some professions (e.g. counselling) do not have their own professional organizations.
    B.   An exception may be made at the discretion of the Membership Committee for a person not holding a professional degree, but who has demonstrated the ability to function at an academic level, and has had an exceptional amount of applicable personal experience.

2. KNOWLEDGE OF MEDIATION THEORY AND SKILLS
    A basic knowledge of theory and skills as set out in the "Optimum Standards" appendix is essential, but for the purpose of application for membership, or continuing membership, an applicant/member must show that he or she has:
    A.   Taken five days or 40 hours of mediation training taught by a recognized mediator or approved by the Ontario Association for Family Mediation, Family Mediation Canada, or equivalent.

The 40 hours of mediation training needs to include a minimum of five hours in each of the following categories:*

    (i) Conflict resolution theories;

    (ii) Psychological issues in separation, divorce, and family dynamics;

    (iii) Issues and needs of children in separation and divorce;

    (iv) Mediation process and techniques;

    (v) Family Law including custody, support, asset evaluation and distribution, and taxation as it relates to separation and divorce; and

    (vi) Family economics (not required if the basic training is limited to custody mediation).

OR

B.   Taught such a course him/herself; or

C.   Had an exceptional amount of applicable practical experience.

An O.A.F.M. member must continue his/her mediation education through attending courses and workshops and reading about new developments in the field.

3.   EXPERIENCE AND CONSULTATION/SUPERVISION IN THE ACTUAL PRACTICE OF MEDIATION

An O.A.F.M. practising mediator must:

A.   Have at least two years of relevant work experience; and

B.   Have mediated a minimum of five cases to the point of agreement. It is preferable that the mediator consult with or be supervised by a practising O.A.F.M. mediator.

If the applicant lacks the minimum qualifications outlined in 1, 2 and 3 above, he/she shall submit a resumé and meet with the Membership Committee to discuss his/her acceptability for membership on an individual basis.

4.   STANDARDS OF PRACTICE

Each applicant/member must commit himself/herself and adhere strictly to the O.A.F.M. Code of Professional Conduct as a Standard of Practice. No mediator shall venture into an area of practice beyond his/her own area of expertise.

It is important to note that anyone can become a member of the Ontario Association for Family Mediation; however, in order to qualify for the membership category entitled "Practising Mediator", an individual would have to meet the criteria set out above. The Alberta Family Mediation Society has adopted a similar set of standards and in addition requires that a practising mediator have mediator liability insurance.

---

*   These categories are those suggested by the Academy of Family Mediators as requirements of basic mediation training for people applying for full membership in that organization.)

ANNOTATED BIBLIOGRAPHY

Baker-Jackson, M., Bergman, K., Ferrick, G., Hovsepian, V., Garcia, J., and Hulbert, R. "Ethical Standards for Court-Connected Mediators." In "Making Ethical Decisions," edited by J.A. Lemmon. (1985), 8 *Mediation Quarterly* 67. This article outlines the significant qualifications in terms of knowledge, training and experience for public sector mediators.

Barsky, M. "Emotional Needs and Dysfunctional Communication as Blocks to Mediation." In "Successful Techniques for Mediating Family Breakups," edited by J.A. Lemmon. (1983), 2 *Mediation Quarterly* 55.

Berg, A.G. "The Attorney as Divorce Mediator." In "Successful Techniques for Mediating Family Breakups," edited by J.A. Lemmon. (1983), 2 *Mediation Quarterly* 21. This article deals with practical suggestions for developing a mediation practice that would be useful for both a family lawyer and a mental health professional.

Bernard, S.E., Folger, J., Weingarten, H., and Zumeta, Z. "The Neutral Mediator: Value Dilemmas in Divorce Mediation." In "Ethics, Standards and Professional Challenges," edited by J.A. Lemmon. (1984), 4 *Mediation Quarterly* 61. This chapter considers both a neutral and interventionist approach to mediation in the light of ethical considerations.

Bishop, T.A. "Mediation Standards: An Ethical Safety Net." In "Ethics, Standards and Professional Challenges," edited by J.A. Lemmon. (1984), 4 *Mediation Quarterly* 5. This article discusses the American Bar Association's Standards of Practice for Family Mediators and their implications for lawyers who are in practice as mediators.

Cramer, C., and Schoeneman, R. "A Court Mediation Model with an Eye Toward Standards." In "Making Ethical Decisions," edited by J.A. Lemmon. (1985), 8 *Mediation Quarterly* 33. This chapter looks at the typical stages of reaching an agreement and discusses how the mediator can follow accepted standards at each stage of the process.

Dibble, C. "Bargaining in Family Mediation: Ethical Considerations." In "Ethics, Standards and Professional Challenges," edited by J.A. Lemmon. (1984), 4 *Mediation Quarterly* 75. This article considers both the dangers and benefits of bargaining in family mediation and addresses the role of the mediator.

Engram, P., and Markowitz, J. "Ethical Issues in Mediation: Divorce and Labour Compared." In "Making Ethical Decisions," edited by J.A. Lemmon. (1985), 8 *Mediation Quarterly* 19. This article examines the ethical procedures for divorce mediators by comparing divorce mediation to labour mediation.

Folberg, J., and Taylor A. *Mediation: A Comprehensive Guide to Resolving Conflicts without Litigation.* San Francisco: Jossey-Bass Inc., Publishers, 1984. See particularly Part Four, "Mediation As a Profession — Educational, Ethical and Practical Dimensions," page 233. See also chapter 10, "Ethical, Professional and Legal Issues," page 244. This chapter contains a comprehensive exploration of ethics, standards of practice, confidentiality and mediator liability.

Goldberg, S.D., Green, E.D., and Sander, F.E.A. "A Dialogue on Legal Representation in Divorce Mediation." In "Making Ethical Decisions," edited by J.A. Lemmon. (1985), 8 *Mediation Quarterly* 5.

Haynes, J.M. *Divorce Mediation: A Practical Guide for Therapists and Counsellors.* New York: Springer Publishing Company, 1981. See in particular Part II, "The Mediation Process," and chapter 4 "Factors Affecting the Process," page 47.

Landau, B. "Identity Crisis: Mediation, Lawyers and Mental Health Professionals." (1985), 11 *Therapy Now* 9. This article explores the role conflicts experienced by lawyers and mental health professionals in relation to mediation and custody assessments.

Lande, J. "Mediation Paradigms and Professional Identities." In "Ethics, Standards and Professional Challenges," edited by J.A. Lemmon. (1984), 4 *Mediation Quarterly* 19. This article considers how mediation principles derived from general theories of dispute resolution may conflict with the American Bar Association's Standards of Practice for Family Mediators.

Lemmon, J.A., ed. "Ethics, Standards and Professional Challenges." (1984), 4 *Mediation Quarterly.*

and

Lemmon, J.A., ed. "Making Ethical Decisions." (1985), 8 *Mediation Quarterly.* These two editions of the journal were devoted to ethical issues and contain a number of articles by well-recognized mediators. In addition, they outline draft codes of conduct adopted by organizations in the United States.

Milne, A. "The Development of Parameters of Practice for Divorce Mediation." In "Ethics, Standards and Professional Challenges," edited by J.A. Lemmon. (1984), 4 *Mediation Quarterly* 49. This article considers various practice principles that would best serve the client, the mediator and the practice of mediation.

Milne, A. "Model Standards of Practice for Family and Divorce Mediation." In "Making Ethical Decisions," edited by J.A. Lemmon. (1985), 8 *Mediation Quarterly* 73. This chapter contains guidelines for practice for both court-connected and private family mediators. These are included in a draft code prepared by the Association of Family and Conciliation Courts in 1983-84.

Perlmutter, F. "Ethical Issues in Family Mediation: A Social Perspective." In "Making Ethical Decisions," edited by J.A. Lemmon. (1985), 8 *Mediation Quarterly* 99. This article focuses particularly on mediation services for low-income families.

Pirie, A.J. "The Lawyer as Mediator: Professional Responsibility Problems or Profession Problems?" (1985), 63 *Canadian Bar Review* 279. This author outlines the important ethical issues for lawyers who are acting as mediators to consider and makes recommendations that the Bar Associations not overly regulate mediation by lawyers at this point in time.

Samuels, M.D., and Shawn, J.A. "The Role of a Lawyer Outside the Mediation Process." In "Successful Techniques for Mediating Family Breakups," edited by J.A. Lemmon. (1983), 2 *Mediation Quarterly* 13. This article considers the role of the non-mediating attorney before, during and after mediation. It provides specific guidelines for practice by mediators at each stage of the process.

Saposnek, D. "Strategies in Child Custody Mediation: A Family Systems Approach." In "Successful Techniques for Mediating Family Breakups," edited by J.A. Lemmon. (1984), 2 *Mediation Quarterly* 29. This is a practical guide for handling communication between the parties during mediation.

Saposnek, D. *Mediating Child Custody Disputes.* San Francisco: Jossey-Bass Inc., Publishers, 1983. See Part V, "Challenges and Professional Issues," particularly chapter 13, "Ethics, Values and Morals in Mediation," page 257. Saposnek, D. "What Is Fair in Child Custody Mediation." In "Making Ethical Decisions," edited by J.A. Lemmon. (1985), 8 *Mediation Quarterly* 9. This article examines the concept of fairness from different perspectives — individual, family, sociopolitical, cultural and moral — and considers whether this would result in different recommendations.

Silberman, L.J. "Professional Responsibility Problems of Divorce Mediation." (1982), 16 *Family Law Quarterly* 107. This article outlines the response of the various Bar Associations in the United States to lawyers acting as mediators.

Chapter Nine

Mediation in Practice: Conclusion

A. BY AGREEMENT OF THE PARTIES

If the parties reach an agreement on one or more issues, the mediator prepares a report containing the specific terms agreed to by the parties.

The form of the mediator's report should be worked out in discussions with both counsel and the parties, preferably at the beginning of mediation, so that all parties are clear about what they will receive from the mediator. For the purpose of this chapter, the report will be called a *memorandum of separation* (some mediators have a different designation, such as *resolutions* or *draft agreement*).

If the parties have not initiated court proceedings and are hoping to arrive at a full separation agreement with respect to all of the issues in dispute, then the issues resolved in mediation can be incorporated into the separation agreement.

If one or both parties have initiated court proceedings, then the issues resolved in mediation can be incorporated into minutes of settlement that would be filed with the court on consent in order to terminate the legal proceedings.

(1) MEMORANDUM OF SEPARATION

This document should outline in clear, unambiguous language the specific agreement reached on those issues sent to mediation.

One of the factors that contributes to couples returning to court to relitigate agreements is the lack of precision of the wording in the agreement. It is very important that the mediator state as clearly and specifically as possible what responsibilities or privileges each party will have. If the parties are to share responsibilities and privileges, it should be clear:

- what responsibilities;
- what privileges;

- under what circumstances;
- with what notice to the other party;
- whether the responsibility is something that a particular spouse is required to do or whether it is something that the spouse can be requested to do, if he or she is available;
- what will happen if one party is unable or unwilling to fulfill a responsibility or accept a privilege.

In general, it is preferable to set out:

- specific times for access visits on weekends, during the week, on statutory holidays, during school breaks and at other times;
- specific times for pickup and delivery;
- whether the parties intend to permit additional access time on request.

The mediator can explain to the parties that in the future, once they are more comfortable with each other's involvement, they can behave in a more flexible way with respect to access times. However, at the beginning, particularly with clients who do not trust each other, a schedule that clarifies their respective rights and obligations is usually helpful.

It is very important to include the parties' intentions with respect to changes in custody or access arrangements in the event that the parties move more than a certain number of miles apart. Families are very mobile, and one or both spouses may move due to a job, a new relationship, for economic or other reasons. An arrangement that has worked well for a number of years may suddenly grind to a stop because a party wishes to move out of the city or even out of the province or country. It is important to anticipate that this may happen and to include a provision to cover this possibility. Many cases end up in litigation when this situation is not anticipated.

In cases of financial mediation, it is important to consider material changes in the parties' circumstances, such as:

- the loss of a job,
- obtaining employment for a previously unemployed spouse,
- the effect of illness or long-term disability,
- the death of a spouse, or
- the remarriage of one or both spouses.

All of these factors could constitute a material change of circumstances that should trigger a re-examination of the original agreement. The process that the parties wish to follow when there is a material change in circumstances should be included in the agreement.

If the parties have agreed to mediate a new arrangement in the event that there is a material change in circumstances (such as remarriage or a move to a new province), the agreement should state how the mediator will be chosen and how the mediator's fees will be shared. That is, will one party pay the full cost, will the fees be shared 50-50 or will the fees be paid in proportion to income at the time?

It may be desirable to have an interim agreement, possibly for three to six months, before completing a final agreement. This would give the parties a chance to evaluate whatever plan they have chosen, both in terms of the best interests of the child and their own needs. An interim agreement would also give the parties an opportunity to adjust to the separation. At the time set for termination of the agreement, the parties could return to mediation to review the contents of the interim agreement and decide whether to continue with it indefinitely, for a further period of time, or whether to make appropriate changes. A time-limited agreement may be preferable in the following circumstances:

- if the child's needs, wishes and/or stage of development change, it may be desirable to reconsider the previous parenting plan;
- if the parties' circumstances change such that a review is warranted;
- if the parties do not have independent legal advice, a time-limited agreement would limit the effect of any adverse legal consequences.

If one or both parties refuse to obtain independent legal advice, it is strongly recommended that the mediator not witness the signature of the parties on the memorandum of separation. If both parties have solicitors, it is recommended that the memorandum of separation be signed in the respective lawyers' offices.

Unless the mediator is a trained lawyer, the mediator should not attempt to draft a separation agreement for the parties. This is because:

- the mediator may not appreciate the implications of certain clauses dealing with custody, financial matters, and releases in terms of their legal significance for the parties;
- the mediator could be sued if one or both parties are prejudiced as a result of clauses that are included in or omitted from the agreement;
- the legal position of one or both clients could be adversely affected because of the mediator's lack of legal training;
- the mediator could be charged under provincial legislation with the unauthorized practice of law.

Some lawyers hold the view that even if the mediator is a lawyer he or she should not draft the complete separation agreement because:

- the mediator may only be dealing with some of the issues in dispute and therefore not have adequate information with respect to all of the issues and their implications for both parties that normally would be included in a complete agreement;
- drafting a separation agreement may create some role confusion in the client's mind about whether the mediator is acting as a mediator or a lawyer;

- the solicitors for the clients may feel the mediator is usurping their role.

This issue should be fully discussed with both the clients and their solicitors in advance to clarify the expectations of all parties. In fact, the lawyer and clients may wish to have the mediator draw up specific clauses of the separation agreement relating to mediation because:

- the mediator who is legally trained both understands the nature of the agreement reached and can express the client's wishes most clearly by adopting a "legal" style of writing;
- the parties are saved the expense of having one or both lawyers who were not present during the discussions try to draft these particular clauses.

The best advice is to clarify what is expected of the mediator in advance to avoid possible confusion or problems at a later time.

In addition to the memorandum of separation, the mediator should prepare a brief report. If the parties have initiated legal proceedings, then the brief report would be sent to the judge along with the minutes of settlement and a copy of the memorandum of separation.

The memorandum of separation should be sent to the parties and to their legal counsel, prior to signing, so that the clients can obtain independent legal advice.

Both in the memorandum of separation and in the brief report, the mediator should indicate that the parties have been strongly advised to obtain independent legal advice prior to signing any agreement.

This brief report should contain the following types of information:

- a statement of the issues that were sent to mediation;
- a statement of which issues were resolved and which issues are still in dispute;
- who was seen during the mediation, how often, in what combinations and for what total period of time;
- a summary of the terms of the memorandum of separation and some additional explanation or encouragement for the parties with respect to implementing the memorandum of separation;
- the intention of the parties when arriving at an agreement;
- the basic responsibilities and privileges of each parent in the context of the best interests of the children;
- any significant concerns or possible obstacles that were identified during the mediation that may affect the ability of one or both parties to carry out the terms of the agreement, along with any suggestions for handling these difficulties if they should arise.

The mediator should indicate that he or she would be available to assist the parties should there be some initial difficulties in implementing the agreement or should difficulties arise in the future due to a material change in circumstance or developmental changes in the children. The covering report should also encourage in the parties to overlook their own differences as spouses in order to co-operate in the best interests of their children. This is particularly important in situations where both parents want to maintain a close and loving relationship with the children.

(2) SEPARATION AGREEMENT

The mediator should send the parties and counsel a copy of the memorandum of separation, which can be incorporated into a full separation agreement.

A separation agreement usually takes into consideration a number of issues that were not discussed during the mediation process and is likely to include a number of clauses not dealt with in mediation.

Once certain issues have been agreed upon during mediation, the clients and their counsel usually continue to negotiate other related issues. For example, if the mediation involved custody and access issues, the lawyers might deal with financial matters and would then draft a separation agreement including clauses with respect to:

- child support
- spousal support
- cost of living increase in support
- division of property
- possession and ownership of the matrimonial home
- division of debts
- material change in circumstances
- share of pension funds
- releases with respect to future claims and liabilities.

It is hoped that the mediation process will set the tone for co-operative and reasonable bargaining with respect to issues that are not covered by mediation.

The mediator should communicate to the lawyers any approaches that might prove helpful in maintaining a co-operative atmosphere. If the remaining issues are dealt with in an adversarial manner, it may undermine the parties' trust in each other and their willingness to fulfill their agreement on the issues that were sent to mediation.

Under the new Ontario *Rules of Civil Procedure,* O. Reg. 560/84, the parties are encouraged to disclose information to each other fully and at an early stage. This is to minimize suspiciousness and distrust and encourage settlement.

It is important to note that there is no onus on a spouse residing in Ontario to request disclosure of relevant financial information; rather there is an obligation on both spouses to provide the other spouse with full and complete disclosure. The penalty for failing to disclose is that any domestic contract, such as a separation agreement, can be set aside by a court because one party failed to disclose significant assets, debts or liabilities to the other. In addition, certain procedural steps are now required in civil cases, particularly family law cases, to encourage a negotiated settlement rather than an adversarial battle. For example, all contested matters must be heard in a pretrial conference prior to proceeding to litigation. These new rules should encourage new practices among lawyers and should make the approach of family law lawyers more compatible with the type of approach and objectives used by the mediator.

(3) Minutes of Settlement

If one or more parties have initiated litigation, then those issues that have been resolved in mediation can be finalized in minutes of settlement. This document is filed with the court, and in most cases, the judge will sign an order in keeping with the terms of the minutes of settlement.

In the event that there are still outstanding issues that have not been resolved, partial minutes of settlement can be filed with the court that deal with only those issues that have been settled.

B. PARTIAL AGREEMENT OR NO AGREEMENT BY THE PARTIES

In the event that the parties fail to agree on one or more of the issues in dispute, the mediator or one or both parties may terminate the mediation process. One or both lawyers may recommend that mediation terminate, but the decision is made by the clients or mediator.

(1) By the Mediator

The mediator may decide to terminate the mediation process, prior to an agreement, for various reasons, such as:

- unequal bargaining power, which can arise because of many factors such as:

  one party has achieved an emotional divorce, while the other party is still longing for reconciliation;

  one party has a good grasp of relevant information with respect to the issues in dispute; however, the other party has very little knowledge or information about the issues in dispute (this arises particularly with financial matters);

  one party uses emotional duress on the other party, for example, threats of physical violence, harassment, refusal to pay support, threatened legal action for custody, or withholding of access;

  differences in education;

  differences in financial status;

differences in emotional stability;

differences in motivation for ending the marriage (for example, desire to remarry or guilt regarding marriage breakdown).

- the mediator feels that one party is delaying the mediation in order to take advantage of a status quo situation (that is, one party may have *de facto* custody of the children and believe it is to his or her advantage to delay mediation);
- the parties may be so hostile to each other that the mediation is unlikely to be productive and may even be destructive of the emotional health of one of the parties;
- one party may be willing to enter an agreement that the mediator feels is detrimental to the well-being of the children. The mediator should exercise this discretion very cautiously. In mediation, the emphasis should be on private ordering, that is, allowing the parties to arrive at a bargain that they feel is reasonable and acceptable. However, if a mediator participates in what is really an unconscionable transaction, then the mediator, on ethical grounds, should withdraw. This is particularly true when there is a risk to children. In any event, if the mediator suspected abuse or neglect of children, the mediator would have a statutory duty to report to the child welfare authorities. This duty should be explained to the parents;
- one party fails to make proper financial disclosure or in fact misleads the other party with respect to finances;
- one party may refuse to pay the mediator's fees within a reasonable period of time.

In the event that the mediator plans to terminate mediation without agreement by the parties, the mediator should inform the parties of the decision to terminate and should then contact counsel. The mediator should explain to both the parties and counsel the basis for the termination.

If the mediation is open mediation, then the mediator should prepare a report with respect to the mediation process. If the mediator has been asked for recommendations, then the mediator should include recommendations with respect to the issues in dispute as was agreed upon. In preparing the report the mediator should indicate:

- the amount of time spent in mediation;
- who was seen and the reasons for termination;
- a statement as to whether it would be desirable for the mediation to continue at a future date and under what circumstances;
- constructive suggestions on how to deal with the major obstacles to a mediated solution.

(2) BY THE PARTY(IES)

One or both parties may decide to terminate the mediation process because of:

- perceived bias by the mediator, for example, with respect to the sex, age, ethnics or racial group, socioeconomic status or religious preference of a party;
- a lack of confidence or trust in the mediator or the other party;
- a personality conflict with the mediator;
- discomfort during the mediation process, particularly in meetings with the other party;
- perceived inequality of bargaining power;
- a belief that the mediator is not acting in an impartial manner;
- a belief that the mediator does not have a sufficient understanding of the children's needs;
- a belief that the other party is using the delay to his or her advantage.

If one or both parties decide to terminate, this should be discussed directly with the mediator to see whether the issue(s) can be resolved. If the party still has some concerns, the party should discuss the matter with his or her lawyer.

The mediator should be open to hearing comments and criticisms about his or her process, and where the concerns are justified, the mediator should endeavour to change his or her behaviour in order to meet the needs of the parties, but this should not be done so as to please one party over another. If the mediator believes that certain changes would be desirable, these changes should be discussed first with the other spouse, so that it will not appear that one spouse is manipulating the mediator.

If the party is still not satisfied, then he or she should terminate the mediation and the party's lawyer should draft a letter to the mediator and the opposite lawyer indicating the reasons for the withdrawal.

The letter should also contain an indication of circumstances, if any, under which mediation could be resumed.

(3) By the Lawyer(s)

Mediation can only be terminated by the client or the mediator. The lawyer can advise his or her client to terminate and raise concerns with the mediator, but it is not the lawyer's prerogative to make that decision. Certainly, it would be responsible conduct for the lawyer to voice his or her concerns with the client and the mediator if:

- the lawyer believed that the mediator had a bias on an issue that was highly relevant to the mediation, for example, with respect to:
    the sex of the custodial parent
    the age of the custodial parent
    religious preference
    sexual orientation
    racial or ethnic group
    socioeconomic status;

- the lawyer was concerned that the other party was taking advantage of the mediation process either for delay or for initiating legal proceedings that were in direct conflict with the mediation process. For example, one lawyer might suspect that the other spouse was dissipating or transferring assets to prevent them being shared with the other spouse;
- the lawyer might lose confidence in the procedure followed by the mediator.

In the event that the lawyer wishes the mediation process to terminate, the lawyer should first discuss his or her concerns with the client. The lawyer should attempt to determine whether the concerns he or she has are in fact perceived by the client or perceived by other individuals who are involved in the mediation process. If the lawyer is not satisfied, the lawyer should discuss the concerns directly with the mediator. Prior to taking any action to terminate the mediation, the lawyer should obtain instructions from the client on the client's wishes.

The lawyer should point out to the client the possible consequence that if one party withdraws from mediation, it may appear that that party is unwilling to co-operate or that that party has something to hide. If the lawyer feels that the risks of continuing the mediation are greater than the risks of stopping, then the lawyer should advise the client to terminate.

C. REPORTS

(1) CLOSED MEDIATION

In closed mediation, the mediator only reports in detail on the issues that were resolved during mediation. In this case, a memorandum of separation is drawn up by the mediator specifying the issues that were agreed to.

For those issues where agreement was not reached, the mediator simply states "agreement was not reached on the following issues" and lists the issues.

In closed mediation, the mediator does not report on the process and does not make any recommendations.

In closed mediation cases, the mediator usually has an agreement with the parties or a court order specifying that he or she would not be called to court as an expert witness to give evidence on behalf of either party.

(2) OPEN MEDIATION

The mediator makes a report with respect to all issues sent to mediation, whether or not they were resolved.

The content of the report depends on the open mediation agreement. This report may contain one or more of the following:

- a report on issues that are resolved;
- for those issues that are not resolved, a statement by the mediator about the process followed and the obstacles to an agreement;
- recommendations by the mediator about the resolution of the issues that are still in dispute.

The mediator should discuss the nature of the report requested with the parties prior to beginning the mediation. That is, is the mediator expected to prepare a report with recommendations in the event that mediation is not completely successful?

For those issues that were resolved by the parties, the mediator would usually not make a personal comment about the agreement reached. Exceptions to this would be if the court has ordered the mediator to provide an opinion on the adequacy of the settlement reached or if the mediator is concerned that the agreement created some danger for the children. The report would usually focus on those issues where agreement was not reached. In these cases, if the mediator has been requested to make recommendations, the mediator should set out a fair, reasonable and workable plan for the parties and the court to consider.

ANNOTATED BIBLIOGRAPHY

Bartoletti, M.; Bourke, P. and MacDonald, E.M. "The Supportive Separation System: A Joint Legal and Marital Counselling Alternative". In *Therapy with Remarriage Families,* edited by L. Messinger. Rockville: Aspen Publications, 1982. In this chapter, the authors (trained respectively in psychology, social work and law) present a collaborative approach to comprehensive mediation within a private practice setting.

Coogler, O.J. *Structured Mediation and Divorce Settlement: A Handbook for Marital Mediators.* Toronto: Lexington Books, D.C. Heath and Company, 1978. See particularly chapter 7, "The Marital Settlement Agreement," at page 63.

Folberg, J., and Taylor, A. *Mediation: A Comprehensive Guide to Resolving Conflicts without Litigation.* San Francisco: Jossey-Bass Publishers, 1984. This book contains a discussion about preparing the settlement agreement. See particularly Part Two "Mediation Stages, Concepts and Skills," chapter 3, "Stages in the Mediation Process," at page 38.

Haynes, J.M. *Divorce Mediation: A Practical Guide for Therapists and Counsellors.* New York: Springer Publishing Company, 1981. See particularly Part IV, "Conclusion," chapter 7, "Some Implications for Practice," at page 127.

Saposnek, D. *Mediating Child Custody Disputes.* San Francisco: Jossey-Bass Publishers, 1983. This book contains a helpful discussion with respect to drafting a mediation agreement. See particularly Part II, "Structuring the Mediation Process," chapter 5, "Drafting the Mediation Agreement," at page 97.

Chapter Ten

Custody Assessments

A. ASSESSMENT PROCEDURE

(1) MEDIATION — THE FIRST STEP

A chapter on custody assessments has been included in this book because the authors take the position that the first step in a custody assessment should be an attempt to mediate the issues in dispute. Mediation should be tried first for the following reasons:

- Parents should be encouraged to take responsibility for their children, and parents are in the best position to know their children and understand what parenting arrangement would be in the best interests of their children.
- If the assessor does not attempt mediation as a first step, then the parties are almost inevitably headed for an adversarial court battle. Such a battle is not in the children's best interests, nor in the parent's best interests.
- If the parties do succeed in reaching a settlement with the assistance of a mediator, they are more likely to accept the result and not to relitigate in the future.
- A mediated settlement is likely to save the parties considerable emotional strain as well as considerable expense.

(2) THE PURPOSE OF A CUSTODY ASSESSMENT

In conducting a custody assessment, it is important to decide what is the purpose of the assessment. That is, is the purpose to determine which is the best parent? Or, is the purpose to determine a parenting plan that would be in the best interests of the children? There is a fundamental difference in attitude between these two initial starting points. If the assessor considers the purpose to be determining the best parent, then the following assumptions might apply:

- The assessor probably presumes that the result will be sole custody to one of the two parents (as opposed to a joint custody or shared parenting arrangement).
- The assessor will attempt to determine which parent is better than the other — for example, in financial status, educational achievement, job security, or personality strengths.
- The assessor probably emphasizes a clinically oriented assessment process. Information gathering is likely to be through psychological testing and individual interviews, as opposed to joint meetings of both parents.
- The assessor will probably spend very little time with the spouses together trying to mediate a co-operative parenting plan.
- The assessor will probably place more emphasis on the stated or perceived preference of the children for one parent over the other.
- It is highly likely that the assessor will prepare a full custody assessment report, which will be submitted to the parties and the court.
- The case is likely to proceed to trial with the assessor called as a witness by the parent who is "preferred" in the assessment report.

On the other hand, if the assessor starts from the premise that the purpose of an assessment is to develop a shared parenting plan that is in the best interests of the children, then the assumptions are somewhat different, namely:

- The assessor is likely to place a great deal of emphasis on attempting to mediate a settlement.
- The assessor is likely to take the position that it is important for the children to have a warm and loving relationship with both parents and that the most desired outcome is an arrangement that maximizes the children's opportunity to spend time with both parents in an atmosphere of reduced tension.
- The assessor is likely to spend considerable time with the children determining the way in which they relate to both parents, and then with both parents together to consider various alternatives for co-operating so as to meet the children's needs, interests and wishes.
- The assessor is likely to focus more on the future of the parenting relationship than on the past or even the present. That is, the assessor will be interested in determining to what extent both parents are willing to share parental responsibilities and are competent to carry these out.
- The assessment will focus more on the communication between the parents and their ability and willingness to co-operate in the interests of their children.

- The assessor is more likely to explore the possibility of a joint custody or shared parenting arrangement, particularly in cases where there are two reasonably competent parents who have some ability to set aside their individual differences in the interests of the children. In some cases, the parents dislike each other intensely, live very different lifestyles, but recognize that they both love the children, are loved by the children and on this basis are prepared to co-operate in their parenting.
- The assessor is likely to focus on factors that might undermine the co-operation or make a shared parenting arrangement more difficult, such as considerable distance between the parents, unwillingness to share the transportation, the attitude of a new spouse that may obstruct co-operation, a poor parent-child relationship, distrust or fears of abuse between the spouses.
- The assessor will encourage the parties to reach their own settlement and not proceed to court, and in many cases will not need to prepare a detailed custody assessment. The more usual result would be a memorandum of separation by the assessor followed by minutes of settlement prepared by the solicitor.

(3) DIFFERENCES BETWEEN MEDIATION AND ASSESSMENTS

In what way is an assessment different from mediation?

In an assessment, unlike closed mediation, the assessor is asked to prepare a report containing his or her observations, opinions and recommendations. This may occur whether or not the parties reach an agreement. In closed mediation, the mediator prepares a report only with respect to those issues resolved in mediation. The mediator does not include his or her observations, opinions or recommendations.

In open mediation, the mediator may prepare a report that is similar to an assessment, although possibly not as detailed, and will only include recommendations if this is specifically requested by the parties. A report in open mediation would include the mediator's observations with respect to issues that were not resolved.

Mediation is a process that essentially emphasizes the private ordering of dispute resolution. That is, the parties are expected to resolve their own difficulties by arriving at a voluntary settlement. An assessment is a process whereby an impartial expert makes recommendations that are then considered by a judge who makes a decision for the parties on how their dispute will be resolved. There is no requirement that the parties accept the assessor's recommendations, and the final resolution is imposed by the court.

The assessment report will carry considerable weight with the court, and for this reason the assessor must spend additional time, which would not be needed in mediation, learning about the special needs, interests, wishes and stage of development of the children and about the capacity of the parents to parent and co-operate with each other.

An assessment focuses on what information an assessor needs in order to arrive at a recommendation; whereas mediation focuses on what information the parties need in order to resolve their dispute on their own.

An assessor must do a complete and thorough investigation, including contacts with a number of collateral sources to ensure that the procedure followed meets acceptable professional standards and to ensure that his or her report is considered credible by the court. A mediator who is not being asked for recommendations does not need to carry out an extensive investigation.

(4) ASSESSMENT INTERVIEWS

The following are basic guidelines for the types of interviews and data collection that are usually carried out in an assessment.

(a) Meeting of Assessor and Both Counsel

The objectives of this meeting are the same as those set out in Chapter Five with respect to mediation, and in addition:

- It is important for the assessor to clarify with counsel that he or she will be attempting to mediate a settlement as a first step in the procedure. The assessor also needs to clarify with counsel what will be expected of him or her if the mediation effort is successful. That is, will the assessor still be expected to prepare a full custody assessment or will a memorandum of separation with a brief report be adequate?
- It is recommended that an assessor not prepare a full assessment report unless it is required by the court for the following reasons:
  The assessment report is likely to be lengthy and more costly than the memorandum of separation and a brief report.
  A full custody assessment often includes information that could be upsetting to one or both parties and will likely weaken rather than encourage co-operative parenting. Many parents feel defensive, somewhat humiliated and often considerably distressed at having their weaknesses exposed.
  The information contained in a full assessment report may be used by one or both parties as further ammunition for their continued battle with each other.
- If a settlement is reached, it is best to emphasize the positive results and state what the parties did that was good, rather than expose their weaknesses. The settlement itself may be undermined by disputes over details in an assessment report.
- The assessor should clarify the fact that if an assessment report is

prepared, the assessor would agree to be called as a witness by either party and would be willing to be cross-examined by both.

- The assessor should clarify the payment of fees during the assessment process, for the preparation of a report or agreement and for a court appearance as an expert witness. It is desirable to have all fees shared throughout, so that there is no suggestion that the assessor has produced a favourable report for the party who is paying his or her fees. This is also in keeping with the assessor's position that he or she is concerned with the best interests of the children and is impartial as between the parties.

(b) Meeting of Assessor and Both Parties Together

See Chapter Five for a discussion of the objectives of this meeting, and in addition:

- The assessor should explain to the parties that they will be encouraged to develop a co-operative parenting plan on their own rather than leaving the decision with respect to their children to strangers such as the assessor or a judge.
- The assessor should clarify with the parents what will happen in the event that they do reach an agreement. That is, the assessor may prepare a memorandum of separation and a brief report rather than an assessment report, unless the assessment report is required by the court.
- The assessor should explain the implications with respect to fees if the parties settle versus if the parties fail to settle and an assessment report and expert witness testimony are required. If at all possible, the assessor should ask the parties to share his or her fees for the entire process. If this is not possible, or if one party will pay the majority of the fees, the assessor should obtain an agreement in writing that the other party will not raise the issue of who paid the fees to suggest bias by the assessor in favour of the spouse who paid.

(c) Meeting of Assessor with Each Party Separately

Some assessors prefer to meet with the parties separately initially and then hold a joint meeting at some other time.

This issue was discussed in Chapter Five with respect to mediation, and the discussion is relevant to assessments.

(d) Home Visit

In a custody assessment, it is strongly recommended that the assessor meet the children in their home environment. This is important for the following reasons:

- Children are far more comfortable in a familiar setting, and communication with the assessor will be enhanced.
- It is more likely that a child will show normalized behaviour in a family setting than in the assessor's office. Also the child is likely to be far less anxious and more communicative.
- A home visit provides the assessor with considerable information about the family's lifestyle and the extent to which the family is child-oriented. This information is more difficult to obtain in an office setting.
- The assessor is able to evaluate parenting ability more accurately in a home setting than in an office interview. For example, the assessor has an opportunity to observe the type of nutrition given the children, the adequacy of stimulation available, the appropriateness of the living arrangements and the desirability of the neighbourhood. In addition, it is more likely that the assessor will observe typical family patterns and discipline techniques in a home setting.
- The assessor should visit with the children in each parent's home in order to observe differences in the home environment and parent-child relationships.
- The assessor may choose to hold a number of meetings in the home on the day of each home visit, such as:
  with both parents and the children,
  with one parent and the children,
  with all children together,
  with each child separately,
  with each parent separately,*
  with the children with one parent and a new partner,
  with the new partner alone,*
  with a regular babysitter alone,*
  with extended family members who are directly involved in the care of the children alone.*

It is recommended that the first home visit be in the home where the children spend the majority of their time. The aim is to make the children feel as comfortable as possible when meeting the assessor and engaging in the asssessment interviews. The same procedure should be followed during the second home visit with the non-custodial parent.

(e) Meeting with the Parties Together on One or More Occasions

Additional meetings with both parties may be necessary, prior to reaching an agreement or preparing a report for such reasons as:

---

* These meetings could be held at the office on a different day if preferred or if necessary because of time constraints.

- to offer the parents information as to the childrens' response to the separation,
- to improve the parents' ability to communicate about parenting issues,
- to determine whether the parents can work out their own parenting plan for sharing responsibilities and time with the children.

Additional meetings may be needed with the children with one or both parents or with one child and a particular parent, with parents and their new partners, or with the entire family.

In difficult cases, a second evaluator could be used to provide independent observations of the children, parents, new partners or other significant figures.

(5) COMMENTS WITH RESPECT TO HOME VISITS

The assessor should discuss with both parents prior to a home visit how the visit will be explained to the children. The children should be told essentially that the assessor is a professional person whom the parents have asked to help them work out a parenting plan that will be in the best interests of the children. During the visit, the assessor will be spending time with both the parents and the children. The children should be told prior to the visit that it is all right for them to talk to the assessor and to say whatever they are feeling or thinking about the marriage breakdown and about the parenting plans for the future. The children should also be told that while their views will be considered, their parents or, in the alternative, a judge will be making the final decision.

Prior to speaking to the children, it is important to ensure that the children have been told by both parents that they are free to say whatever they wish to the assessor, that the parents' feelings will not be hurt by what they may say, and that there will be no negative repercussions for them.

It is usually best to hold a meeting of both parents together with the children, or at least one parent with the children, prior to seeing the children individually. The children need some time to become comfortable in the presence of the assessor, and the assessor needs some context of family interaction before beginning the individual sessions with each child.

The assessor should ensure that the meetings with each child are held in private and in a setting where the child is most comfortable. Usually children select their bedroom as a place to meet.

During the home visit the assessor needs to be tuned into such things as:

- whether there is affection shown between the parents and each child;
- whether there are appropriate toys and educational stimulation;
- the standard of cleanliness in the home;
- whether nutritious meals and snacks are served;

- whether there are pictures of the children, trophies or other items that indicate the value of the children to the parent;
- the daily routines for the children;
- whether the children are fearful, clinging to the parent or independent and confident in meeting strangers;
- the parent-child interaction, that is, whether the parent gives each child praise, encourages independence, sets reasonable limits, values the child's suggestions and opinions or is critical, controlling, uses lax or excessive discipline and minimizes the child's contribution.

The assessor should observe the interaction between the siblings to determine whether the siblings are supportive of each other or vying for attention: Do they include or exclude each other? Do they bicker or get along reasonably well? Does the parent intervene in an appropriate way when necessary with the children?

The assessor should eat one meal with the family, if possible, and observe:

- how nutritious the meal is;
- the types of limits and expectations with respect to table manners;
- whether the children are comfortable and participate in the conversation or are ignored and uncomfortable.

The assessor should observe the quality of interaction between the children and other significant figures who are to be interviewed, in terms of how they are greeted by the children, whether there is any display of affection or whether they are largely ignored.

At the end of the day, before the assessor leaves, it is desirable to hold a brief meeting between the children and the parent(s) just to sum up the day and ensure that everyone is clear about the next step in the process. The next step may be a home visit at the other spouse's home, and the children should be informed about when this will occur and what the purpose of the meeting will be. This will make the children more relaxed for the second visit.

(6) Collateral Sources

In addition to interview information, the assessor needs to collect information from external sources that have relevant and, it is hoped, reliable information with respect to the needs, interests and stage of development of the children, as well as the parenting capacity of both parents. Such information can be collected through reports, telephone conversations and, if necessary, direct visits with such sources as:

- the school
- the family doctor
- other mental health professionals

- the Children's Aid Society
- the public health nurse
- the employer.

(7) STANDARDS OF PRACTICE

As with mediation, it is important for the mediator to establish that he or she:

- has appropriate qualifications with respect to education, training and experience;
- adheres to a professional code of conduct as set out by his or her professional discipline; and
- adheres to a code of conduct established by a recognized professional organization for mediators and/or assessors.

The credibility or weight given to an assessment report will be determined by its thoroughness and its conformity with ethical standards. The court will be particularly interested in the following types of infomation:

- the amount of time spent in the total assessment process;
- who was interviewed, in what combination of persons, for how long and on how many occasions;
- what collateral sources were contacted;
- whether significant allegations were followed up, for example, with respect to alcohol or drug abuse, emotional disturbance or criminal behaviour;
- whether the assessor attempted to resolve the dispute through mediation prior to making recommendations;
- whether the assessor explained the nature of the recommendations to the parties and counsel prior to submitting the report to court (and possibly prior to preparing the report);
- whether the report was up to date; that is, did the assessor update his or her observations close to the time of the trial;
- whether the report was thorough; and
- whether the assessor presented a fair and balanced account of the parties in the report and in the testimony given in court.

B. PREPARATION OF CUSTODY ASSESSMENT REPORTS

In the event that the parties fail to resolve their dispute and a full assessment report is required, the following types of information should be included:

(i) Referral sources

The report should state whether this is a court-ordered assessment or one that is being conducted on the consent of the parties. The report should indicate whether the parties jointly selected the assessor or whether the assessor was selected by one of the parties over the opposition of the other. If the recommendation for an assessment was made by an external agency, such as the Children's Aid Society, this should be indicated.

(ii) Reasons for Referral

The report should indicate whether the referral was made to help the parents develop a co-operative parenting plan, select one parent in preference to the other, investigate allegations of child abuse, alcoholism, mental disorder or for some other reason(s). The events leading to the referral should be stated clearly.

It should also be clear whether the report was prepared for a contested custody trial, a child welfare trial or because one or both parents wished to review existing custody and access arrangements.

(iii) Objective of the Assessment

The report should set out the questions to be answered by the assessment. For example, is the primary concern the best parenting arrangements or is the issue restricted to the most appropriate access schedule or the involvement of a new partner in the children's lives?

(iv) Qualifications of Assessor

The report should contain a brief summary of the assessor's qualifications and a full *curriculum vitae* should be attached to the report.

(v) Assessment Process

The report should state who was seen or spoken to and for how long and what materials, reports or court documents were reviewed. This information can be included in paragraph or chart format.

(vi) Family History

The report should contain relevant family history; that is, information that pertains to the objectives of the assessment. This may include a history of the marriage, the early parenting of the child, the reasons for the marriage breakdown, if relevant, the present parenting plan and any difficulties or positive features of the present plan.

(vii) History of the Child and Assessor's Observations

This section should include information with respect to the child's physical, psychological, social, emotional and educational development. Included should be information with respect to the child's strengths and weaknesses, as well as special needs and abilities.

(viii) Summary of Observations of the Family and of Information from Other Sources

The report should contain a summary of family dynamics in relation to possible parenting arrangements, and should summarize the relevant information from such sources as the schoolteacher, family doctor and other involved professionals.

(ix) Discussion of Alternative Parenting Arrangements

The report should discuss viable parenting options in light of the objectives of the assessment. The relative strengths and weaknesses of the alternatives should be considered.

(x) Recommendations

The assessor may then wish to set out in specific terms the final recommendations with respect to the involvement of each parent in the child's life. This can include such recommendations as:

- sole versus joint custody;
- the primary residence of the child (if any);
- the amount of time to be spent with each parent, including the specific days and times for access;
- the manner in which parental responsibilities and privileges should be shared such as health care, educational planning, religious training and access to information;
- what should occur if one parent moves out of the jurisdiction or far enough away such that the access arrangements are no longer feasible;
- the method of dispute resolution to be used if the parents have a further dispute with respect to custody of or access to the children.

It is important for the assessor to indicate to both the parties and counsel that he or she will be available to meet with one or both parties prior to the trial date:

- to discuss the recommendations;
- to make a further attempt at settlement;
- to refer one or both parties for professional assistance, such as counselling or treatment for alcohol abuse;
- for additional information with respect to the needs of the children and how both parents can meet these needs.

The assessor should maintain a position of impartiality as between the parents and should remember throughout this process that the primary task is to devise a parenting plan that will be in the best interests of the children. A good assessment report is not one that helps one parent win and destroys the other parent, but rather one that makes constructive, reasonable recommendations that will eventually lead to a reduction of tension and an improvement in relationships between the children and both parents.

(xi) Rationale for Recommendations

The assessor should set out in this section the criteria that he or she is applying in making recommendations. Also, the assessor should summarize those key facts and observations with respect to each criterion that is relevant to a recommendation. For example, if the stability of the child's living arrangements is an important factor to the assessor, the report should make this clear. A summary should be given of the relevant facts and observations with respect to how each parent would affect the stability of the child's living arrangements. For example, one parent might be a professional musician and plan to take the child on extended world tours with nannies and tutors available. The other parent might be engaged in employment that does not require travelling and that would result in the child growing up in a familiar community, near friends and extended family members. The assessor should indicate how the different parenting plans would impact on the child's stability.

ANNOTATED BIBLIOGRAPHY

Gardner, R. *Family Evaluation in Child Custody Litigation.* New Jersey: Creative Therapeutics, 1982. This is a practical guide to performing custody assessments and includes a very useful discussion about the interview process, including who to interview, what information to collect, and also how to prepare a report.

Keeney, B. P., ed. *Diagnosis and Assessment in Family Therapy.* Rockville: Aspen Publications, 1983. A collection of papers by some of the foremost family therapists and diagnosticians in the United States and Canada, describing how to make family assessments more comprehensive.

Mayhew, C., and Raiford, K. *Guidelines for Court Connected Child Custody Evaluations.* U.S. Association of Family and Conciliation Courts, 1986. These standards were adopted by the Association of Conciliation Courts in 1986.

Perry, Ruth, ed. *Custody Disputes Evaluation and Intervention.* Toronto: Lexington Books, 1985. This book contains a number of interesting chapters written by experienced professionals with respect to the theory and practice of custody assessments.

Raiford, K. "Custody Evaluations: Standards and Procedures of the Los Angeles County Superior Court." (1985), 23 *Conciliation Courts Review* 57. This article sets out the standards of practice followed in the Conciliation Court in California.

Skafte, D. *Child Custody Evaluations: A Practical Guide.* California: Sage Publications Inc., 1986. This book is an informative, highly readable guide for those preparing custody evaluations.

Chapter Eleven

The Mediator/Assessor as Expert Witness

A. EXPERT TESTIMONY

It is important to consider the circumstances under which a mediator or an assessor might have to appear in court prior to beginning the mediation process. It should be clear to the clients and the mediator that the mediator could be subpoenaed to court to testify if he or she was involved in one of the following procedures:

- *open mediation or an assessment where the mediation or assessment has been court ordered.* Pursuant to ss. 30(7) and 31(5) (en. 1982, c. 20, s. 1) of the Ontario *Children's Law Reform Act,* R.S.O. 1980, c. 68, the mediator/assessor is required to submit a report to court, and the mediator can be summonsed by one or both parties as a witness, and the other party or parties may cross-examine the mediator/assessor on the contents of the report. In this case, the mediator/assessor might be called to appear in court even if the parties have come to an agreement on all issues. This would occur if the judge wanted additional information on how the agreement was arrived at, whether the clients appeared to have equal bargaining power and, therefore, whether the agreement was reached voluntarily. The mediator might be asked to comment on the fairness of the agreement by either counsel or the judge.
- *open mediation or an assessment where the parties do not reach an agreement on one or more issues.* The mediator/assessor may be summonsed by one or more parties to appear in court. The other party or parties may then cross-examine the mediator/assessor on the mediation process and the contents of any report that was written. This could occur whether or not the mediation or assessment was court ordered.

In the case of closed mediation, where the mediation was court ordered pursuant to a statute that permitted closed mediation, it is unlikely that the mediator would be summonsed to appear in court. For example, a statute such as the Ontario *Children's Law Reform Act,* ss. 31(4)(*b*) and 31(7), permits closed mediation and establishes a statutory privilege for any communication made during the course of mediation. That is, s. 31(7) states with respect to closed mediation that

> 31(7) . . . evidence of anything said or of any admission or communication made in the course of the mediation is not admissible in any proceeding except with the consent of all parties to the proceeding in which the order was made under subsection (1).

It is not clear whether the mediator could be summonsed to give evidence in a proceeding that was not under the statute that permitted closed mediation. For example, it is not clear whether the mediator could be required to testify in child welfare proceedings or perhaps in proceedings under the *Criminal Code.* These statutes do not confer any special statutory privilege on the mediator. Similarly, unless there is an order pursuant to s. 10(4) or (5) of the new *Divorce Act, 1985,* the mediator could be called as a witness in divorce proceedings and compelled to reveal what would otherwise be confidential communications. Section 31(7) of the Ontario *Children's Law Reform Act* does say that any admission or communication made in the course of mediation is not admissible in *any proceeding* except with the consent of all parties to the proceeding, but to date there has been no case law to indicate whether that statutory privilege would be respected in proceedings under another statute. It is unlikely that privilege would attach to these other proceedings, particularly in a child welfare case where the primary concern is the best interests of the child. It is important for mediators to understand and to communicate to clients any limitations on the confidentiality they can promise their clients.

- *closed mediation that is arranged by agreement, that is, not pursuant to a court order for closed mediation.* The mediator/assessor may have an oral or written agreement with the parties and/or their counsel that the mediation is to be closed. This means that any admission or communication made during the course of the mediation is to be confidential and the mediator is not to be called as an expert witness in any proceeding. If this agreement is not made pursuant to an order under a statute such as the Ontario *Children's Law Reform Act,* which has provision for closed mediation, then the communications may not be kept confidential in subsequent litigation. In these circumstances, it is possible that the mediator could claim a privilege based on the common law protection extended to settlement negotiations that take place when litigation is pending or contemplated. However, the mediator could not guarantee clients that he or she would not be required to testify if subpoenaed. It is important for mediators to explain to clients that they cannot guarantee confidentiality to their clients.

(1) SUBPOENA

A mediator/assessor may appear in court on consent; that is, if the mediator/assessor has been called as a witness by one or more parties, the mediator/assessor may agree to appear without the need for a subpoena.

Regardless of whether the mediator/assessor is prepared to appear without a subpoena, the party or parties wishing to call the mediator/assessor may issue a subpoena, which is a court document that requires that the mediator/assessor appear on a particular day, at a particular time, at a particular place in order to give testimony with respect to particular proceedings. If the mediator/assessor is subpoenaed, the subpoena usually requires that the mediator/assessor bring all relevant notes and documents with him or her.

With respect to any notes made on the file, it is not permissible for the mediator/assessor to keep a separate personal file and an official office file. Any notes made during the course of the mediation/assessment process would have to be brought to the court.

The subpoena is a legal document requiring the attendance of the mediator/assessor and must be served personally on the mediator/assessor.

The party issuing the subpoena is usually under an obligation to provide conduct money to the mediator/assessor, and without the provision of conduct money, the subpoena is not valid.

If the mediator/assessor is served with a subpoena, then it would be a contempt of court if the mediator/assessor failed to appear. The consequences of being found guilty of contempt of court are a fine and/or a jail sentence, depending on the particular statute or jurisdiction.

(2) PRIVILEGE

The term *privilege* is often confused with *confidentiality*. It is very important that both the mediator/assessor and the clients and their counsel understand the difference between these terms and are clear about whether the relationship is a privileged relationship or a confidential one. For the relationship to be privileged,

- there must be statutory protection, such as under the Ontario *Children's Law Reform Act,* the British Columbia *Family Relations Act,* R.S.B.C. 1979, c. 121, or the new *Divorce Act, 1985,* S.C. 1986, c. 4. For a statutory privilege to apply, there must be a court order pursuant to the relevant statute; or
- there must be a relevant common law privilege. For example, there is a common law privilege that protects settlement negotiations when litigation is pending or contemplated. Several recent court decisions in Ontario and British Columbia, as well as in the United States and England, have ruled that mediation discussions that were entered

into for the purpose of settling issues that were the subject of pending litigation were privileged. Recourse to the common law privilege may be available in cases where no statutory privilege applies; or
- the court may make a finding that it is in the public interest to protect certain communications. Wigmore has established four fundamental conditions which must be met before privilege will be extended to communications. These are:

1. The communications must originate in a *confidence* that they will not be disclosed.
2. This element of *confidentiality must be essential* to the full and satisfactory maintenance of the relation between the parties.
3. The *relation* must be one which in the opinion of the community ought to be sedulously *fostered*.
4. The *injury* which would inure to the relation by the disclosure of the communications must be *greater than the benefit* thereby gained for the correct disposal of the litigation (8 Wigmore on Evidence, §2285).

If the relationship is privileged, then any communications or admissions made during the course of the mediation may only be disclosed if all of the parties to the communication consent to the disclosure.

The privilege belongs to the clients, rather than the mediator. Therefore, if both clients wish to waive the privilege, they may do so and the mediator may disclose the contents of their communication.

(3) CONFIDENTIALITY

Confidentiality is a legal, moral and ethical duty to keep certain matters secret or confidential. Most mental health professionals and other professionals have an ethical duty, often set out in professional codes of conduct, to maintain a confidential relationship with their clients. That is, they are bound not to disclose any communications made during professional contacts, with certain exceptions.

There may be a conflict between privilege and confidentiality in that professional communications may not be privileged, even though the professional has promised to keep information confidential. For example, a doctor, psychologist or social worker may be compelled to testify, even though his or her professional relationship is based on confidentiality. Only the solicitor-client relationship is protected by privilege. However, the court has the discretionary power to exclude confidential communications if the court concludes that there are strong public policy reasons for doing so.

It should be made clear to clients that there can be no protection for confidential communications if there is a concern about possible abuse to children.

It is very important for the mediator, the clients and their counsel to consider the issues of confidentiality and privilege prior to the mediation beginning. The following issues should be clarified:

- whether the appointment of the mediator is pursuant to a statute that confers privilege or whether it is by agreement of the parties;
- whether the mediation is open or closed. If it is closed mediation pursuant to a statute that confers privilege, then the communications will be privileged.

Once these issues are decided, then:

- if the mediation is by agreement of the parties (not pursuant to a court order), the agreement should include a specific reference to a "without prejudice" relationship based on the common law privilege afforded settlement negotiations;
- if the mediation is open or if an assessment is requested, the agreement should indicate that the communications will not be privileged. However, the relationship would still be confidential in the sense of most professional-client relationships.

The confidentiality belongs to the clients, rather than the mediator. Therefore, if both clients wish to waive the confidentiality, they may do so and the mediator may disclose the contents of their communication.

B. QUALIFICATIONS OF AN EXPERT WITNESS

The general rule in litigation is that the judge is the trier of fact. That is, the judge draws inferences from the evidence presented in court and reaches a decision on the issues in dispute.

In making decisions in cases involving custody of or access to children, the court often relies on opinion evidence given by expert witnesses. These expert witnesses are not bound by the same evidentiary restrictions as ordinary witnesses. That is, expert witnesses (those who establish special qualifications for dealing with the issues in dispute) are permitted to include hearsay in their evidence. In addition, the expert witness is permitted to draw inferences based on facts, hearsay, research findings and other sources for arriving at an opinion. The process used by an expert in drawing inferences is very similar to the judicial role and is very much broader than the usual role of a witness. Because of the special latitude given the expert, it is important that the expert have the necessary qualifications for giving opinion evidence. The more qualified the mediator/assessor, the more likely the trier of fact (the judge) will permit the witness to give an expert opinion and will give weight or credibility to that expert opinion.

The expert has to establish his or her expertise in the following areas:

(1) EDUCATION

The mediator/assessor should have:

- a post-graduate degree in a mental health field, such as psychology, social work, psychiatry or counselling;

- ongoing attendance at relevant educational programs and conferences to upgrade skills and information with respect to mediation and assessments;
- up-to-date knowledge of the mediation/assessment literature, as well as literature on child development, parenting skills and the impact of separation and divorce on families.

(2) TRAINING

The mediator/assessor should have:

- completed a training program conducted by recognized authorities on mediation and assessments or have taught such a program;
- ongoing contact with a peer group of competent professionals for the purpose of case consultation, sharing of information and supervision.

(3) EXPERIENCE

The mediator/assessor should:

- have an ongoing professional practice with mediation and/or assessment cases;
- belong to a recognized professional organization for mediators and/or assessors;
- have published articles or research findings in professional newsletters, journals or books for mediators and/or assessors or have spoken at conferences or seminars attended by other professionals.

(4) METHODS OF PRACTICE AND CODE OF CONDUCT

The mediator/assessor should:

- conduct the mediations and/or custody assessments according to well-recognized standards of practice within the profession;
- be prepared to outline the methodology used and be able to justify this methodology on the basis of the generally accepted standards of practice in the field and the needs of the particular case;
- subscribe to a code of conduct set out by his or her professional discipline (e.g., psychology, psychiatry or social work) and in addition adhere to a code of conduct for mediators and/or assessors as set out by a recognized professional organization for mediators and/or assessors.

The mediator/assessor should provide the clients, their counsel and the court (if relevant) with an up-to-date *curriculum vitae* that outlines all of the qualifications as set out above that are relevant for conducting mediation or assessments.

In the event that the parties are unable to agree on an individual to conduct an assessment, the court should have sufficient information to determine which individual is most qualified for the task.

C. GUIDELINES FOR GIVING TESTIMONY IN COURT

In mediation/assessment cases, the expert is usually attempting to determine what is in the best interests of the children, and does not view himself or herself as acting for any of the parties. The expert performs something of an *amicus curiae* role, that is, a friend of the court. Given the impartial role of the mediator/assessor, he or she should be very careful to maintain that neutral stance and not be drawn into taking particular positions because they are of benefit to one of the parties.

Prior to trial, it is important that the mediator/assessor offer the parties and counsel an opportunity to meet with him or her in order to give the mediator/assessor any relevant, up-to-date information. This opportunity should be offered to both sides.

In a number of cases that go to court, a settlement can be reached during the course of the trial by one or both counsel or the judge asking for a brief recess for the parties to meet and see whether any of the issues can be resolved. The mediator/assessor should indicate to the judge and to the parties and their counsel that he or she will be available, during the course of the trial, if this might prove helpful in reaching a settlement. This again underlines the impartial role of the mediator/assessor.

If the expert is to testify, the first task is to determine whether the expert is qualified to give opinion evidence. That is, opposing counsel may argue that the court should not accept a witness's report or testimony as that of an expert. If counsel are successful, then the mediator/assessor will not be able to give opinion evidence and will not be able to rely on any hearsay in his or her testimony.

It is important that the mediator/assessor bring an up-to-date *curriculum vitae* to court and be prepared to respond to questions about why in general and specifically in this case he or she should be permitted to give expert testimony.

The judge will weigh the mediator/assessor's credibility and this credibility will depend on such factors as:

- the qualifications of the mediator/assessor;
- the methodology used in the case and how closely this methodology approximates to the standards in the field;
- the code of ethics followed;
- the factual basis from which the mediator/assessor drew his or her conclusions;
- the mediator/assessor's appearance. The mediator/assessor should always appear in court well dressed and well groomed;

- the impression of impartiality as opposed to partiality. Was the mediator/assessor paid exclusively by one side? If so, was this agreed to by the parties in advance? Did the mediator/assessor see both sides in the dispute and did the mediator/assessor spend approximately equal amounts of time with each? Were the mediator/assessor's facts gathered from a variety of sources, including independent sources, or were the facts gathered primarily from those with a stake in the proceedings, that is, supporters of one party?

The mediator/assessor must be prepared to testify in court if a report has been submitted and to be cross-examined on this report. Unless there is a statutory exception to being called, the mediator/assessor should expect to be called as a witness and give *viva voce* evidence.

Following the establishment of the credentials of the professional, the party who called the mediator/assessor will ask questions. This is known as the examination-in-chief. The counsel conducting the examination is not permitted to ask leading questions. That is, the counsel cannot ask questions suggesting a particular answer. The questions must be open ended, and it is wise for the mediator/assessor to meet with the counsel who will be doing the examination-in-chief in advance of court in order to determine those areas that will be covered.

The mediator/assessor will next be cross-examined by the opposing counsel(s). The purpose of cross-examination is to reduce the credibility of the expert's opinion. It is permissible when cross-examining to suggest answers or to lead the witness, but it is not permissible to badger the witness.

When being cross-examined, it is important to remain professional and unemotional. Do not take the questions personally and do not respond with sarcasm or hostility. It is always permissible to ask for a question to be repeated. If you do not know the answer to a question or if a question is outside of the area considered by the mediation or assessment, it is wise to state that directly.

Do not argue with the questioner and do not interrupt while the questions are being asked.

Expect to have your answers cut off short. The cross-examiner will try to stop you from talking when you are saying things that are not helpful to the opposing party. Remember the counsel who conducted the examination-in-chief will have an opportunity to ask certain questions at a later time during the re-examination.

When giving testimony, speak slowly and clearly so that it is easier for the court reporter and the judge to make notes about your testimony. It is very irritating to the judge to have to keep reminding the expert witness to speak up and slow down, so observe this courtesy.

It is required that you take your entire file to court, that is, your report, as well as any notes made during interviews or telephone conversations. In addition, you should take all reports, documents or other materials that were relied on as a basis for the mediation/assessment report.

Please note that your file will likely be examined by both counsel prior to asking you questions in court.

If you do not have notes made from interview conversations, you can expect that your report will have greatly reduced credibility. If you rely on your memory for details of conversations and interviews, the judge is likely to put far less weight on your ultimate report and recommendations than if careful notes were made during sessions.

When asked about opinions or recommendations, it is very important to remember to state the factual basis for your recommendations. If the basis for your opinion is solely hearsay, and if that hearsay information comes from a biased source, then again your recommendations will have little weight.

If the expert is asked a question and cannot remember the answer or the facts on which an answer would be based, it is permissible to use notes to refresh his or her memory. If the expert wishes to look at notes, then it must be established that the notes were made contemporaneously with the event; that is, the notes were made at the time or very close to the time of interviews or conversations and therefore are likely to be accurate. In addition, it must be established that the notes were made personally by the mediator/assessor.

If the mediator/assessor asks to see notes to refresh his or her memory, then counsel are likely to ask to see those notes. The notes should be in the mediator/assessor's personal handwriting, not dictated notes that were subsequently typed, because these notes may not be acceptable.

Many mental health professionals have a considerable fear of testifying in court. They are afraid of being humiliated, badgered and asked questions they perceive to be irrelevant to the best interests of children. In addition, appearances at court are often inconvenient and disrupt a busy practice. Professionals often have to wait hours, if not days, to be called, and this causes further inconvenience and discomfort.

Many mental health professionals are critical of the legal system, because it appears that an adversarial approach is harmful, rather than helpful, to the family as a whole. It often appears to the mediator/assessor that the purpose of counsel is to cause psychological damage to the other party, rather than to find a solution to the problem that would be the most satisfactory for the children and even for the family as a whole.

It is important for the mediator/assessor to understand that the purpose of the court procedure is not to arrive at a therapeutic outcome. The purpose of the court system is to arrive at the truth, and the premise of our court system is that the truth is best obtained by a battle of two strongly partisan adversaries, namely, counsel. There is a growing awareness that the adversarial process is not the most suitable for family law matters, and therefore there is a gradual change in attitude and approach, both in the legislation and the actual court practice.

Both the legislation and courtroom procedure are moving away from matrimonial fault as a basis for deciding family law disputes. However, it is still the role of counsel for the party who is not satisfied with the mediator/assessor's report to try to reduce the report's weight in the eyes of the court as a means of promoting his or her client's position.

Because of the great weight and latitude normally given to experts' reports, it is important that the report and expert opinion be capable of withstanding a strong test as to their credibility. Instead of looking at this as a personal attack, the mediator/assessor should welcome the opportunity to have his or her facts and opinions tested thoroughly by the court process as a safety check. In the event that the report is based on poorly researched facts, on biased opinions, or on insufficient time with the parties, it is important for the family to have a weak report exposed. Similarly, if a report has been prepared on the basis of a thorough examination and the recommendations are carefully thought out, then the mediator/assessor and all of the parties concerned are likely to have more confidence in it. It is in the public interest to have these reports, which are given such great weight by the courts, thoroughly tested.

ANNOTATED BIBLIOGRAPHY

Kirkpatrick, G.J. "Should Mediators Have a Confidentiality Privilege?" In "Legal and Family Perspectives in Divorce Mediation." (1985), 9 *Mediation Quarterly* 85. This article examines the question of the limitations on the expert refusing to testify in court. It considers the balance between the right to privacy and the court's need to know.

Moir, D. "The Clinician As a Witness." Paper presented at the Association of Conciliation Courts Conference, Toronto, 1983.

Sopinka, J., and Lederman, S. *The Law of Evidence in Civil Cases.* Toronto: Butterworths, 1974. This is the leading text on the law of evidence in civil cases.

Ziskin, J. *Coping with Psychiatric and Psychological Testimony,* vols. 1 and 2. California: Law and Psychology Press, 1981 (Supplement, 1983). This book offers a strong critique of expert evidence in child custody cases, as well as in criminal and personal injury cases. The author is a psychologist and a lawyer and uses both professional backgrounds to prepare the lawyer for cross-examination of the mental health expert. This book would be very valuable for both mental health professionals and lawyers dealing with contested custody cases.

LIST OF APPENDICES

1A. Letter from Mediator: Willingness to Act — Mediation
1B. Letter from Mediator/Assessor: Willingness to Act — Custody Assessment

2A. Outline of Mediation Procedure
2B. Outline of Custody Assessment Procedure

3. Client Questionnaire

4A. Retainer Contract: Closed Mediation
4B. Retainer Contract: Open Mediation/Assessment

5A. Consent to Release Information
5B. Covering Letter re Consent to Release Information
5C. Memo to File re Consents

6. Letter to Solicitor from Mediator

7A. Sample Clauses: Memorandum of Separation — Custody and Access
7B. Sample Clauses: Memorandum of Separation — Support

8. Interim Agreement Without Prejudice

9A. The Code of Professional Conduct of the Law Society of Upper Canada
9B. Code of Ethics — Ontario Association for Family Mediation — Code of Professional Conduct
9C. Model Standards of Practice for Family and Divorce Mediation
9D. Family Mediation Canada — Code of Professional Conduct

10. Checklist for Interviews and Contacts During Mediation/ Assessment

11. Outline of Custody Assessment Report

APPENDIX 1A

LETTER FROM MEDIATOR: Willingness to Act —

Mediation

LETTER TO LAWYERS
(Referral Source)

MEDIATOR   ADDRESS
                                                                                    DATE

LAWYER'S NAME
AND ADDRESS

Dear Solicitor,*

Re: Mediation – Client's Name

I am writing to indicate that I would be willing to offer mediation services in this case.

I would like to explain briefly the service I would offer. I would be retained by both the husband and the wife, and my goal would be to help them arrive at a voluntary agreement on those issues that they wish to submit to mediation. My experience and that of my colleagues indicates that when a solution is reached by the parties themselves, the solution is more likely to be carried out in practice.

I would be prepared to offer either open or closed mediation, depending on the wishes of both parties. In either case, if the parties reach an agreement on all issues sent to mediation, I would prepare a Memorandum of Separation setting out the agreement reached.

If the parties select open mediation and they do not reach agreement on one or more issues, I would prepare a Memorandum of Separation on those issues that were resolved and a report reviewing the mediation process for those issues that were not resolved.

If closed mediation is selected and the parties do not reach agreement on one or more issues, I would prepare a Memorandum of Separation on those issues that were resolved and a statement specifying which issues were not resolved. There would be no review of the mediation process in closed mediation.

I would submit my report and Memorandum of Separation to both counsel and both clients and, if the mediation was court ordered, to the court for review prior to the court hearing.

In the case of open mediation I would be prepared to appear in court and be cross-examined by one or both counsel on the information obtained

---

* This letter could be adapted for use with clients.

during open mediation. In the case of closed mediation I would not be prepared to appear in court to testify, as the communications made are confidential.

Please find attached my *curriculum vitae* and an outline of the general procedure I follow in mediation. Please note that the procedure may vary according to the issues to be mediated and the circumstances of the particular case.

My fee is $ per hour for interviews, preparing a Memorandum of Separation and/or a report. An additional fee is required for preparation for court and attendance as an expert witness, should this be necessary.

With respect to payment of my fees, my policy is that both spouses share the cost equally, if possible, because I want to ensure that both of them perceive me as objective and impartial. I will ask that counsel undertake the responsibility of paying my fees and I will ask for a retainer before beginning.

I am looking forward to assisting your client in arriving at a satisfactory resolution of the issues submitted to mediation. If I am retained I would hold an initial meeting with both counsel to clarify the issues to be mediated and to determine whether open or closed mediation is desired.

Yours sincerely,

MEDIATOR

Encl

APPENDIX 1B

LETTER FROM MEDIATOR/ASSESSOR: Willingness to Act — Custody Assessment

LETTER TO LAWYERS
(Referral Source)

ASSESSOR   ADDRESS
                                                                            DATE

LAWYER'S NAME
AND ADDRESS

Dear Solicitor,*

Re: Custody Assessment – Client's Name

I am writing to indicate that I would be willing to carry out a custody assessment in this case.

I would like to explain briefly the service I would offer. I would be retained by both the husband and the wife, and my initial goal would be to help them as parents arrive at a resolution that they both are comfortable with and that reflects the needs and interests of their child(ren). My experience and that of my colleagues indicates that when a solution is reached by the parties themselves, the solution is more likely to be enforced. If the parties do reach an agreement, I would draft a Memorandum of Separation and send copies to both counsel and both parties. In addition, I would prepare a brief report outlining some suggestions for implementing and maintaining the agreed-upon plan.

If the husband and wife cannot arrive at a resolution to their difficulties, then I would prepare a full custody assessment report containing my recommendations for the plan that would best meet the child(ren)'s needs. This report would be submitted to counsel and to the court, and I would be willing to be called to court to testify.

Please find attached my *curriculum vitae* and an outline of the general procedure that I follow in conducting custody assessments. Of course, the procedure would have to be modified to cover the needs of the particular case.

My fee is $ per hour for interviews and preparation of a report. I charge an additional fee for preparation for court and attendance as an expert witness, should this be necessary.

With respect to payment for my services, my policy is that both spouses share the cost equally, if possible, because I want to ensure that

---

* This letter could be adapted for use with clients.

both of them perceive me as objective and impartial. I will ask that counsel undertake the responsibility of paying my fees and I will ask for a retainer before beginning.

If I am retained, I would hold an initial meeting with both counsel to clarify the issues to be mediated and to determine whether open or closed mediation is desired. I am looking forward to assisting your client in arriving at a satisfactory resolution of the custody and access issues. Please feel free to contact me should you have any questions about my policies or procedures.

Yours sincerely,

ASSESSOR

Encl

APPENDIX 2A

OUTLINE OF MEDIATION PROCEDURE

As a general outline, my procedure in mediation is as follows:

(a) *Meet with counsel for the parties* in order to:

- establish whether mediation will be open or closed;
- clarify what issues are to be mediated;
- clarify payment of fees;
- permit counsel, in each other's presence, to explain which factors they feel are particularly significant in the case.

(b) *Meet with the parties together* to:

- explain the mediator's role as an objective, impartial professional as between the parents;
- encourage the parents to consider the best interests of the child(ren) in reaching a resolution to the issues in dispute;
- discuss the differences between open and closed mediation in order to determine the parties' preference;
- improve the communication between the parents;
- assist the parents to identify the issues and encourage them to work toward their own resolution of the issues in dispute, particularly where children are involved.

(c) *Meet with each parent individually.*

(d) *Meet with the child(ren) individually, with siblings* (if any) and together *with each parent* (this is necessary for custody and access mediation only).

(e) *Meet with other significant adults* who will be playing a caretaking role, such as new and common law spouses, grandparents, and other caretakers (this may only be necessary in custody and access mediation).

(f) *Request information from relevant sources* such as schools, family doctors, mental health professionals, accountants, property appraisers, etc.

(g) Prepare a Memorandum of Separation and/or report.

In my experience, mediation takes approximately fifteen hours of interviews. It is difficult to judge the exact number of hours because this depends on the number of issues to be mediated, the type of issues, the complexity of the situation, the number of parties involved and the willingness of the parties to reach a voluntary agreement. Preparation of a Memorandum of Separation and/or report requires additional time.

APPENDIX 2B

OUTLINE OF CUSTODY ASSESSMENT PROCEDURE

As a general outline, my procedure in custody assessments is as follows:

(a) *Meet with counsel for the parties* to:

- clarify what the assessor's role will be;
- establish whether open mediation is to be attempted at the outset of the assessment;
- permit counsel, in each other's presence, to explain which factors they feel are particularly significant in the case;
- ask counsel to provide affidavits, notices of motion, transcripts of evidence, professional reports and other documents relevant to the assessment issues;
- clarify the payment of fees, including fees for the preparation of a report, court preparation and attendance as an expert witness.

(b) *Meet with the parties together* to:

- explain the assessor's role as an objective, impartial professional as between the parents;
- clarify whether mediation is to be attempted as an initial step;
- encourage the parents to develop a parenting plan whereby they share parental responsibilities and visitation with the child(ren) that is in the best interests of the child(ren);
- clarify the assessor's role, that is, to represent the best interests of the child(ren) in the event that the parents are not able to agree on a shared parenting plan;
- clarify the procedure to be followed in the assessment, including who is to be interviewed, in what location and on how many occasions;
- obtain the names of persons and agencies who have reliable and relevant information with respect to parenting capacity and the needs and interests of the child(ren).

(c) *Meet with each parent individually.*

(d) *Meet with the child(ren) individually, with siblings* (if any), and together *with each parent.*

(e) *Meet with other significant adults* who will be playing a caretaking role, such as new and common law spouses, grandparents, and other caretakers.

(f) *Request information from relevant sources* such as schools, family doctors, mental health professionals, etc.

(g) *Conduct home visits* to observe:

- the child(ren) interacting with each parent and stepparents, siblings and stepsiblings;
- the neighbourhood setting of each home;
- the household routines as they pertain to the child(ren);
- the standards of cleanliness, nutrition and disciplinary limits set.

(h) *Arrange for psychological testing* of the child(ren) and adults if necessary.

(i) *Prepare a Memorandum of Separation and/or an assessment report.*

In my experience, I find that custody assessments take approximately twenty to thirty hours of interviews and data collection. It is difficult to judge the exact number of hours because this depends on the complexity of the case, the seriousness of the concerns with respect to parenting capacity, the number of individuals involved and the willingness of the parties to resolve the issues by agreement. Preparation of a Memorandum of Separation and/or an assessment report requires additional time.

APPENDIX 3
CLIENT QUESTIONNAIRE

DATE

REFERRED BY

1. HUSBAND

Name: _____

Home Address: _____   Business Address: _____

Mail to: Home _____   Business: _____

Home
telephone: ( )_____   Business
telephone: ( )_____

Occupation: _____   Full time _____
                                 Part time _____ (hrs.)

Number of years at present place of employment: _____

Approximate net amount of income from employment: _____

Approximate net amount of income from other sources: _____

Date of birth: ____ / ____ / ____   Place of birth: _____

Length of residence in Ontario _____   Canada _____

Solicitor: _____   Telephone: _____

Address: _____

2. WIFE

Name: _____

Home Address: _____   Business Address: _____

Mail to: Home _____   Business: _____

Home
telephone: (___) _____   Business
telephone: (___) _____

Occupation: _____   Full time _____
Part time _____ (hrs.)

_____

Number of years at present place of employment: _____   _____

Approximate net amount of income from employment: _____

Approximate net amount of income from other sources: _____

Date of birth: ____/____/____   Place of birth: _____

Length of residence in Ontario _____   Canada _____

Solicitor: _____   Telephone: _____

Address: _____

MARITAL INFORMATION

Date of marriage/relationship: ____/____/____   City of marriage: _____

Date of
present separation: _____   Date of
previous separations: _____

_____

Present marital status: Married/ Common law/ Separated/ Divorced/
Widowed/ Single/

Has a divorce petition been filed?   Yes   No (If yes by: Husband   Wife)

Are/did you attend marital/family counselling: Yes   No
If yes, Name _____   From: _____

Address _____   To: _____

                              Telephone: _____

Are you interested in a reconciliation: Wife: Yes   No
                                          Husband: Yes   No

Are you interested in marital counselling: Yes No

Did you attend individual counselling?

Wife: Yes   No
If yes, Name: _____   Telephone: _____

Address: _____

_____

Husband: Yes   No
If yes, Name: _____   Telephone: _____

Address: _____

_____

CHILDREN OF PRESENT MARRIAGE/RELATIONSHIP

Beginning with the oldest child

Name	Age	Birthdate D M Y	Residing With	Grade	School
_____	__	__/__/__	_____	____	____
_____	__	__/__/__	_____	____	____
_____	__	__/__/__	_____	____	____
_____	__	__/__/__	_____	____	____
_____	__	__/__/__	_____	____	____

_____ ____ _/ _/_ _____ _____ _____

_____ ____ _/ _/_ _____ _____ _____

_____ ____ _/ _/_ _____ _____ _____

Doctor for: Husband/Wife/Child # 1, 2, 3, 4

G.P./SPECIALIST

Name: _____ Telephone: _____

Address: _____

Name: _____ Telephone: _____

Address: _____

Name: _____ Telephone _____

Address: _____

Name: _____ Telephone _____

Address: _____

Name: _____ Telephone _____

Address: _____

BABYSITTER/PRINCIPAL CARETAKER

Name: _____ Telephone _____

Address: _____

COUNSELLOR/THERAPIST FOR CHILD (REN)

Name: _____ Telephone _____

Address: _____

Counsellor for: _____

Others: _____

PREVIOUS RELATIONSHIPS

Have you been married before?

Wife   Yes   No

(If yes)   Date of marriage/divorce/death _____

Husband Yes   No

(If yes)   Date of marriage/divorce/death _____

CHILDREN FROM PREVIOUS MARRIAGE/RELATIONSHIP

Place an * beside any of the children involved in the present dispute.

Name	Age	Birthdate	Residing With	Grade	School
Wife:		D M Y			
_____	___	_/_/_	_____	_____	_____
_____	___	_/_/_	_____	_____	_____
_____	___	_/_/_	_____	_____	_____
_____	___	_/_/_	_____	_____	_____
Husband:					
_____	___	_/_/_	_____	_____	_____
_____	___	_/_/_	_____	_____	_____
_____	___	_/_/_	_____	_____	_____
_____	___	_/_/_	_____	_____	_____
_____	___	_/_/_	_____	_____	_____

PREVIOUS RELATIONSHIP(S)

Are you paying/receiving spousal support?   Yes   No
(If yes), Amount _____

Are you paying/receiving child support: Yes   No
(If yes), amount _____

NEW RELATIONSHIPS

Does husband have a new partner? — If yes: residing together? Yes No

Name: _____

Telephone: _____

Does new partner have children?   Yes   No
(If yes), residing with husband?   Yes   No

<u>Names of Children:</u>   <u>Age</u>

_____   _____

_____   _____

_____   _____

_____   _____

Are you paying/receiving financial assistance in the new relationship?
      Yes   No

Does wife have a new partner? — If yes: residing together? Yes No

Name: _____

Telephone: _____

Does new partner have children?   Yes   No
(If yes), residing with wife?   Yes   No

<u>Names of Children:</u>   <u>Age</u>

_____   _____

_____   _____

_____   _____

_____   _____

Are you paying/receiving financial assistance in the new relationship?
Yes   No

Do you anticipate a dispute regarding:
Custody/Access/Child support/Spousal support/Possession of the matrimonial home/Division of property/Debts/Other? _____

_____

Custody: Present custodial arrangement — Sole custody to _____
                                          Joint custody
                                          (shared parenting)

Desired custody arrangement: Sole custody to _____
                                          Joint custody
                                          (shared parenting)

Describe present visitation schedule

Weekends #   1 / 2 / 3 / 4 / 5   With Mother Father
                    From: _____   To: _____

Weekdays (Week 1)   M / T / W / T / F /

With   / / / / /

Weekdays (Week 2)   M / T / W / T / F /

With   / / / / /

Weekdays (Week 3)   M / T / W / T / F /

With   / / / / /

Weekdays (Week 4)   M / T / W / T / F /

With   / / / / /

Do you spend: Too much time/ Too little time / The right amount of time / with each child?

Comment: _____

Spousal Support

Are you presently — Paying / Receiving / Spousal support? If yes, how much per month $ _____ .

Payments are made Regularly/Irregularly

Child Support per Child:

Are you presently — Paying / Receiving / Child support. If yes, how much per month $ _____ per child. (Number of children) _____ .

Payments are made: Regularly/Irregularly

Other Contributions To Living Expenses — Explain

_____

_____

I would like: Possession of the matrimonial home / Sale of the matrimonial home / Other _____

Other Assets: Have been divided / Have not been divided / Explain:

_____

Significant Debts of Husband   *Significant Debts of Wife*

_____   _____

_____   _____

APPENDIX 4A

RETAINER CONTRACT: Closed Mediation

RE: (CLIENTS' NAMES)

1. It is hereby agreed that (mediator's name) is retained to act as mediator with respect to the family law issues arising out of the marriage breakdown of the parties identified above. The issues to be mediated include, but are not limited to:

- custody of and access to the child(ren) of the marriage
- division of property
- child and spousal support.

2. It is acknowledged that the mediator is an impartial third party whose role is to assist the husband and the wife to negotiate a voluntary settlement of the issues arising as a result of their marriage breakdown, based on full and frank disclosure between them.

3. It is agreed that the best interests of the child(ren) will be the primary consideration for:

- resolving the issues of custody and access, and
- developing a shared parenting plan.

4. The parties are strongly advised to obtain independent legal advice, particularly prior to signing any written Agreement to ensure that they are fully informed of their legal rights and obligations and the legal implications of such an Agreement.

5. In attempting to bring about an agreement, the mediator will meet with the husband and wife for joint sessions and, on occasion, individual sessions. The mediator will have the right at any time to include in the mediation the child(ren) or any other significant third party, such as a new partner, grandparents, other relatives, legal counsel, a chartered accountant, or other significant involved persons as the mediator deems necessary.

6. The mediator may obtain information from relevant sources and may consult such persons and read such reports, records or documents as the mediator deems necessary for arriving at an agreement.

7. It is agreed that the parties will:

- make full disclosure of all relevant information reasonably required for the mediator to understand the issues being mediated;
- execute any consent forms necessary for the mediator to obtain relevant information.

8. If the parties reach agreement on any issues, the mediator will prepare a

Memorandum of Separation with respect to those issues for consideration by the parties and their respective counsel.

9. It is understood that:

- anything said or any admission or communication made in the course of mediation is not admissible in any legal proceeding;
- the mediator will not be called as a witness by or on behalf of either party in any legal proceeding;
- the mediator may be required by the court to testify despite this agreement to the contrary;
- if the parties do not reach an agreement through mediation on any specified issue, that will be so reported by the mediator.

10. Neither the husband nor the wife nor anyone acting on their behalf will take any fresh steps in the legal proceedings between the parties with respect to those issues that are being mediated.

11. The mediator will not voluntarily disclose any written or oral communications that have taken place during the mediation process except:

- the mediator may disclose information with the written Consent or Direction of both the husband and the wife;
- the mediator may share any information or concerns arising during the mediation process with either party.

12. It is agreed that:

- The parties will share equally the fees and disbursements incurred by the mediator for all services provided with respect to the mediation and preparation of any documents or reports, including but not limited to time for interviews, reading reports and documentation, telephone conversations with the clients, lawyers, or other collateral sources, preparing correspondence and other relevant activities. Disbursements and other out-of-pocket expenses incurred by the mediator, such as for photocopying, long-distance telephone calls and messenger services will be billed additionally. Travel time will be billed at a reduced rate.
- A retainer in the amount of $ will be paid by each party prior to the commencement of mediation.
- Interim accounts shall be sent to the parties and payments shall be due when an account is rendered.
- The hourly rate shall be $ per hour and is subject to change upon notice by the mediator.
- Interest will be charged on all accounts outstanding after 30 (thirty) days at the prime interest rate at the time the account is rendered.
- Clients will be billed for appointments that are cancelled if there is less than 24 (twenty-four) hours' notice prior to cancellation.

- Counsel for the parties agree that they shall guarantee payment of the mediators account in the same proportion as the parties are required to pay according to this Retainer.

13. Each of the undersigned acknowledges that he/she has read this Retainer and agrees to be bound by the terms set out above.

DATED at   this   day of   , 19 .

SIGNED in the presence of

_____   _____

                             WIFE

_____   _____

                             HUSBAND

_____   _____

                             MEDIATOR

Note: In the event that the mediator wishes to have counsel for the parties guarantee his/her fees, the following clauses should be substituted for above clause 13.

13. Counsel for the parties agree that they shall guarantee payment of the mediator's account in the same proportion as the parties are required to pay according to this Retainer.

14. Each of the undersigned acknowledges that he/she had read this Retainer and agrees to be bound by the terms set out above.

DATED at   this   day of   , 19 .

SIGNED in the presence of

_____   _____

                             SOLICITOR'S NAME
                             Solicitor for Mrs.

_____   _____

                             SOLICITOR'S NAME
                             Solicitor for Mr.

_____   _____

                             MEDIATOR

APPENDIX 4B

RETAINER CONTRACT: Open Mediation*/Assessment

RE: (CLIENTS' NAMES)

1. It is hereby agreed that (Assessor/Mediator's name) is retained to act as the Assessor/Mediator** with respect to the family law issues arising out of the marriage breakdown of the parties identified above. The issues include:

- custody of, and
- access to

the child(ren) of the marriage.

2. It is acknowledged that the Assessor is an impartial third party whose role is to assist the parties to negotiate a parenting plan. In the event that the parents are not able to arrive at a voluntary settlement, the Assessor will perform a complete evaluation in order to arrive at recommendations for a parenting plan that will be in the best interests of the child.

3. The parties are strongly advised to obtain independent legal advice, particularly prior to signing any written agreement, to ensure that they are fully informed of their legal rights and obligations and the legal implications of such an agreement.

4. In attempting to bring about an agreement, the Assessor will meet with the Husband and Wife for joint sessions and on occasion for individual sessions. The Assessor will have the right at any time to include in the mediation/assessment*** process the child(ren) or any other significant third party, such as a new partner, grandparents, other relatives, legal counsel or other significant involved persons as the Assessor deems necessary.

5. The Assessor may obtain information from relevant sources and may consult such persons and read such reports, records or documents as she deems necessary.

---

* If open mediation is to be conducted, then issues other than custody and access may be included. Recommendations are usually not made following open mediation unless specifically requested by the parties.

** For the remainder of this Retainer, the Assessor/Mediator will be referred to as the "Assessor" and this will be interpreted to mean Assessor/Mediator.

*** For the remainder of this Retainer, a mediation/assessment will be referred to be as an "assessment" and this will be interpreted to mean mediation/assessment.

6. It is agreed that the parties will:

- make full disclosure of all relevant information reasonably required for the Assessor to understand the issues presented, including full and complete disclosure of each party's financial circumstances.

7. It is further agreed that the Husband and Wife will execute any consent forms necessary for the Assessor to obtain relevant information.

8. If the parties reach agreement on one or more issues, the Assessor shall prepare a Memorandum of Separation with respect to those issues for consideration by the parties and their respective counsel.

9. It is understood that if an agreement is reached on all issues that:

- anything said or any admission or communication made in the course of the assessment is not admissible in the pending or any other legal proceeding, and
- the Assessor will not be called as a witness by or on behalf of either party in any legal proceeding.

10. If the parties fail to agree on one or more issues it is understood that:

- the Assessor will prepare a report outlining the Assessor's recommendations,
- anything said or any admission or communication made in the course of the assessment may be used in the report,
- the Assessor may be called as a witness by either party in a legal proceeding and would be open to cross-examination by either counsel.

11. Copies of the report will be distributed to both counsel, both parties and the court at least two weeks prior to the court date.

12. It is agreed that:

- The parties will share equally the fees and disbursements incurred by the Assessor for all services provided with respect to the assessment and preparation of any documents or reports, including but not limited to time for interviews, reading reports and documentation, telephone conversations with the clients, lawyers, or other collateral sources, preparing correspondence and other relevant activities. Disbursements and other out-of-pocket expenses incurred by the Assessor, such as for photocopying, long-distance telephone calls and messenger services will be billed additionally. Travel time will be billed at a reduced rate.
- A retainer in the amount of $ will be paid by each party prior to the commencement of the assessment;
- Interim accounts shall be sent to the parties and payments shall be due when an account is rendered;

- The hourly rate shall be $ per hour and is subject to change upon notice by the Assessor;
- Interest will be charged on all accounts outstanding after 30 (thirty) days at the prime interest rate at the time the account is rendered;
- Clients will be billed for appointments that are cancelled if there is less than 24 (twenty-four) hours' notice prior to cancellation.
- Counsel for the parties agree that they shall guarantee payment of the Assessor's account in the same proportion as the parties are required to pay according to this Retainer.

13. Neither the husband nor the wife nor anyone acting on their behalf will take any fresh steps in the legal proceedings between the parties with respect to those issues that are being assessed.

14. The report will not be released until all outstanding professional fees and disbursements related to the assessment have been paid in full.

15. In the event that the Assessor is called to court, a separate fee shall be required for preparation and attendance as an expert witness. This fee shall be paid in advance by the Husband and Wife in equal shares.

16. Each of the undersigned acknowledges that he/she has read this Retainer and agrees to be bound by the terms set out above.

      DATED at   this   day of   , 19 .

SIGNED in the presence of

_____   _____

                                              WIFE

_____   _____

                                              HUSBAND

_____

                                            ASSESSOR

Note: The following clauses should be substituted for above clause 16 to ensure that counsel guarantee payment of the Assessor's account.

16. Counsel for the parties agree that they shall guarantee payment of the Assessor's account in the same proportion as the parties are required to pay according to this Retainer.

17. Each of the undersigned and the Assessor acknowledge that he/she has read this Retainer and agrees to be bound by the terms set out above.

DATED at   this   day of   , 19   .

SIGNED in the presence of

_____

_____
SOLICITOR
Solicitor for Mrs.

_____

_____
SOLICITOR
SOLICITOR FOR MR.

_____

_____
ASSESSOR

APPENDIX 5A
CONSENT TO RELEASE INFORMATION

TO: Principal, School

FROM: Mr. and Mrs. _____

RE: Child's Name

I/WE HEREBY AUTHORIZE AND DIRECT you to release information relevant to school performance and adjustment respecting the above-named child(ren) to our (Mediator/Assessor) (name) _____ (address) _____ , as (he/she) may require.

AND FOR DOING SO this shall be your good and sufficient authority.

DATED at   this   day of   19 .

_____

_____

APPENDIX 5B
COVERING LETTER RE CONSENT
TO RELEASE INFORMATION

DATE

ADDRESS OF ABC PUBLIC SCHOOL

Dear:

Re: Name

I have been retained by Mr. and Mrs.   as a Mediator/ Assessor to assist with respect to marital difficulties. Enclosed please find a Release of Information form duly signed by Mr. and Mrs.   . I would greatly appreciate your contacting me by telephone as soon as possible to discuss information you may have with respect to the child's school performance and adjustment.

Yours sincerely,

MEDIATOR/ASSESSOR

Encl.

APPENDIX 5C
MEMO TO FILE RE CONSENTS

CONSENT FORMS SENT TO

Name: _____   Date Sent: _____

Contact made: Yes   No   Telephone: _____

Name: _____   Date Sent: _____

Contact made: Yes   No   Telephone: _____

Name: _____   Date Sent: _____

Contact made: Yes   No   Telephone: _____

Name: _____   Date Sent: _____

Contact made: Yes   No   Telephone: _____

Name: _____   Date Sent: _____

Contact made: Yes   No   Telephone: _____

Name: _____   Date Sent: _____

Contact made: Yes   No   Telephone: _____

APPENDIX 6

LETTER TO SOLICITOR FROM MEDIATOR

Dear Solicitor,

I am pleased to report that the parties have reached an agreement with respect to sharing parental rights, responsibilities and time with the children. In arriving at their agreement, the parties participated in the following process: They were seen in a combination of individual and joint sessions. In addition, each parent was seen with the children, and the children were seen both individually and in a sibling group. New partners were interviewed, the school, family doctor and relevant mental health professionals were contacted with respect to information about parenting arrangements, the needs and interests of the children and the sharing of parental responsibilities. During the mediation process, meetings were held with the solicitors and feedback was given as necessary. All documents and reports provided by the solicitors were reviewed by the mediator.

I have enclosed a copy of the Memorandum of Separation drafted with respect to those issues sent to mediation. Please note that the terms set out below do not constitute a full Separation Agreement. The solicitors may incorporate the terms in the Memorandum of Separation or similar terms into a full Separation Agreement. If one or both parties wishes to make some changes with respect to the issues sent to mediation, I would be more than happy to discuss this with both the parties and the lawyers and then make modifications based on those discussions.

I have enjoyed working with both the parties and counsel and would be more than willing to offer assistance in the future should there be a change in circumstances or should some difficulty arise that might be best dealt with through mediation. I would appreciate receiving a copy of the final Agreement for my files, once it has been negotiated with the assistance of the lawyers.

Thank you for your co-operation in this matter.

Yours sincerely,

MEDIATOR

APPENDIX 7A

SAMPLE CLAUSES: Memorandum of Separation —

Custody and Access

MEMORANDUM OF SEPARATION made this   day of
19

BETWEEN:

HUSBAND

– and –

WIFE

1. Definitions

In this Agreement:

1.1 "Cohabit" means to live together in a conjugal relationship whether inside or outside marriage;

1.2 "Husband" means   who is one of the parties to this Agreement;

1.3 "Wife" means   who is one of the parties to this Agreement;

1.4 "Children's Law Reform Act" means the *Children's Law Reform Act,* R.S.O. 1980, Chapter 68, as amended, and any successor;

1.5 "Divorce Act" means the *Divorce Act, 1985,* and any successor;

1.6 "Family Law Act, 1986" means the *Family Law Act,* S.O. 1986, Chapter 4, and any successor.

2. Background

2.1 The parties were married to each other in the City of   , in the County of   , Province of   , on the   day of   , 19   .

2.2 The husband and wife have two children of the marriage, namely   born on the   day of   , 19   and   born on the   day of   , 19   .

2.3 The husband and wife have been living separate and apart since   and agree to live separate and apart for the rest of their lives and to settle by this Agreement all the rights and obligations that they have or may otherwise acquire concerning custody of and access to their children.

2.4 The husband and wife agree to be bound by the terms of this Agreement.

3. *Freedom from the Other*

Neither the husband nor the wife will molest, annoy, harass or in any way interfere with the other or attempt to compel the other to cohabit or live with him or her.

4. *Custody*

4.1 The husband and wife acknowledge that the other is a devoted loving parent and that it is in the best interests of the children to have a close relationship with both parents.

4.2 As a result the husband and wife agree to have joint custody of the children.

4.2.01   The husband and wife agree that joint custody means that:

4.2.02   The children's best interests will always be paramount in making decisions with regard to the considerations in paragraph 4.

4.2.03   The husband and wife will consult each other on significant decisions with respect to the children's education, medical care, dental care and mental health care and with respect to significant expenditures respecting the children where both parties will be contributing to such expenditures.

4.2.04   The husband and wife both have a right to receive significant information with respect to the children's education, medical care, dental care and mental health care, including the right to receive school report cards and to hold interviews with the children's teachers and school principals.

4.2.05   The husband and wife both have a right to attend any extra-curricular activities involving the children.

4.2.06   The husband and wife agree to share parenting responsibilities, for example, taking the children to doctor appointments, dentist appointments, other professional appointments, extracurricular activities and other programs or appointments. Such arrangements should be made by mutual agreement on the basis of the needs of the children and the ability of each parent to take on such responsibilities.

4.2.07   The primary residence of the children will be with the wife, and the husband will have the right to visit frequently with both children together and at times with each child separately. Visits will include, but not be limited to, the following times:

    (a) Every other weekend from Friday at 5:00 p.m. until Sunday at 8:00 p.m..

    (b) Two evenings each week to be arranged by mutual consent of the parents.

    (c) Additional access times to include both days and overnights, during the Christmas school break, the mid-winter school break and the summer school break, such times to be arranged by the parents, in accordance with the father's work schedule and the needs and interests of the children.

4.2.08 Terms of access to the father may be varied upon at least 48 hours' notice to the other party where it is shown that it would be in the best interests of the child or children to vary such period of access, and such request for alteration of the period of access will not be unreasonably withheld by either party, unless it is in the best interests of the child or children not to accede to such a request.

4.2.09 The primary day-to-day responsibility for the guidance and upbringing of the children shall be exercised by the parent with whom the children are residing at any particular time.

4.2.10 Neither the husband nor the wife will remove the children from the Province of Ontario without the consent in writing of the other parent, except for a brief vacation, and such consent will not be unreasonably withheld. The husband and wife agree to give the other parent notice if the children are removed from the Province of Ontario for a brief vacation and such notice shall include the location and duration of the vacation.

4.2.11 If either the husband or wife move to a new location, the parent who moves agrees to inform the other parent of the new address.

4.2.12 If either the husband or the wife move to a new location such that the aforementioned access schedule cannot be followed, then the parties agree that any new access schedule should be based on the principle of maintaining a close relationship between the children and both parents. The primary residence shall continue to be with the wife, and the husband and wife agree to meet and discuss a revised access schedule.

4.2.13 If one parent predeceases the other, the residence of the children and the day-to-day care and control of the children shall be with the surviving parent.

4.2.14 (a) In the event the husband or wife cannot agree on the issues of custody of and access to the children, they agree first to give each other written notice of the nature of the disagreement.

(b) If no agreement has been reached 30 clear days after notice has been given, the parties agree to participate in mediation in order to resolve any dispute. The mediator shall be chosen by consent of the husband and wife and the husband and wife agree to share the cost of mediation equally.

(c) If no agreement has been reached through mediation with respect to the issues of custody of and access to the children, the husband and wife may then confer with their respective solicitors to settle what, if any, variations should be made.

(d) If no agreement is reached through mediation or their respective solicitors, either the husband or the wife may make an application pursuant to the *Children's Law Reform Act* or the *Divorce Act* to determine these issues.

4.2.15   The husband and wife agree to attend at the office of   ,
the mediator, for the purpose of reviewing the terms of this Agreement with respect to the issues of custody of and access to the children six months from the date of signing this Agreement.

5. *Independent Legal Advice and Disclosure*

The husband and wife each acknowledge that he or she:
   (a) has had independent legal advice;
   (b) understands his or her respective rights and obligations un-
        der this agreement;
   (c) has made full disclosure of all relevant information to the
        other; and
   (d) is signing this Agreement voluntarily.

6. *Execution*

TO EVIDENCE THIS AGREEMENT the husband and wife have each signed this Agreement under seal.

SIGNED, SEALED AND DELIVERED   )
)
   In the presence of   )
)
_____   )   _____
WITNESS TO SIGNATURE   )   HUSBAND
)
)
)
)
_____   )   _____
WITNESS TO SIGNATURE   )   WIFE
)
)

APPENDIX 7B

SAMPLE CLAUSES: Memorandum of Separation — Support

THIS IS A MEMORANDUM OF AGREEMENT made this   day of   , 19   .

BETWEEN:

HUSBAND

and

WIFE

1. Definitions

In this Agreement:

1.1 "Cohabit" means to live together in a conjugal relationship whether inside or outside marriage;

1.2 "Divorce Act" means the *Divorce Act, 1985* or its successor;

1.3 "Husband" means   , who is one of the parties to this Agreement;

1.4 "Family Law Act, 1986" means the *Family Law Act,* S.O. 1986, c. 4 or its successor;

1.5 "Property" means any interest, present or future, vested or contingent, in real or personal property;

1.6 "Net Family Property" means net family property as that term is defined by the *Family Law Act* or its successor;

1.7 "Wife" means   , who is one of the parties to this Agreement.

2. Background

2.1 The parties married each other on   , in the City of   , Ontario.

2.2 The parties are the parents of   , born on   , 19   ;
         , born on   , 19   ;   , born on   , 19   and   , born on   , 19   .

2.3 The parties have been living separate and apart since May   , 19   . On that date the matrimonial home was sold. The parties continued to live separate and apart under the same roof until the date of closing which occurred on   , 19   . There is no reasonable prospect of their resuming cohabitation.

2.4 By this Agreement, the parties wish to settle all their rights and obligations which they have or may acquire in the future with respect to possession, ownership and division of their property; support and maintenance of themselves; and any equalization of net family properties.

3. Agreement

3.1 Each of the parties agrees to be bound by the provisions of this Agreement.

4. Domestic Contract

4.1 Each of the parties acknowledges that this Agreement is entered into under Section 54 of the *Family Law Act, 1986,* and is a domestic contract which prevails over matters provided for in the *Family Law Act* or its successor.

5. Living Separate and Apart

The parties will continue to live separate and apart for the rest of their lives.

6. Freedom from the Other

Neither party will molest, annoy, harass or in any way interfere with the other, or attempt to compel the other to cohabit or live with him or her.

7. Financial Provision

See Appendix A (at page 236).

7.1 Commencing on June 1, 19   and on the first day of each month thereafter, the Husband will pay to the Wife for the support and maintenance of the Wife the sum of $940.00 (Nine Hundred and Forty Dollars) in advance until one or more of the following occurs:
  (a) the Wife remarries,
  (b) the Wife cohabits with another man,
  (c) the Wife is no longer employed full-time,
  (d) the Wife dies,
  (e) the Husband dies.
7.1.01   If the Wife is not employed, then on the first day of each month in which the Wife is not employed, the Husband will pay to the Wife for the support and maintenance of the Wife the sum of $1,500.00 (Fifteen Hundred Dollars) in advance until one or more of the following occurs:
  (a) the Wife remarries,
  (b) the Wife cohabits with another man,
  (c) the Wife dies,
  (d) the Husband dies.
7.1.02   If the Wife is employed part-time, then the amount of spousal support paid by the Husband to the Wife shall be determined by subtracting the Wife's net monthly income from $1,500.00 (Fifteen Hundred Dollars), and the amount remaining is the amount that the Husband shall pay to the Wife for the support and maintenance of the Wife until one or more of the following occurs:

    (a) the Wife remarries,

    (b) the Wife cohabits with another man,

    (c) the Wife dies,

    (d) the Husband dies.

8. *Cost of Living Adjustment*

8.1 The amount of the monthly maintenance and support payments that the Husband is required to make to the Wife for the support and maintenance of the Wife pursuant to the provisions of this Agreement will be increased or decreased with each unit of increase or decrease in the Consumer Price Index provided that:

8.1.01   The amount of increase or decrease in such payments will be directly proportionate to the increase or decrease in the Consumer Price Index published by Statistics Canada under the heading "All Items Toronto Area." For the purpose of this Agreement, the Consumer Price Index at the date of the Agreement is 132.7 and is based on the Consumer Price Index for 1981 equalling 100.

8.1.02   However, any increase or decrease will be made once a year only and becomes effective on the 1st day of June in each year, commencing on the 1st day of June, 19   and will be based upon the Consumer Price Index published immediately prior to the effective date of adjustment.

8.1.03   Any increase will be the lesser of:

    (a) the percentage increase in the Consumer Price Index as calculated above; and,

    (b) the Husband's percentage increase in his total gross income for all sources. If the Husband chooses to rely on this subsection he will, no later than May 1st in each year, produce to the Wife a copy of his tax returns for the two immediately preceding years, which will form the basis of the calculation of his percentage increase in his gross income from all sources. If in any year the Husband fails to provide the income tax returns to the Wife, then the increase on July 1st of that year will be in accordance with the increase in the Consumer Price Index.

9. *Material Change in Circumstances*

9.1 The parties intend section 7 of this Agreement to be final, except for variation because of a material change in circumstances.

9.2 If a material change in circumstances takes place, only the provisions in section 7 of this Agreement may be varied.

9.3 A material change in circumstance includes, but is not limited to:

    (a) the Husband loses his employment,

    (b) the Wife loses her employment,

(c) the Husband remarries,

(d) the wife remarries

(e) the Wife cohabits with another man,

(f) the Husband is disabled,

(g) the Wife is disabled,

(h) the Husband dies,

(i) the Wife dies.

9.4 The party seeking a variation will give to the other a notice of the variation he or she is seeking and the parties may then confer with each other either personally or through their respective solicitors to settle what, if any, variation should be made.

9.5 In the event that the Husband or Wife cannot agree on the issue of spousal support, they agree first to give each other written notice of the nature of the disagreement and then to participate in mediation in order to resolve any dispute. The mediator shall be chosen by consent of the parties, and the parties agree to share the cost of mediation equally.

9.6 If no Agreement has been reached 30 clear days after notice has been given under section 9.3, variation relating to spousal support may be determined at the instance of either party by an application pursuant to the *Family Law Act, 1986* or the *Divorce Act, 1985* or their successors.

10. Cottage Property

10.1 The parties acknowledge that title to the cottage property located at
,   ,   Township in the County of
, in the Province of   , is held in name of the Wife alone.

10.2 The Husband hereby releases to the Wife any and all interest he may now have or may afterwards acquire in the cottage property, whether possessory or proprietary, as and for a lump sum settlement as a portion of the equalization payment owed to the Wife by the Husband.

10.3 The Wife will have exclusive possession of the cottage property.

10.4 The Wife will pay all insurance premiums, mortgage payments, taxes and other expenses related to the cottage property and will indemnify the Husband from all liability relating to the cottage property.

11. Equalization Payment

11.1 Upon the signing of this Agreement the Wife will pay to the Husband $16,000.00 (Sixteen Thousand Dollars) and the Husband will transfer to the Wife $19,100.00 (Nineteen Thousand and One Hundred Dollars) of RRSP's presently held in the Husband's name in full and final settlement of any claim that either party may have, now or in the future, to an equalization of their net family property.

12. Attribution of Income Tax

12.1 The parties agree that if for any reason there is attribution of taxable capital gains between them under the provisions of the *Income Tax Act*

(Canada) or any similar Federal or Provincial legislation for the period after execution of this Agreement, the transferor spouse will be indemnified and saved harmless by the transferee spouse for any resulting increase in income tax liability.

12.2 The parties agree that if for any reason there is income attribution between them under the provisions of the *Income Tax Act* (Canada) or any similar Federal or Provincial legislation for the period after the execution of this Agreement, the transferor spouse will be indemnified and saved harmless by the transferee spouse for any resulting increase in income tax liability.

13. Life Insurance

13.1 The Husband acknowledges that he presently carries a policy of life insurance on his life with   in the amount of $68,000.00 (Sixty Eight Thousand Dollars). The Husband agrees to maintain this policy with the Wife as sole irrevocable beneficiary for as long as she lives.

13.2 The Husband acknowledges that his life is presently insured through his employer   . The policy provides a death benefit of two times his salary at date of death and an additional amount to cover voluntary personal accident insurance. The Husband agrees to maintain this policy with his Wife as beneficiary for as long as his Wife lives.

13.3 The Husband warrants that he has irrevocably designated the Wife as the sole beneficiary under the policies set out and that he has filed a designation with the relevant companies pursuant to the provisions of the *Insurance Act*. The Husband will give the Wife a true copy of the designation within 14 days from the execution of this Agreement.

13.4 The Husband will, while eligible to do so, maintain the policies in force whether he does so through renewal from time to time or otherwise, and will pay or cause to be paid the premiums required on the policies as the premiums fall due. The Husband agrees that if he becomes ineligible to maintain this coverage, he will immediately obtain replacement coverage for the plans or policies (ensuring that there is no gap in coverage beyond his control) to the extent available at similar cost, and will maintain the replacement coverage and will pay the required premiums as they fall due and so on for each succeeding policy. The Husband agrees that he will maintain the Wife as sole beneficiary of the policies for as long as she lives.

13.5 The Wife agrees that when she dies the Husband may deal with these policies as he wishes free from any claim by her estate and her personal representative will give and execute any consent or other document then required to enable the husband to deal with the policies.

13.6 Within 14 days of the Wife's demanding it, the Husband will deliver proof to her that the policies are in good standing. If the Husband defaults in payment of the premiums and the policies are no longer in good standing, the Wife may pay any premiums and may recover them from the

Husband together with all her costs and expenses including her solicitor-and-client costs.

13.7 If the Husband dies without this insurance in effect, his obligation to pay support or maintenance pursuant to this Agreement will survive his death (notwithstanding section 7 of this Agreement) and will be a first charge on his estate.

13.8 The parties acknowledge that the Husband's maintaining this life insurance is to provide a fund out of which support and maintenance may be payable to the Wife in the event of the Husband's death. The support and maintenance payments, however, are not limited to this fund.

14. Release Against Property

14.1 Except as provided in this Agreement, each of the parties releases and discharges all rights and claims each now has or may afterward acquire relating to property in which the other has or had an interest, including all rights and claims involving:

  (a) possession of property;
  (b) ownership of property;
  (c) division of property;
  (d) compensation for contributions of any kind, or an interest in property for contributions of any kind, and
  (e) equalization payments of any kind,

under the *Family Law Act, 1986* or its successor.

14.2 Each party acknowledges that neither holds any property in trust for the other, whether by way of resulting trust or any other type of trust.

15. Release Against Support and Maintenance

15.1 Except as provided in this Agreement, each of the parties releases and discharges the other from all rights to and claims for support and maintenance that he or she has or may have under the laws of any jurisdiction, in particular all rights to and claims for support and maintenance that he or she has, may have or may acquire in the future under the *Family Law Act, 1986* and the *Divorce Act, 1985* or their successors.

16. Pension Plan

16.1 The parties acknowledge that each is aware of the amendments to the *Canada Pension Plan Act* whereby pension credits earned by one or both spouses during their years of marriage may be divided equally upon marriage dissolution. Both the parties agree that upon marriage dissolution either can make an application to any Canada Pension Plan District or Local Office for a credit sharing of Canada Pension Plan Benefits resulting in the division of pension credits between them.

16.2 The parties agree that the pension credits earned by the Husband at the   from the date of his employment in   , 19   until the date of separation on   , 19   form part of the Husband's net family property. The parties further agree that the Wife shall be paid a one-half interest in the pension credits accumulated during this period at the time when the Husband receives his pension credits.

17. *General Release*

Each of the parties accepts the provisions of this Agreement in full satisfaction of all claims and causes of action each now has or may acquire including, but not limited to, claims and causes of action for maintenance, support, interim maintenance or interim support, possession of or title to or an interest in property, equalization of net family property or equalization payments of any kind or any other claim arising out of the marriage of the Husband and the Wife except for causes of action arising under this Agreement or for a Divorce Judgment. Nothing in this Agreement bars any action or proceeding by either party to enforce any of the provisions of this Agreement.

18. *Separation Agreement to Survive Divorce*

If either party obtains a decree of divorce, all the provisions of this Agreement will survive and continue in force. If some of the provisions of this Agreement are included in the Divorce Judgment, the remaining provisions will be severed and will survive and continue in effect.

19. *Ninety-day Trial Cohabitation*

If at any future time, the parties, with their mutual consent, cohabit as Husband and Wife for a period or periods of less than ninety days with reconciliation as the primary purpose of the cohabitation, the provisions contained in this Agreement will not be affected except as provided in this section. If the parties with their mutual consent cohabit as Husband and Wife for a period totalling more than ninety days with reconciliation as the primary purpose of the cohabitation, the provisions contained in this Agreement will become void, except that nothing in this section will affect or invalidate any payment, conveyance or act made or done pursuant to the provisions of this Agreement.

20. *Applicable Law and Interpretation*

20.1 This Agreement is governed by and is to be construed and enforced in accordance with the internal laws of the Province of Ontario as those laws apply to contracts made in Ontario to be wholly performed in Ontario by persons domiciled in Ontario.

20.2 If any provision of any statute of any jurisdiction invalidates or voids this Agreement, or any amendments to it, as a domestic contract, it is the intention of the parties that each provision of this Agreement or any amendments to it be construed as a separate contract under ordinary contract law and enforceable as such.

20.3 The invalidity or unenforceability of any provision of this Agreement will not affect the validity or enforceability of any other provision but the contract will be construed as if such invalid provision were omitted.

20.4 The parties agree that there are no representations, warranties, collateral agreements or conditions affecting this Agreement other than as expressed in this Agreement.

20.5 The provisions of this Agreement are for the benefit of and are binding on the parties and their respective heirs, executors, administrators and assigns.

21. *Amendments*

The parties may amend any of the provisions of this Agreement either by a separate written Agreement or by endorsing the amendment on this Agreement, which amendment, in either form, must be signed by both parties and witnessed.

22. *Execution of Other Documents*

The parties will execute any document or documents reasonably required from time to time to give effect to the provisions and intent of this agreement.

23. *Financial Disclosure*

23.1 Each of the parties acknowledges that
   (a) his or her significant assets, debts or other liabilities existing when this Agreement was made have been disclosed to the other party;
   (b) he or she has made such investigation of the financial circumstances of the other as he or she considers reasonable;
   (c) he or she is satisfied with the information furnished and disclosure made.

24. *Independent Legal Advice*

24.1 The parties acknowledge that each of them:
   (a) has had independent legal advice, or the opportunity to obtain independent legal advice;
   (b) understands his or her rights and obligations under this Agreement and the nature and consequences of this Agreement;
   (c) is signing this Agreement voluntarily.

25. *Legal Fees*

25.1 The Husband and Wife have agreed to pay for their own legal fees incurred in relation to their matrimonial dispute to date and for the negotiation and preparation of this Agreement.

25.2 The parties further agree that they will share equally the mediator's fees and disbursements incurred in the preparation of this Agreement.

26. Execution

TO EVIDENCE THIS AGREEMENT the husband and wife have each signed this Agreement under seal.

SIGNED, SEALED AND DELIVERED	)	
	)	
In the presence of	)	
	)	
_____	)	_____
WITNESS TO SIGNATURE	)	HUSBAND
	)	
	)	
	)	
	)	
	)	
_____	)	_____
WITNESS TO SIGNATURE	)	WIFE
	)	
	)	

APPENDIX A
EFFECTIVE TAXATION:
THE EFFECT OF TAXATION ON SUPPORT PAYMENTS

IF THE HUSBAND PAYS TO THE WIFE:

TAX DEDUCTIONS & HEADINGS	$940.00 per month	$1,500.00 per month	$1,600.00 per month	$1,800.00 per month
Employment income	$49,000.00	$49,000.00	$49,000.00	$49,000.00
Basic personal exemption	4,140.00	4,140.00	4,140.00	4,140.00
Exemption for dependent child	1,420.00	1,420.00	1,420.00	1,420.00
Support payments	11,280.00	18,000.00	19,200.00	21,600.00
Employment expense deduction	500.00	500.00	500.00	500.00
RRSP ($3,500.00)	3,500.00	3,500.00	3,500.00	3,500.00

TOTAL DEDUCTIONS	20,840.00	27,560.00	28,760.00	31,160.00
Taxable income	28,160.00	21,440.00	20,240.00	17,840.00
Net tax payable	5,615.50	3,973.30	3,697.30	3,154.00
NET INCOME AFTER TAXES	22,544.50	17,466.10	16,542.70	15,788.10

IF WIFE RECEIVES:

TAX DEDUCTIONS & HEADINGS	$940.00 per month	$1,500.00 per month	$1,600.00 per month	$1,800.00 per month
Income	15,300.00 11,280.00 26,580.00	18,000.00	19,200.00	21,600.00
DEDUCTIONS Basic personal exemption	4,140.00	4,140.00	4,140.00	4,140.00
Employee expense deduction	500.00			
TOTAL DEDUCTIONS	4,640.00	4,140.00	4,140.00	4,140.00
Taxable income	21,940.00	13,860.00	15,060.00	17,460.00
Net tax payable	3,377.65	2,221.50	2,598.00	3,078.00
NET INCOME AFTER TAXES	18,562.35	11,638.50	12,462.00	14,382.00

APPENDIX 8

INTERIM AGREEMENT WITHOUT PREJUDICE

THIS IS AN INTERIM AGREEMENT made this   day of   , 19   .

BETWEEN:

HUSBAND

– and –

WIFE

WHEREAS unhappy differences have arisen between the parties hereto;

AND WHEREAS they are in the process of negotiating an agreement for settlement of all rights and liabilities against and to each other and with reference to the property and estate of the other;

AND WHEREAS the parties have agreed to live separate and apart from each other for the future, and have in fact lived separate and apart under the same roof continuously since the   of   and plan to live in separate residences as of the   day of   19 ,

AND WHEREAS the husband and wife were married in the City of   in the Borough of   in the Province of Ontario on the   day of   , 19   ;

AND WHEREAS the husband and wife have two children of the marriage, namely   , born on the   day of   , 19   and   , born on the   day of   , 19   ;

AND WHEREAS the parties hereto have agreed to enter into an Interim Agreement to have effect until determined by one of the parties or until all issues between them at the present time have been settled;

NOW THEREFORE THIS AGREEMENT WITNESSETH that in consideration of the premises and the mutual covenants of the said parties they have agreed as follows:

1. The husband and wife will henceforth live separate and apart from each other and neither of them will directly or indirectly molest or disturb or annoy or interfere with the other or the other's business in any manner whatsoever.

2. The husband and wife shall have joint custody of the children of the marriage and the children shall have their primary residence with the father.

3. The husband and wife agree that joint custody means
    (a) that they will share the responsibility for the children and make major decisions about the welfare of the children jointly. Such decisions may include, but are not limited to, decisions with respect to: dental care, medical care, religion, friendships, education and vocation.
    (b) the parents will share all information with each other with respect to, but not limited to, the following areas: dental care, medical care, religion, friendships, education and vocation.

4. The mother will have access to the children at, but not limited to, the following times:
    (a) from Wednesday after school until Thursday morning, at which time the mother shall deliver the children to school;
    (b) every second weekend after school on Friday until Monday morning, at which time the mother shall deliver the children to school;
    (c) additional time to be arranged by mutual consent of the parties.
    (d) at least one week during the summer vacation, with additional time to be arranged by mutual consent;
    (e) at least twenty-four (24) hours during the period from Christmas Eve to Boxing Day. Christmas morning on alternate years;
    (f) time during the school winter break to be arranged by mutual consent of the parties.

5. The terms of access to the wife may be varied upon at least 48 hours' notice to the other party where it is shown that it would be in the best interests of the child or children to vary such period of access, and such request for alteration of the period of access will not be unreasonably withheld by either party, unless it is in the best interests of the child or children not to accede to such a request.

6. Neither party shall remove the children of the marriage from the Province of Ontario without the written consent of the other, except for the purpose of a brief vacation. In the event that either party wishes to remove the children from the Province of Ontario for a brief vacation, he or she shall notify the other parent about the location and dates for the vacation.

7. In the event that the parties cannot agree on matters related to custody of or access to the children, both the husband and wife agree to seek family mediation prior to litigating the issues in dispute. The parties agree to share the cost of such mediation services equally.

8. Commencing on the first day of   , 19   and on the first day of each subsequent month, the wife will pay to the husband for the support and maintenance of the children of the marriage One Thousand Dollars ($1,000.00) until such time as a final agreement is reached as to the support and maintenance for the spouse and children of the marriage.

9. The husband and wife agree that this Agreement shall terminate upon the earlier of
   (a) 90 (ninety) days from the date of signing this Agreement;
   (b) upon the signing of a written Separation Agreement in full settlement of their respective rights and liabilities against and to each other and with reference to the property and estate of the other;
   (c) upon receipt by the solicitor of the husband of a letter from the wife or the wife's solicitor, advising that the wife terminates this Agreement;
   (d) upon receipt by the solicitor of the wife of a letter from the husband or the husband's solicitor, advising that the husband terminates this Agreement.

10. This Agreement is without prejudice to the rights of the parties and shall not be referred to in any subsequent proceeding.

IN WITNESS WHEREOF the parties hereto have set their hands and seals

SIGNED, SEALED AND DELIVERED)
)
        In the presence of   )
)
)
)
)
_____) _____
) HUSBAND
)
)
_____) _____
) WIFE

APPENDIX 9A

THE CODE OF PROFESSIONAL CONDUCT
OF THE LAW SOCIETY OF UPPER CANADA

The following are specific rules for lawyers who act as mediators in Ontario.

INTEGRITY

RULE 1

The lawyer must discharge his duties to his client, the court, members of the public and his fellow members of the profession with integrity.

Commentary

1. Integrity is the fundamental quality of any person who seeks to practise as a member of the legal profession. If the client is in any doubt as to his lawyer's trustworthiness, the essential element in the true lawyer-client relationship will be missing. If the lawyer is lacking in personal integrity, his usefulness to his client and his reputation within the profession will be destroyed regardless of how competent a lawyer he may be.

2. Dishonourable or questionable conduct on the part of the lawyer in either his private life or his professional activities will reflect adversely to a greater or lesser degree upon the integrity of the profession and the administration of law and justice as a whole. If the conduct, whether within or outside the professional sphere, is such that knowledge of it would be likely to impair a client's trust in the lawyer as a professional consultant, the Society may be justified in taking disciplinary action.

3. Generally speaking however, the Society will not be concerned with the purely private or extra-professional activities of a lawyer which do not bring his professional integrity or competence into question.

IMPARTIALITY AND
CONFLICT OF INTEREST

RULE 5

The lawyer must not advise or represent both sides of a dispute and, save after adequate disclosure to and with the consent of the client or prospective client concerned, he should not act or continue to act in a matter when there is or there is likely to be a conflicting interest. A conflicting interest is one which would be likely to affect adversely the judgment of the lawyer on behalf of or his loyalty to a client or prospective client or which the lawyer might be prompted to prefer to the interests of a client or prospective client.

Commentary

. . . . .

10. The Rule will not prevent a lawyer from arbitrating or settling, or attempting to arbitrate or settle, a dispute between two or more clients or former clients who are sui juris and who wish to submit the dispute to him.

OUTSIDE INTERESTS AND THE PRACTICE OF LAW

RULE 6

The lawyer who engages in another profession, business or occupation concurrently with the practice of law must not allow such outside interest to jeopardize his professional integrity, independence or competence.

Commentary

1. The term "outside interest" covers the widest possible range and includes activities which may overlap or be connected with the practice of law, such as for example, engaging in the mortgage business, acting as a director of a client corporation, or writing on legal subjects, as well as activities not so connected, such as, for example, careers in business, politics, broadcasting, and the performing arts. In each case the question of whether the lawyer may be permitted to engage in the outside interest, and, if so, to what extent will be subject to any applicable law or rule of the Society.

2. The lawyer must not allow his involvement in an outside interest to impair the exercise of his independent professional judgment on behalf of his clients.

3. Where the lawyer's outside interest is not related to the legal services that he performs for clients, ethical considerations will usually not arise unless his conduct might bring him or the profession into disrepute, or his activities impair his competence as, for example, where the outside interest might so occupy his time that his client's interests would suffer from his inattention or unpreparedness.

LAW SOCIETY OF UPPER CANADA
COMMUNIQUE

24 October, 1986

* More and more members of the profession are serving as mediators primarily in the Family Law area but in other areas as well. Convocation adopted a new Rule 25 which was recommended by the Professional Conduct Committee. The Rule has been supplemented by guidelines which are set out in the Communiqué Plus. The new Rule reads: "The lawyer who functions as a mediator must ensure that the parties to the mediation process understand fully that the function being discharged is not part of the traditional practice of law and that the lawyer is not acting as a lawyer for either party. The lawyer as mediator acts to assist the parties to resolve the matters in issue."

The commentary that follows the Rule stresses that at the outset the parties to the mediation should be told that communications involved in the mediation are not covered by solicitor/client privilege and that the lawyer acting as mediator should not give legal advice, as distinct from legal information, but advise and encourage the parties to seek the advice of separate counsel, particularly with respect to a draft contract prepared by the mediator.

Kenneth Jarvis, Secretary.

COMMUNIQUE PLUS

Number 13   24th October, 1986

FAMILY LAW MEDIATION

The following are the Guidelines for Lawyer/Mediators:

1.   The lawyer/mediator or any partner or associate of such lawyer/mediator, should not undertake mediation with any person whom he or she has previously represented or to whom he or she has given any prior legal advice relating to the matters to be mediated. If there has been any previous contact with either one or both of the parties on an unrelated matter, this should be disclosed to both parties and the mediation should proceed only on the written consent of both of them.[1]

2.   The lawyer/mediator should inform the parties before the mediation commences that he or she will be functioning as a mediator and not as a lawyer for either or both parties to mediation.[2] The differences between the two roles, i.e. as neutral facilitator and as advocate, should be fully explained. The parties should also be informed at this time that because no solicitor/client relationship exists, no solicitor/client privilege will attach to any communications made during the mediation process.[3] The parties should be asked to sign a written acknowledgement of the above.[4]

3.   The parties to mediation should be encouraged to obtain independent legal counsel, preferably before mediation commences, but in any event, before a final agreement is reached.[5] Independent counsel should be asked to advise each spouse separately with respect to his or her legal rights and entitlements, give a legal opinion as to the range of probable dispositions by the court if the matters were litigated, to act as coaches for each party throughout the mediation process, to review and advise the spouses with respect to the adequacy of the financial disclosure received from the other spouse, to review and swear to the accuracy of their own client's financial disclosure, and finally, to review and advise with respect to the draft agreement and the effect of any release clauses contained therein. The spouses should be informed by the mediator of the risks of proceeding without independent counsel.

4.   An agreement should be obtained by the mediator in the initial mediation session with respect to the confidentiality of the mediation sessions, including whether or not the mediator will be expected to submit a report or to testify in court if agreement is not reached by parties on some or all issues. If the mediation is open, the parties should agree as to whether the mediator's report will contain recommendations. If closed, the parties should be warned that no privilege exists for mediation unless, in Ontario, mediation has been ordered by a court on the consent of the parties. If so, the mediator may be required to testify despite the spouses' voluntary agreement to the contrary. Ideally, agreement with respect to the confidentiality of the mediation sessions should be made in writing.[6]

5.   The mediating spouses should agree to make full financial disclosure to each other during mediation, and undertake not to hide or dispose of any assets, cancel or change any beneficiaries of life insurance policies, or take any further steps in legal proceedings while the mediation is in process. They should also be informed of and asked to acknowledge the risks inherent in mediation, such as the development of a status quo with respect to custody, or the establishment of a standard for the level of spousal and/ or child support.

6.   All of the above mentioned consents, undertakings and acknowledgements should be contained in a written mediation contract, signed by both spouses and the mediator.[7] The written contract should also contain a statement identifying the issues to be mediated, the conduct of the sessions, the terms and responsibility for payment, and the circumstances under which mediation can be terminated by either spouse or the mediator. A copy of the fully executed mediation contract should be given to each spouse and the original retained by the mediator.

7.   In oder to maintain an appearance of neutrality, the lawyer/mediator should avoid giving legal advice and should dispense only general legal

information, in the presence of both spouses during the mediation process.[8] The spouses should be referred to their independent solicitors for any specific legal advice requested or required. Pamphlets and brochures on custody, support and the division of property, and the income tax consequences of separation and divorce may be made available by way of information in the mediator's office, if desired. The mediator should be available as a referral source for other experts who may be required from time to time in the course of mediation, such as accountants and appraisers.

8.   The lawyer/mediator should stay within his or her own area of competence and should not attempt to mediate highly contentious child custody disputes without knowledge of child development and psychology, and training in counselling techniques, or unless co-mediating with a mental health professional.

9.   Before holding him or herself out as a mediator, the lawyer/mediator should familiarize him or herself with mediation theory and techniques, preferably by enrolling in a course of mediation training led by qualified mediators and/or by a recognized mediation association.

10.   The mediator should terminate mediation if, at any time, he or she believes that the conditions for mediation have been breached, or if, in the opinion of the mediator, one or more of the participants is being harmed or seriously prejudiced by the process.

11.   The lawyer/mediator may prepare a separation agreement in draft form, incorporating the terms of the agreement reached in mediation, but should refrain from discussing the legal effects and implications of the agreement which should be taken by each of the mediating spouses to their respective counsel for review and advice. The mediated agreement, if acceptable, should be executed in the offices of the independent solicitors wherever possible to avoid any appearance of coercion on the part of the mediator.

12.   The lawyer/mediator or any partner or associate, should decline to represent either or both spouses in any subsequent legal matter related to the issues mediated. Rather, the mediator should keep him or herself available as a neutral to assist the parties in future in the event that any modifications are required to the mediated settlement.

13.   If the lawyer co-mediates with a mental health professional, he or she should bill separately for his or her individual services.[9]

14.   To avoid confusion in the minds of mediation clients between lawyer and mediator roles, the lawyer/mediator might consider having separate letterhead, business cards and account stationery for his or her legal and

mediation practices. Separate offices, telephone numbers and office signs would be even stronger evidence of the separation of the two roles but are not required.

---

1. See Rule 5, Commentary 4, which contemplates dual "representation" on the written consent of the parties.
2. Rule 25.
3. Rule 25, Commentary 4.
4. See Standard Mediation Contract, paragraph.
5. Rule 25, Commentary 2
6. See paragraph 9, Standard Mediation Contract.
7. See Standard Mediation Contract.
8. Rule 25, Commentary 5.
9. Rule 10, Commentary 6.

Note The Law Society in British Columbia has established very different rules for lawyer mediators. The Law Societies of Alberta, Saskatchewan and Manitoba are likely to enact rules in the near future that are similar to the B.C. model.

APPENDIX 9B

CODE OF ETHICS —
Ontario Association for Family Mediation
Code of Professional Conduct

1. Foreword

The following rules are intended to govern the relations of family mediators with their clients, their professional colleagues, and the general public so that all will benefit from high standards of practice in family mediation. The rules are to be observed in spirit as well as in practice.

2. Definition of Terms

For the purposes of this code, family mediation is defined as a non-adversarial process in which a qualified and impartial third party (the mediator) helps family members resolve their disputes. The resolution is voluntary and is based on sufficient information and advice for each participant.

In open mediation, if the parties fail to agree voluntarily on one or more issues, the mediator may prepare a report on the mediation and/or make recommendations. In open mediation, such a report may be used in subsequent court proceedings.

In closed mediation, there is no such report or recommendations and the process is entirely confidential.

3. Competence

It is the obligation of anyone acting as a family mediator to ensure that he or she is fully qualified to deal with the specific issues involved.

(a) It is acknowledged that family mediators will have a diversity of education and training, but the obligation to refrain from rendering services outside the limits of the family mediator's qualifications and capabilities remains.

(b) Family mediators shall co-operate with and endeavor to involve other competent professionals where the situation requires it.

(c) Family mediators shall engage in continuing education to ensure that their mediation skills are current and effective.

(d) Family mediators shall perform their service in a conscientious, diligent, and efficient manner in accordance with this code of conduct.

4. Duty of Confidentiality

The mediator shall not voluntarily disclose to anyone not a party to the mediation any information obtained through the mediation process except:

(a) non-identifying information for research or educational purposes; or

(b) with the written consent of the parties to the mediation contract; or

(c) where ordered to do so by an appropriate judicial authority or required to do so by law; or

(d) where the information discloses an actual or potential threat to human life or safety or a proposed breach of the Criminal Code of Canada.

If mediation is open, communications made in the course of the mediation and the mediator's report and recommendations may be disclosed to a third party only for the purposes of resolving the dispute whether by litigation or otherwise.

While closed mediation imposes the intention and the duty of confidentiality on the mediator, it cannot confer privilege, and the mediator should advise the parties that the intended confidentiality cannot be guaranteed.

5. Impartiality

The mediator has a duty to be impartial in relation to the participants. Impartiality requires that the mediator shall not have preconceived opinions in favour of or against one person or the other.

(a) The mediator shall disclose to the participants any biases he or she may have relating to the issues to be mediated.

(b) The mediator will refrain from mediating in cases where the mediator knows there has been any significant prior involvement by the mediator or any partner or associate of the mediator with one of the participants except after full disclosure of the involvement to, and express consent by, the other participant(s). The role of the mediator should be distinguished from the earlier relationship.

(c) A lawyer-mediator, or any partner or associate of such lawyer-mediator, shall not represent either party during or after the mediation process in any contested legal matters arising out of the issues discussed in the mediation.

(d) The perception of partiality on the part of the mediator by one or both participants does not in itself require the mediator to withdraw. In these circumstances, it is only the duty of the mediator to advise the participants of their right to terminate the mediation.

6. Agreement to Mediate

The mediator has a duty to explain the mediation process clearly to the participants before reaching an agreement to mediate. In particular, the mediator shall do the following:

(a) define mediation, distinguishing it from other methods of dispute resolution and from therapy and marriage counselling;

(b) determine the appropriateness of mediation for the participants in light of their particular circumstances;

(c) discuss the differences between closed mediation, open mediation and assessment, and the implications of each, and require the parties to choose open or closed mediation;

(d) advise participants that either of them or the mediator has the right to suspend or terminate the process at any time;

(e) explain the cost of mediation and reach an agreement with the participants regarding payment. It is inappropriate for the mediator to charge a contingency fee or to base the fee on the outcome of the mediation process;

(f) advise the participants of the role of independent legal advice in accordance with paragraph 9 of this code. In the event the mediator is a lawyer, the lawyer-mediator shall inform the participants that he or she cannot represent either or both of them in any legal action relating to their marriage except uncontested proceedings where both parties consent after receiving independent legal advice;

(g) discuss with the participants the mediator's specific procedures and practices;

(h) recommend that the agreement to mediate be written and signed by the parties and the mediator.

7. Potential Problems in Mediation

It is the duty of the mediator to advise the participants of potential problems that may arise during mediation. Some of these problems include:

(a) the possibility that one or both spouses may use the time during the mediation to dissipate or conceal assets;

(b) the fact that a status quo may be developing with respect to the custody of the children so that the non-custodial parent may be prejudiced in any future custody claim in the courts, notwithstanding any agreement to the contrary;

(c) the fact that information disclosed during the mediation may be used against a participant in the event of subsequent legal proceedings.

  (i) Even if the information disclosed directly in the mediation is confidential, it may open up lines of inquiry or reveal other information which might not otherwise have come to light in any subsequent litigation.

(ii) A judicial authority may require disclosure of information revealed during mediation.

8. Availability of Information and Advice

It is the duty of the mediator to ensure that the mediation participants make decisions based upon sufficient information, knowledge and advice.

(a) Where financial or property issues are involved, the mediator shall obtain an undertaking from the participants to make full and frank disclosure of their financial and other related circumstances at the appropriate time in the mediation process unless the parties otherwise expressly agree. The mediator will assist the participants and their lawyers to achieve this disclosure. It is the ongoing obligation of the mediator to advise the participants to obtain legal advice and assistance in this respect.

(b) If the participants or either of them choose(s) to proceed without independent legal advice, the mediator shall warn them (him or her) of the risks involved in not being represented, including the possibilities that:

(i) the parties may not be making fully informed choices in light of their respective legal rights; and

(ii) the agreement they reach is less likely to be enforced by a court.

9. Independent Legal Advice

It is the obligation of every family mediator to advise clients:

(a) of the availability of independent legal advice for each spouse;

(b) of the advisability of obtaining it from the outset of the mediation;

(c) to obtain independent legal advice prior to signing the mediated agreement.

10. Duty to Minimize Harm or Prejudice to Participants

It is the duty of the mediator to suspend or terminate mediation whenever continuation of the process would harm or prejudice one or more of the participants.

(a) The mediator shall suspend or terminate mediation where the ability or the willingness of either of the participants to effectively participate in the process is lacking.

(b) The mediator shall suspend or terminate mediation when its usefulness is exhausted so that there is no unnecessary expense to the participants from unproductive mediation.

(c) If the mediator has suspended or terminated the process, he or she may suggest that the participants obtain appropriate professional services.

(d) When the mediator believes the agreement being reached is unreasonable, he or she shall so advise the participants.

(e) Notwithstanding impartiality, the mediator has the duty to promote the best interests of the children and to assist the parents to examine the separate and individual needs of each child.

(f) While the mediator has an obligation to minimize the harm or prejudice to participants in the process, it is a fundamental principle of mediation that competent and informed participants can reach an agreement that may not correspond to legal guidelines contained in the relevant statutes or case law or that does not correspond to general community expectations and standards.

(g) The mediator shall see that the participants are reaching agreement freely, voluntarily, and without undue influence.

11. Public Communications

(a) The purpose of public statements concerning family mediation should be:

    (i) to educate the public generally about the process; and

    (ii) to present the process of mediation objectively as one of several methods of dispute resolution in order to help the public make informed judgements and choices.

(b) When advertising professional services, mediators should restrict themselves to matters which educate and inform the public. These could include the following to describe the mediator and the services offered: name, address, telephone number, office hours of the particular mediation service, highest relevant academic degree, relevant training and experience in mediation, appropriate professional affiliations and membership status, and any additional relevant or important consumer information.

(c) Public communications should not imply that membership in the Ontario Association for Family Mediation constitutes certification as a mediator.

12. Duty to Encourage Reporting of Breaches of Code

It is the obligation of family mediators to encourage clients to report in writing real or apparent breaches of this Code forthwith to the Chairman of the Standards and Ethics Committee and/or to the President of the Ontario Association for Family Mediation.

APPENDIX 9C

MODEL STANDARDS OF PRACTICE
FOR FAMILY AND DIVORCE MEDIATION

Symposium on Standards and Practices
for Family and Divorce Mediation
May 22-23, 1984
Denver, Colorado

Introduction

Mediation offers families a means of resolving disputes through a cooperative decision making process. Family and divorce mediation has evolved without the benefit of established standards or guidelines tailored for this distinct new service.

The Association of Family and Conciliation Courts has facilitated the formulation of Model Standards of Practice for Family and Divorce Mediation by serving as the convenor for three symposiums on Divorce Mediation Standards and Ethics. Over forty individuals representing thirty professional organizations attended the first symposium held December, 1982 in San Diego, California.

It was the consensus of the delegates attending this symposium that it was premature to establish a certification procedure for family and divorce mediation but that the development of parameters of practice would assist individual mediators and the development of the practice.

A second symposium was convened in May, 1983, in Toronto, Ontario, Canada to begin to develop a draft of parameters of practice for family and divorce mediators. With the aid of resource materials from participating organizations, delegates discussed the ethical issues of family and divorce mediation as they relate to the client, the mediator, the practice of mediation and its relationship to community and colleagues.

A subcommittee reflecting the field and settings of family and divorce mediation was subsequently appointed to draft model standards of practice. The drafting committee consisted of Christopher Moore, chairperson, Director of Training, Center for Dispute Resolution, Denver, Colorado; Thomas Bishop, member of the ABA Family Law Section Mediation and Arbitration Committee, and in private practice, New London, Connecticut; Clarence Cramer, Director Pinal County, Conciliation Court, Florence, Arizona and President Mediation Association of Southern Arizona; Jay Folberg, President AFCC and Professor of Law, Lewis & Clark Law School, Portland, Oregon; Lois Gold, Vice President Academy of Family Mediators and Director Family Mediation Center, Portland, Oregon; Ann Milne, Chairperson, AFCC Mediation Committee and in private practice,

Madison, Wisconsin; and Patrick Phear, representative of the American Arbitration Association and Director Children's Judicial Resource Council, Cambridge, Massachusetts.

With the financial assistance of the National Institute for Dispute Resolution, the drafting committee met and using resource materials and standards and ethical statements from 18 other organizations prepared a draft of Model Standards of Practice for Family and Divorce Mediation. This draft was distributed to 130 individuals and organizations for comment. Thirty invited delegates attended the third and final symposium in Denver, Colorado May 22-23, 1984 and completed the drafting process.

The development of these Model Standards of Practice reflects the diversity of mediation practices while manifesting the need to provide principles of practice that cross settings and disciplines. They are being distributed to courts, organizations, agencies and individuals for subscription, endorsement or adoption. The Model Standards may also serve as a foundation document for those organizations that must develop their own standards to fit unique services not specifically addressed in this model. The Model Standards of Practice are presented as a means of furthering the practice of family self-determination and embody the principle of mediation as a process of consensus.

Ann Milne, ACSW
Chairperson, AFCC Mediation Committee

Model Standards of Practice
for Family and Divorce Mediation

Preamble

Mediation is a family centered conflict resolution process in which an impartial third party assists the participants to negotiate a consensual and informed settlement. In mediation, whether private or public, decision making authority rests with the parties. The role of the mediator includes reducing the obstacles to communication, maximizing the exploration of alternatives, and addressing the needs of those it is agreed are involved or affected.

Mediation is based on principles of problem solving which focus on the needs and interests of the participants, fairness, privacy, self determination, and the best interests of all family members.

These standards are intended to assist and guide public and private, voluntary and mandatory mediation. It is understood that the manner of implementation and mediator adherence to these standards may be influenced by local law or court rule.

I. *Initiating the Process*

A. Definition and Description of Mediation.

The mediator shall define mediation and describe the differences and similarities between mediation and other procedures for dispute resolution. In defining the process, the mediator shall delineate it from therapy, counselling, custody evaluation, arbitration, and advocacy.

B. Identification of Issues.

The mediator shall elicit sufficient information from the participants so that they can mutually define and agree on the issues to be resolved in mediation.

C. Appropriateness of Mediation.

The mediator shall help the participants evaluate the benefits, risks, and costs of mediation and the alternatives available to them.

D. Mediator's Duty of Disclosure.

1. Biases.

The mediator shall disclose to the participants any biases or strong views relating to the issues to be mediated.

2. Training and Experience.

The mediator's education, training, and experience to mediate the issues should be accurately described to the participants.

E. Procedures.

The mediator shall reach an understanding with the participants regarding the procedures to be followed in mediation. This includes but is not limited to the practice as to separate meetings between a participant and the mediator, confidentiality, use of legal services, the involvement of additional parties, and conditions under which mediation may be terminated.

F. Mutual Duties and Responsibilities.

The mediator and the participants shall agree upon the duties and responsibilities that each is accepting in the mediation process. This may be a written or verbal agreement.

II. *Impartiality and Neutrality*

A. Impartiality.

The mediator is obligated to maintain impartiality toward all participants. Impartiality means freedom from favoritism or bias either in word or action. Impartiality implies a commitment to aid all participants, as opposed to a single individual, in reaching a mutually satisfactory agreement. Impartiality means that a mediator will not play an adversarial role.

The mediator has a responsibility to maintain impartiality while raising questions for the parties to consider as to the fairness, equity, and feasibility of proposed options for settlement.

B. Neutrality.

Neutrality refers to the relationship that the mediator has with the disputing parties. If the mediator feels or any one of the participants states that the mediator's background or personal experiences would prejudice the mediator's performance, the mediator should withdraw from mediation unless all agree to proceed.

1. Prior Relationships.

A mediator's actual or perceived impartiality may be compromised by social or professional relationships with one of the participants at any point in time. The mediator shall not proceed if previous legal or counseling services have been provided to one of the participants. If such services have been provided to both participants, mediation shall not proceed unless the prior relationship has been discussed, the role of the mediator made distinct from the earlier relationship and the participants have been given the opportunity to freely choose to proceed.

2. Relationship to Participants.

The mediator should be aware that post-mediation professional or social relationships may compromise the mediator's continued availability as a neutral third party.

3. Conflicts of Interest.

A mediator should disclose any circumstance to the participants which might cause a conflict of interest.

III. Costs and Fees

A. Explanation of Fees.

The mediator shall explain the fees to be charged for mediation and any related costs and shall agree with the participants on how the fees will be shared and the manner of payment.

B. Reasonable.

When setting fees, the mediator shall ensure that they are explicit, fair, reasonable, and commensurate with the service to be performed. Unearned fees should be promptly returned to the clients.

C. Contingent Fees.

It is inappropriate for a mediator to charge contingent fees or to base fees on the outcome of mediation.

D. Referrals and Commissions.

No commissions, rebates, or similar forms of remuneration shall be given or received for referral of clients for mediation services.

IV. Confidentiality and Exchange of Information

A. Confidentiality.

Confidentiality relates to the full and open disclosure necessary for the mediation process. A mediator shall foster the confidentiality of the process.

1. Limits of Confidentiality.

The mediator shall inform the parties at the initial meeting of limitations on confidentiality such as statutorily or judicially mandated reporting.

2. Appearing in Court.

The mediator shall inform the parties of circumstances under which mediators may be compelled to testify in court.

3. Consequences of Disclosure of Facts Between Parties.

The mediator shall discuss with the participants the potential consequences of their disclosure of facts to each other during the mediation process.

B. Release of Information.

1. The mediator shall obtain the consent of the participants prior to releasing information to others.

2. The mediator shall maintain confidentiality and render anonymous all identifying information when materials are used for research or training purposes.

C. Caucus.

The mediator shall discuss policy regarding confidentiality for individual caucuses. In the event that a mediator, upon the consent of the participants, speaks privately with any person not represented in mediation, including children, the mediator shall define how information received will be used.

D. Storage and Disposal of Records.

The mediator shall maintain confidentiality in the storage and disposal of records.

V. *Full Disclosure*

The mediator shall require that there is disclosure of all relevant information in the mediation process as would reasonably occur in the judicial discovery process.

VI. *Self Determination*

A. Responsibilities of the Participants and the Mediator.

The primary responsibility for the resolution of a dispute rests with the participants. The mediator's obligation is to assist the disputants in reaching an informed and voluntary settlement. At no time shall a mediator coerce a participant into agreement or make a substantive decision for any participant.

B. Responsibility to Third Parties.

The mediator has a responsibility to promote the participants' consideration of the interests of children and other persons affected by the agreement. The mediator also has a duty to assist parents to examine, apart from their own desires, the separate and individual needs of such people. The participants shall be encouraged to seek outside professional consultation when appropriate or when they are otherwise unable to agree on the needs of any individual affected by the agreement.

VII. *Professional Advice*

A. Independent Advice and Information.

The mediator shall encourage and assist the participants to obtain independent expert information and advice when such information is needed to reach an informed agreement or to protect the rights of a participant.

B. Providing Information.

A mediator shall give information only in those areas where qualified by training or experience.

C. Independent Legal Counsel.

When the mediation may affect legal rights or obligations, the mediator shall advise the participants to seek independent legal counsel prior to resolving the issues and in conjunction with formalizing an agreement.

VIII. Parties' Ability to Negotiate

The mediator shall assure that each participant has had an opportunity to understand the implications and ramifications of available options. In the event a participant needs either additional information or assistance in order for the negotiations to proceed in a fair and orderly manner or for an agreement to be reached, the mediator shall refer the individual to appropriate resources.

    A. Procedural.

The mediator has a duty to assure balanced negotiations and should not permit manipulative or intimidating negotiation techniques.

    B. Psychological.

The mediator shall explore whether the participants are capable of participating in informed negotiations. The mediator may postpone mediation and refer the parties to appropriate resources if necessary.

IX. Concluding Mediation

    A. With Agreement.
        1. Full Agreement.

The mediator shall discuss with the participants the process for formalization and implementation of the agreement.

        2. Partial Agreement.

When the participants reach a partial agreement, the mediator shall discuss with them procedures available to resolve the remaining issues.

    B. Without Agreement.
        1. Termination by Participants.

The mediator shall inform the participants of their right to withdraw from mediation at any time and for any reason.

        2. Termination by Mediator.

If the mediator believes that participants are unable or unwilling to meaningfully participate in the process or that a reasonable agreement is unlikely, the mediator may suspend or terminate mediation and should encourage the parties to seek appropriate professional help.

        3. Impasse.

If the participants reach a final impasse, the mediator should not prolong unproductive discussions that would result in emotional and monetary costs to the participants.

X. Training and Education

A. Training.

A mediator shall acquire substantive knowledge and procedural skill in the specialized area of practice. This may include but is not limited to family and human development, family law, divorce procedures, family finances, community resources, the mediation process and professional ethics.

B. Continuing Education.

A mediator shall participate in continuing education and be personally responsible for on-going professional growth. A mediator is encouraged to join with other mediators and members of related professions to promote mutual professional development.

XI. Advertising

A mediator shall make only accurate statements about the mediation process, its costs and benefits, and about the mediator's qualifications.

XII. Relationships with Other Professionals

A. The Responsibility of the Mediator Toward Other Mediators.

1. Relationship with Other Mediators

A mediator should not mediate any dispute which is being mediated by another mediator without first endeavoring to consult with the person or persons conducting such mediation.

2. Co-Mediation.

In those situations where more than one mediator is participating in a particular case, each mediator has a responsibility to keep the others informed of developments essential to a cooperative effort.

B. Relationship with Other Professionals.

A mediator should respect the complementary relationship between mediation and legal, mental health, and other social services and should promote cooperation with other professionals.

XIII. Advancement of Mediation

A. Mediation Service.

A mediator is encouraged to provide some mediation service in the community for nominal or no fee.

B. Promotion of Mediation.

A mediator shall promote the advancement of mediation by encouraging and participating in research, publishing, or other forms of professional and public education.

*Parameters of Practice for Family
and Divorce Mediation*

Resource List

Academy of Family Mediators — Standards of Practice

American Arbitration Association — Family Mediation Rules

American Association for Marriage and Family Therapy — Membership Standards

American Association of Pastoral Counselors — Code of Ethics

American Bar Association, Family Law Section, Standards of Practice for Divorce Mediators, adopted in principle by the Council of the Family Law Section, 7/29/83

American Bar Association, 1982 Annual Meeting, Rule 2.2 Intermediary Comment

American Psychological Association — Ethical Standards of Psychologists

Arizona State Bar Family Law Section — Standards of Practice for Family Mediators

Association of Family and Conciliation Courts — Task Group Report, Education and Training of Mediators

Center for Dispute Resolution, Denver, Colorado, Code of Professional Conduct for Mediators

Family Mediation Association — Proposed Code of Professional Responsibility for Practicing Family Mediators

Massachusetts Council on Family Mediation — Draft Standards

Mediation Association of Southern Arizona — A Proposed Code of Ethics

Mediation Consortium of Washington State — Proposed Standards of Practice for Mediators

Mediation Council of Illinois — Professional Standards of Practice

Michigan Council for Family and Divorce Mediation — Statement of Ethics

National Association of Social Workers — Code of Ethics, Professional Standards

Model Standards of Practice:
Family and Divorce Mediation

Participating Organizations

Academy of Family Mediators
American Academy of Matrimonial Lawyers
American Arbitration Association
American Association for Mediated Divorce
American Association of Pastoral Counselors
American Bar Association Family Law Section, Mediation & Arbitration Committee
American Bar Association Special Committee on Alternative Dispute Resolution
American Psychological Association
Association of Family & Conciliation Courts
Association of Family & Conciliation Courts — California Chapter
British Columbia Judges Committee on Family Law
California State Bar, Family Law Section,
Custody & Visitation Committee
Canadian Federal Government — Department of Justice, Policy & Planning
Center for Dispute Resolution, Denver, Colorado
Children's Judicial Resource Council
Colorado Bar, Family Law Section
Council on Accreditation of Services for Families and Children
Family Mediation Association
Family Mediation Center, Scottsdale, Arizona
Family Mediation Service of Ontario
Hennepin County Court Services
Legal Aid of Quebec
Los Angeles Conciliation Court
Maricopa County Conciliation Court
Mediation Association of Southern Arizona
Mediation Consortium of Washington State
Mediation Council of Illinois
Mediation Institute of California
Minnesota Council of Family Mediation
Montreal Conciliation Court
National Association of Social Workers
National Council on Family Relations
National Institute for Dispute Resolution
Northwest Mediation Service
Ontario Association for Family Mediation
Pima County Superior Court

Pinal County Conciliation Court
San Diego County Superior Court Family Services
Society of Professionals in Dispute Resolution
South Florida Council on Divorce Mediation
Southern California Mediation Network
State Bar of California — Legal Specialization Committee
Wisconsin Association of Family & Divorce Mediators

APPENDIX 9D

FAMILY MEDIATION CANADA
CODE OF PROFESSIONAL CONDUCT

Article 1: Application and Enforcement

1. Membership in Family Mediation Canada requires explicit agreement to abide by:

   (a) this Code of Professional Conduct; and
   (b) the disciplinary procedures and sanctions adopted from time to time by the Standards and Ethics Committee and the Board of Directors of Family Mediation Canada.

2. The following rules are intended to govern the relations of family mediators with their clients, their professional colleagues, and the general public so that all will benefit from high standards of practice in family mediation. Members of Family Mediation Canada shall observe the spirit as well as the letter of provisions in this Code.

3. It is the obligation of family mediators to report and to encourage their clients to report, in writing, real or apparent breaches of this Code forthwith to the Chairperson of the Standards and Ethics Committee and/or to the President of Family Mediation Canada and/or to the President of their provincial or territorial association.

4. Members shall make this Code available to clients or the public upon request.

Article 2: Types of Mediation and Their Meaning

1. For the purposes of this Code, "family mediation" is defined as a non-adversarial, cooperative decision-making process in which a qualified and impartial third party, "the mediator", attempts to help family members resolve their disputes by agreement. The resolution is to be voluntary and based upon sufficient information and advice for each party.

2. The "closed mediation" process is intended to be confidential.

3. The "open mediation" process may result in the mediator preparing a report and/or making recommendations.

Article 3: Goal of Process and Role of Participants

1. The goal of family mediation is a fair and workable agreement, not a settlement at any cost.

2. The primary responsibility for the resolution of a dispute rests with the

parties. At no time shall a mediator coerce the participants into agreement or make a substantive decision for any participant.

3. The mediator's role is that of a facilitator, i.e. to assist the parties to reach an informed and voluntary agreement that is consistent with the needs of their children.

Article 4: Integrity

1. Mediators shall avoid any activity that could create a conflict of interest. They shall not become involved in relationships with clients which might impair their professional judgment or in any way increase the risk of exploiting clients, such as, but not limited to, mediating disputes involving close friends, relatives, colleagues, supervisors or students. It is a violation of this Code to engage in sexual intimacies with a participant in the mediation process.

Article 5: Competence

1. Family mediators shall perform their services in a conscientious, diligent and efficient manner in accordance with this Code.

2. It is the obligation of a member acting as a family mediator to ensure that he or she is qualified to deal with the specific issues involved. Mediators shall acquire substantive knowledge and procedural skills as defined by the Education Committee and adopted by the Board of Directors of Family Mediation Canada.

3. While family mediators have a diversity of education and training, the obligation to refrain from rendering services outside the limits of a mediator's qualifications and capabilities remains.

4. Family mediators shall engage in continuing education to ensure that their mediation skills are current and effective.

Article 6: Inter-Professional Relations

1. A mediator shall respect the complementary relationships among mediation, legal, mental health and other social services. He or she should promote cooperation with other professionals and encourage clients to use other professional resources when appropriate.

2. Where more than one mediator is participating in a particular case, each has the responsibility to keep the other(s) informed of developments in the mediation process essential to a cooperative effort.

Article 7: Confidentiality

1. A mediator shall not voluntarily disclose to anyone who is not a party to

the mediation any information obtained through the mediation process except:

- (a) non-identifying information for research or educational purposes; or
- (b) with the written consent of the parties to the mediation contract; or
- (c) when ordered to do so by a judicial authority with jurisdiction to compel such disclosure, or required to do so by legislation or other law; or
- (d) when the information discloses an actual or potential threat to human life or safety.

2. Any information so divulged shall be limited to what is absolutely necessary to accomplish such purposes.

3. While closed mediation imposes the intention and duty of confidentiality on a mediator, it cannot confer privilege, and the mediator shall advise the parties that the intended confidentiality cannot be guaranteed unless legislative privilege exists.

4. Clients shall be informed, at the outset, of these and other limitations to confidentiality.

5. A mediator shall maintain confidentiality of clients' files and shall ensure that office staff do so as well in the storage and disposal of such records.

Article 8: Impartiality

1. A mediator has a duty to act with impartiality in relation to the participants. Impartiality means freedom from favouritism or bias either in word or in action.

2. Notwithstanding impartiality, a mediator has a duty to restrain parents from coming to arrangements that are perceived by the mediator not to be in the best interests of the children involved, and to withdraw from the mediation if this proves not to be possible.

3. The perception by one or both of the parties that the mediator is partial does not in itself require the mediator to withdraw, but in such circumstances, the mediator shall remind both parties of their right to terminate the mediation.

4. A mediator shall disclose to the participants any biases he or she may have relating to the issues to be mediated and any circumstances which might constitute or cause a conflict of interest, real or perceived, to arise. Such disclosure shall be made as soon as the mediator recognizes the potential or any bias becoming operative or any conflict of interest arising.

5. A mediator shall refrain from mediating in cases where there has been any significant prior involvement between the mediator and one of the participants, unless every other participant expressly consents to the mediation proceeding after there has been full disclosure of such prior involvement. In this case, the role of the mediator should be carefully distinguished from the earlier relationship.

6. A lawyer-mediator, or any partner or associate of such lawyer-mediator, shall not represent either party during or after the mediation process in any related legal matters arising out of the issues discussed in the mediation.

Article 9: Ensuring Fair Negotiations

1. A mediator shall endeavour to ensure that the participants reach agreement freely, voluntarily, without undue influence, and on the basis of informed consent.

2. A mediator shall ensure that each party has had an opportunity to understand the implications and ramifications of available options. In the event that a party needs either additional information or assistance in order for the negotiations to proceed in a fair and orderly manner or for an agreement to be reached, the mediator shall refer the individual to appropriate resources.

3. A mediator shall explore whether the participants are capable of engaging in the mediation process. If a mediator believes that the parties are unable or unwilling to meaningfully participate in the process or that a reasonable agreement is unlikely, the mediator may suspend or terminate mediation and should encourage the parties to seek appropriate professional help.

4. The mediator has a duty to ensure balanced negotiations and shall not permit manipulative or intimidating negotiating techniques. While mediators must be impartial towards the participants, impartiality does not imply neutrality on the issue of fairness. If such negative tactics cannot be eliminated, the mediator has a duty to terminate mediation.

5. It is a fundamental principle of mediation that competent and informed parties can reach an agreement which may not correspond to legal guidelines contained in the relevant statutes or case law or that does not correspond with general community expectations and standards. Although the mediator's role is that of a facilitator and the primary responsibility for the resolution of a dispute rests with the parties, if the mediator finds an agreement or any part of it to be inherently unfair, he or she is expected to indicate his or her nonconcurrence to the parties.

Article 10: Information, Disclosure and Advice

1. It is the duty of a mediator to actively encourage the participants to make decisions based upon sufficient information, knowledge and advice.

2. Where financial or property issues are involved, the mediator shall obtain an undertaking from the parties to make frank and full disclosure of their financial and related circumstances at the appropriate time in the mediation process. The mediator will assist the parties and their advisors to achieve such disclosure. A mediator has an ongoing obligation to advise both parties to obtain legal and other professional advice and assistance in this respect.

3. Every family mediator has an ongoing obligation to advise participants of the desirability and availability of independent legal advice. While neutral legal information may be made available to the parties, each should be encouraged to obtain legal advice.

Article 11: Agreement to Mediate

1. The mediator shall explain the mediation process clearly to the parties before agreeing to mediate their dispute. In particular, the mediator should at the outset:

- (a) define and explain mediation, both closed and open, and distinguish it from reconciliation counselling, therapy, assessment, advocacy, adjudication and arbitration;
- (b) discuss the appropriateness of mediation for the parties in light of their particular circumstances, the benefits and risks of mediation, and the other alternatives open to the parties;
- (c) discuss the differences between closed and open mediation and the implications of each, and if the mediator practices both types, require the parties to choose between closed and open mediation;
- (d) advise the parties that either of them or the mediator has the right to suspend or terminate the process at any time;
- (e) make explicit the costs of mediation and reach an agreement with the parties regarding payment of these costs;
- (f) advise the parties of the role of legal advice in accordance with Article 10 of this Code. If the mediator is also a lawyer, he or she shall inform the parties that he or she cannot represent either or both of them in any related legal action;
- (g) discuss with the parties the mediator's specific procedures and practices, such as when:
    - (i) separate sessions may be held;
    - (ii) there are to be separate communications with the parties or their counsel; and

(iii) other persons are to be involved in the mediation; and

(h) recommend that the agreement to mediate be written and signed by the parties and the mediator.

Article 12: Termination of Mediation

1. It is the duty of a mediator to suspend or terminate mediation whenever continuation of the process is likely to harm or prejudice one or more of the participants, such as when mediation is being misused to:

(a) develop a status quo with respect to the custody of the children; or

(b) to dissipate or conceal assets.

2. A mediator shall suspend or terminate mediation when its usefulness is exhausted.

3. When a mediator believes that an agreement being reached is unreasonable, he or she shall so advise the parties and shall consider withdrawing from the mediation.

4. Mediators have a duty not to withdraw their services except for good cause and upon reasonable notice to the parties.

Article 13: Public Statements and Promotional Activities

1. The purpose of public statements concerning family mediation should be to:

(a) educate the public generally about the process; and

(b) present the process of mediation objectively as one of several methods of dispute resolution in order to help the public make informed judgments and choices.

2. Public communications shall not mislead the public, misrepresent facts, or contain any:

(a) false, fraudulent, misleading or unfair statements;

(b) statements likely to mislead or deceive by making only a partial disclosure of relevant facts; or

(c) statements intended or likely to create false or unjustified expectations of favourable results.

3. When advertising professional services, mediators should restrict themselves to matters which educate and inform the public. These could include the following information to describe the mediator and the services offered: name, address, telephone number, office hours, relevant academic degree(s), relevant training and experience in mediation, appropriate professional affiliations and membership status, advantages of the mediation process, and any additional relevant or important consumer information.

4. Public communications shall not falsely imply that membership in Family Mediation Canada or a provincial or territorial family mediation association constitutes certification as a mediator.

5. Mediators should promote the advancement of mediation by encouraging and/or participating in research, publishing, and other forms of professional and public education.

6. Mediators are encouraged to provide some mediation services to the community for no or nominal charge.

7. Mediators should generally promote a cooperative approach to problem-solving and the welfare of the family as a whole, especially children.

Article 14: Charges for Services

1. At the outset, the mediator shall explain the fees to be charged for mediation and any related costs. He or she shall obtain agreement from the parties as to how the fees are to be shared and the method of payment.

2. No commissions, rebates or similar forms of remuneration shall be given or received for referral of clients for mediation services.

3. It is inappropriate for a mediator to base fees on the outcome of the mediation process.

4. When a retainer has been collected before mediation services were rendered, any unearned fees should be promptly returned to the clients upon the termination of mediation.

November 8, 1986

APPENDIX 10

CHECKLIST FOR INTERVIEWS AND CONTACTS
DURING MEDIATION/ASSESSMENT

ISSUES SENT TO MEDIATION:

CONTACT	CUSTODY AND ACCESS	SUPPORT SPOUSAL & CHILD	PROPERTY DIVISION & OTHER FINANCIAL ISSUES
CHILD #1	✓	?	×
CHILD #2	✓	?	×
CHILD #3	✓	?	×
CHILD #4	✓	?	×
CHILD #5	✓	?	×
CHILD #6	✓	?	×
CHILD #7	✓	?	×
CHILD #8	✓	?	×
CHILD #9	✓	?	×
CHILD #10	✓	?	×
FATHER	✓	✓	✓
MOTHER	✓	✓	✓
FATHER'S LAWYER	✓	✓	✓
MOTHER'S LAWYER	✓	✓	✓
CHILD'S LAWYER	✓	✓	✓
FATHER'S NEW PARTNER	✓	?	?
MOTHER'S NEW PARTNER	✓	?	?
FATHER'S CHILDREN: FROM OTHER RELATIONSHIPS	?	?	?
MOTHER'S CHILDREN FROM OTHER RELATIONSHIPS	?	?	?
FATHER'S PARENT(S)	?	?	?
MOTHER'S PARENT(S)	?	?	?

CONTACT	CUSTODY AND ACCESS	SUPPORT SPOUSAL & CHILD	PROPERTY DIVISION & OTHER FINANCIAL ISSUES
FATHER'S OTHER RELATIVE(S)	?	✕	✕
MOTHER'S OTHER RELATIVE(S)	?	✕	✕
CHILD(REN)'S CARETAKER: (NANNY, DAY CARE CENTRE)	✓	✕	✕
FATHER'S FRIEND(S)	?	✕	✕
MOTHER'S FRIEND(S)	?	✕	✕
MOTHER'S PHYSICIAN(S)	✓	?	✕
FATHER'S PHYSICIAN(S)	✓	?	✕
CHILD(REN)'S PHYSICIAN(S)	✓	?	✕
CHILD(REN)'S SCHOOL(S)	✓✓	✕	✕
PUBLIC HEALTH NURSE	?	✕	✕
OTHER MENTAL HEALTH PROFESSIONALS	✓	?	✕
TAX SPECIALIST	✕	?	?
PENSION ANALYST	✕	?	?
BANK MANAGER	✕	?	?
ACCOUNTANT	✕	?	?
CHILDREN'S AID SOCIETY	?	✕	✕
POLICE	?	✕	✕

OTHER, PLEASE SPECIFY _____

OTHER, PLEASE SPECIFY _____

✓	=	SHOULD BE CONTACTED
?	=	POSSIBLE CONTACT
✕	=	NOT NECESSARY TO CONTACT

APPENDIX 11

OUTLINE OF CUSTODY ASSESSMENT REPORT

1. Referral Sources

2. Reasons for Referral

3. Objectives of the Assessment

4. Qualifications of the Assessor

5. Assessment Process

6. Family History, Including Relevant Marital History, Child Development, and Family Dynamics

7. Summary of Observations of the Family and of Information from Other Sources

8. Discussion of Important Issues

9. Alternative Parenting Arrangements

10. Rationale for the Recommendations

11. Recommendations of Assessor

Index